The History of Art for Kids

by Fred Alien

Illustrated by Julia Kobus

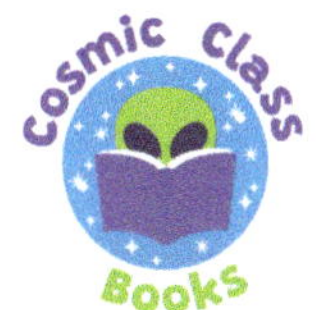

Table of Contents

Welcome to the wonderful world of art!

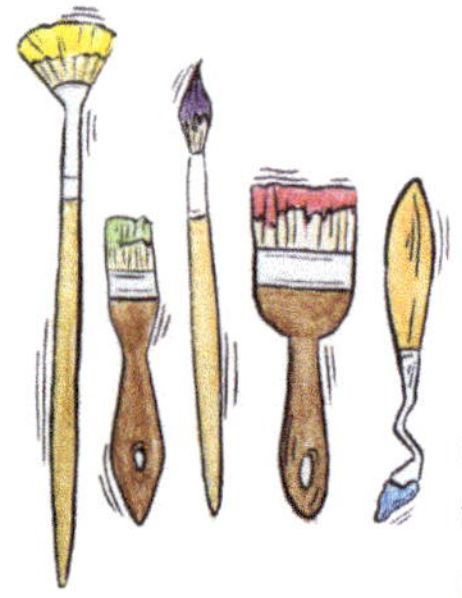

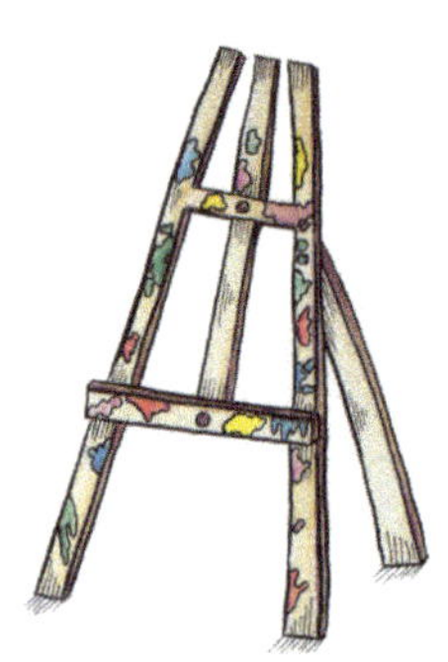

Hey there, Earthlings! I love your wonderful world of art!

It's so nice to meet you. My name is really tricky for humans to say, but you can call me "Fred"!

What's your name?..

I bet you're wondering why an alien like me is talking to you. Well, don't worry. I come in peace! I come from a far corner of the universe and have journeyed across countless lightyears to uncover the secrets of space. Ages ago, I had the pleasure of discovering your beautiful blue planet.

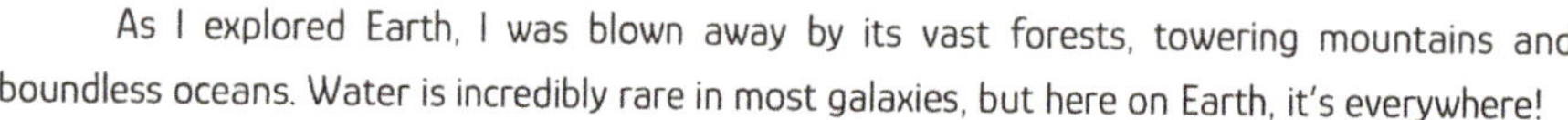

As I explored Earth, I was blown away by its vast forests, towering mountains and boundless oceans. Water is incredibly rare in most galaxies, but here on Earth, it's everywhere!

Do you know what's even rarer than water? Something that I've never encountered anywhere else in the universe, ART! Humans have been creating art for as long as they've existed, and it has always intrigued me!

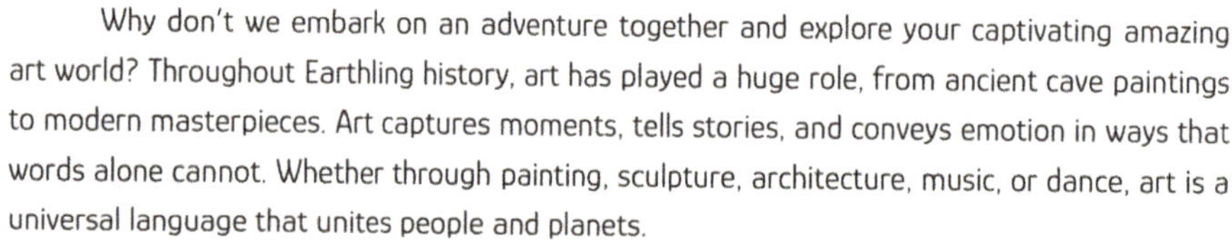

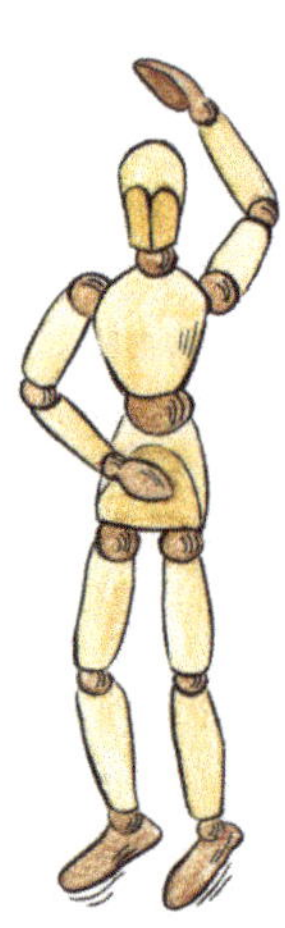

Why don't we embark on an adventure together and explore your captivating amazing art world? Throughout Earthling history, art has played a huge role, from ancient cave paintings to modern masterpieces. Art captures moments, tells stories, and conveys emotion in ways that words alone cannot. Whether through painting, sculpture, architecture, music, or dance, art is a universal language that unites people and planets.

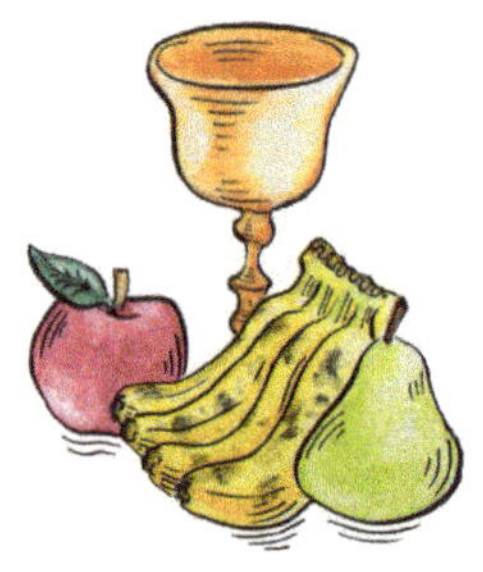

On this journey, we'll dive into a collage of colors, boundless imagination and endless possibilities. We will see how art transcends barriers of language, culture, and galaxy! Let us walk in the footsteps of great human artists who lived long ago and see how they inspired generations long after theirs, and even inspired aliens, like me.

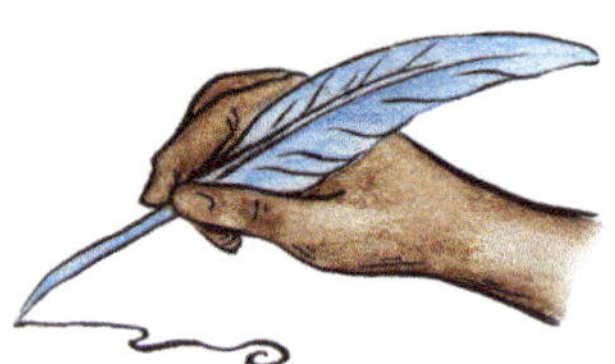

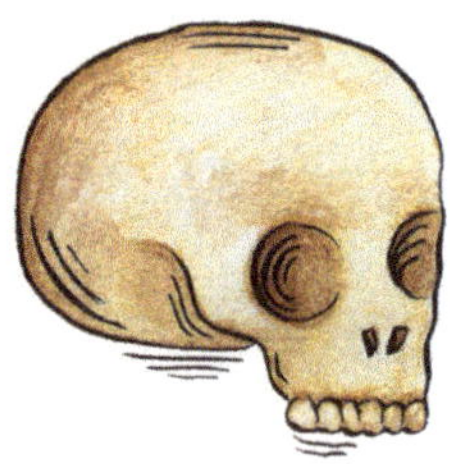

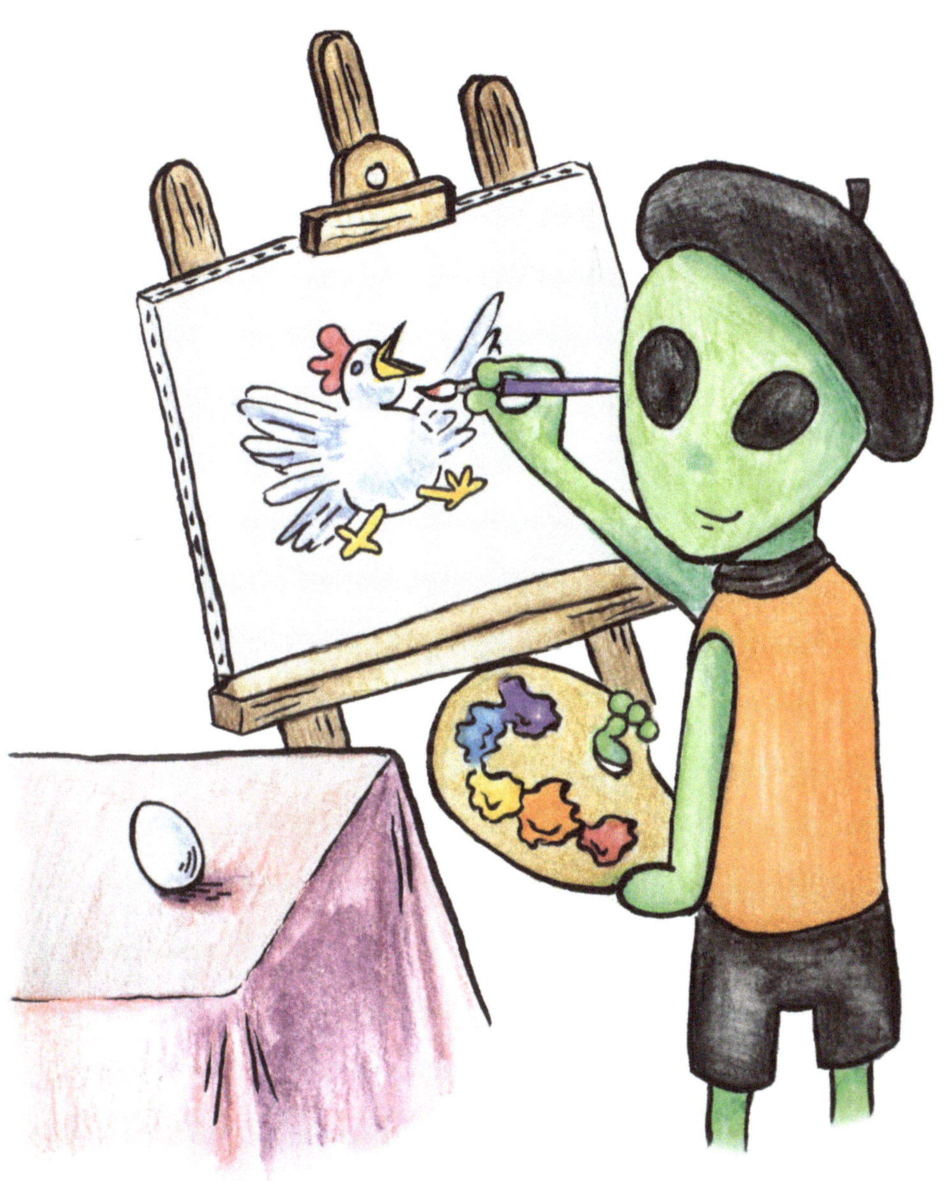

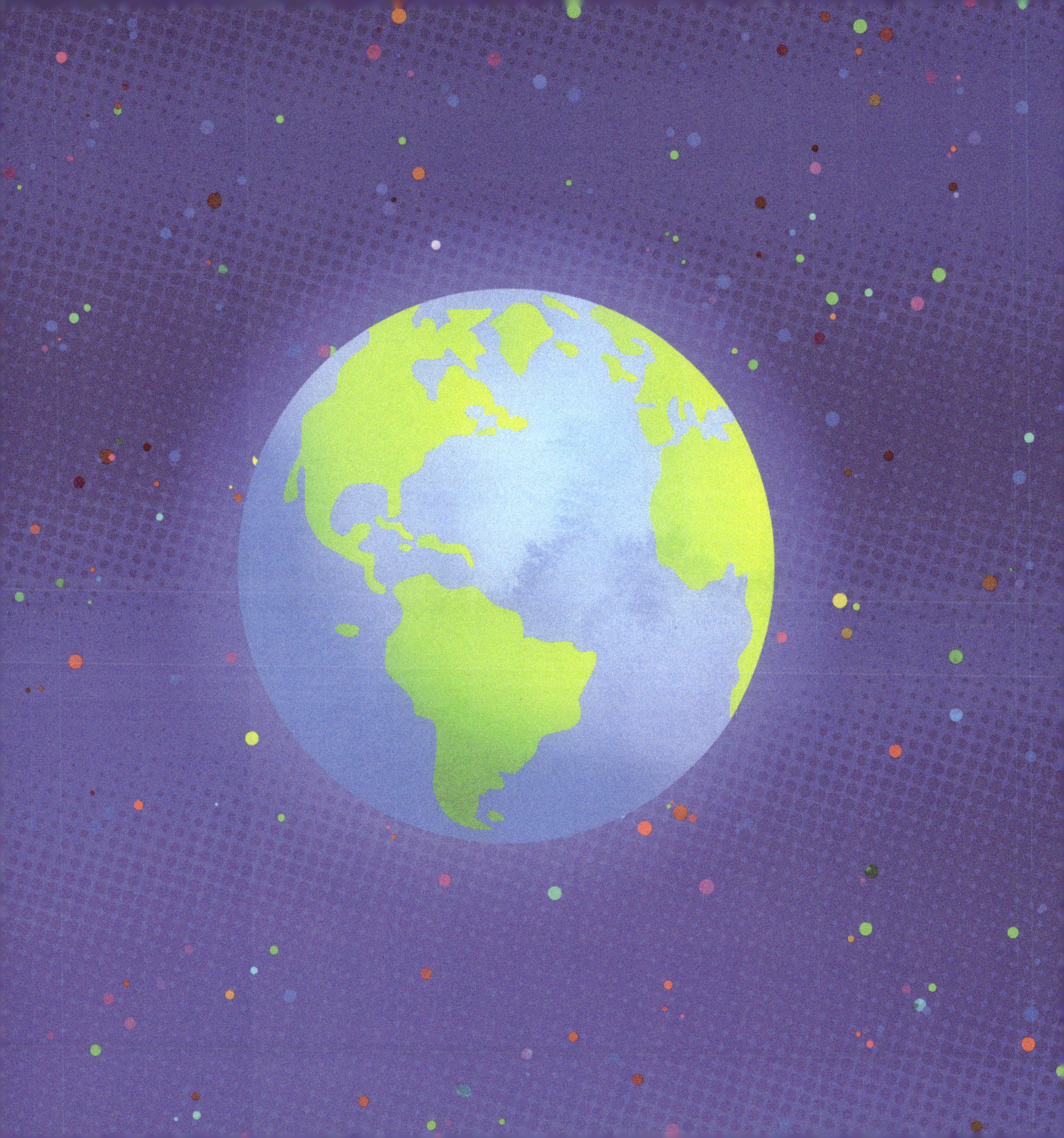

Prehistoric and Ancient Art

Prehistoric Art

WHAT better way to start than from the very beginning? Humans made art a very, very, **very** long time ago, long before they made buildings. Even though we don't know if they danced or sang, we can find lots of visual art that they left behind for us to discover, and it is really amazing.

Some human art is so old that it's hard to believe - Your prehistoric ancestors started making art more than 75,000 years ago! That's older than almost anything else you can imagine. Even though I've been to lots of different places in the universe, I never imagined Earth had such old things. We're lucky that we can still see and appreciate ancient art today.

Lascaux Cave Paintings, circa 14,000 BCE

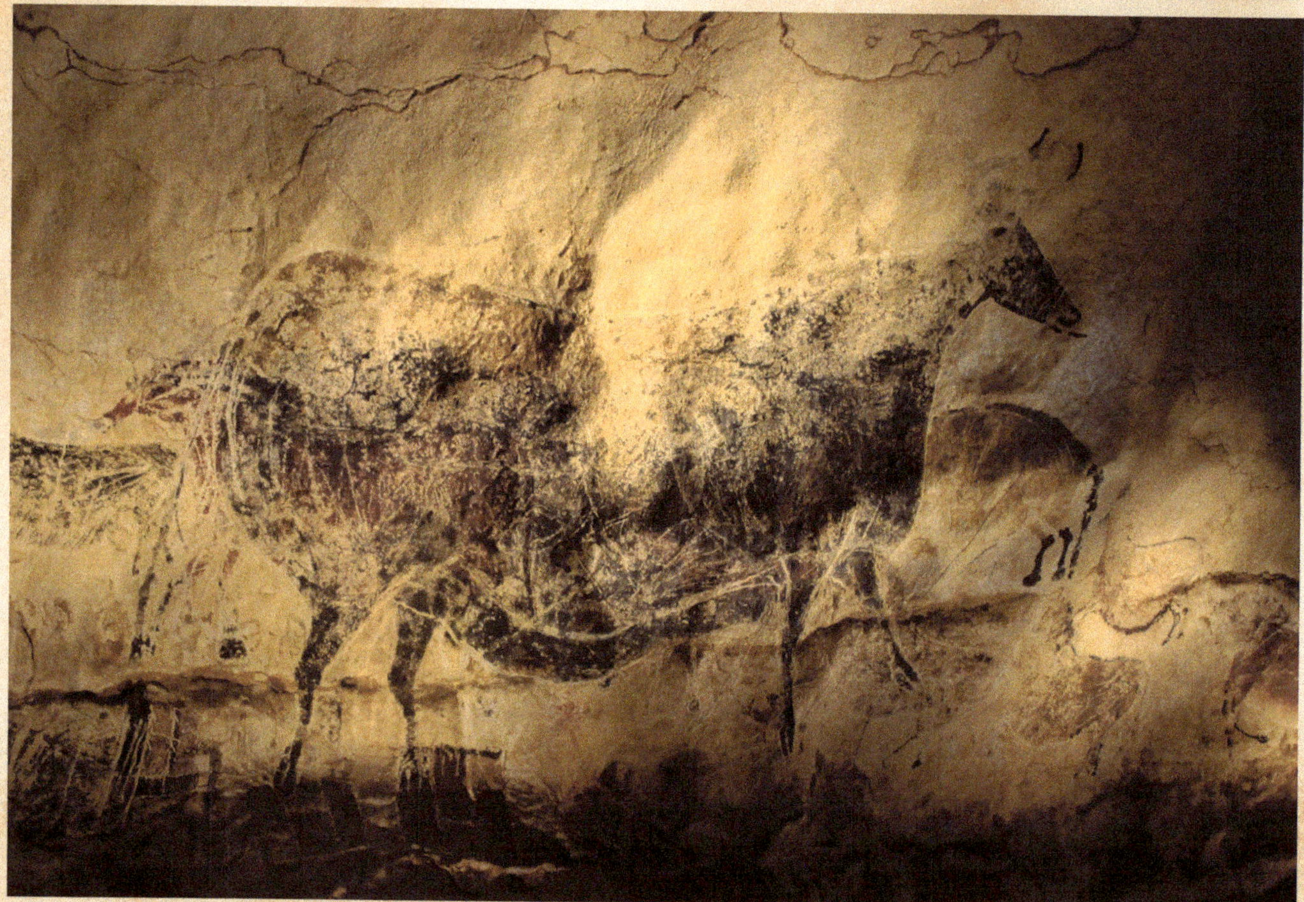

These works of art were often painted on rocks or cave walls, as well as stone engravings called petroglyphs. Prehistoric art can be found all around your beautiful Earth, and its meanings and techniques vary from culture to culture.

For example, in Australia, we can find several paintings of animals like whales, kangaroos, and the extinct Tasmanian tiger. The largest collection of petroglyphs ever discovered can be found in the Murujuga National Park. The Aboriginal Australians created these images for spiritual ceremonies. They would also create paintings and petroglyphs simply to have something beautiful to look at, just as humans do today.

Another incredible series of animal paintings can be found in the Lascaux caves of Dordogne, France. Created around 14,000 BCE, this prehistoric art collection is believed to depict hunting rituals.

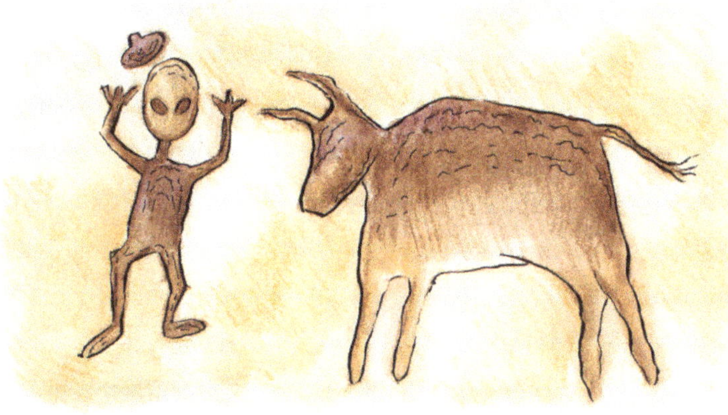

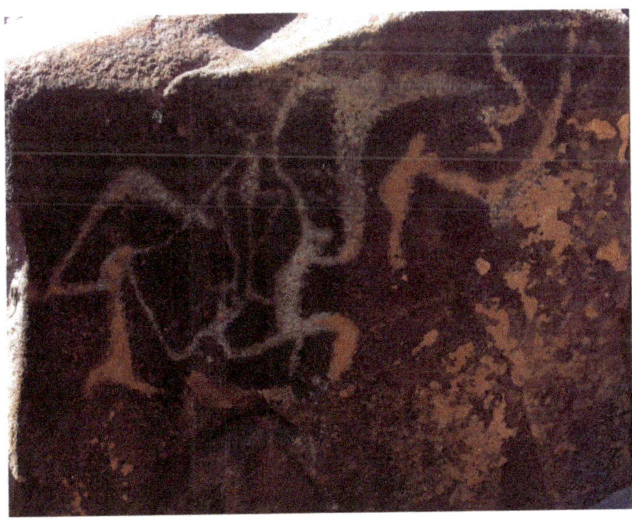

Murujuga Petroglyph, circa 40,000 BCE

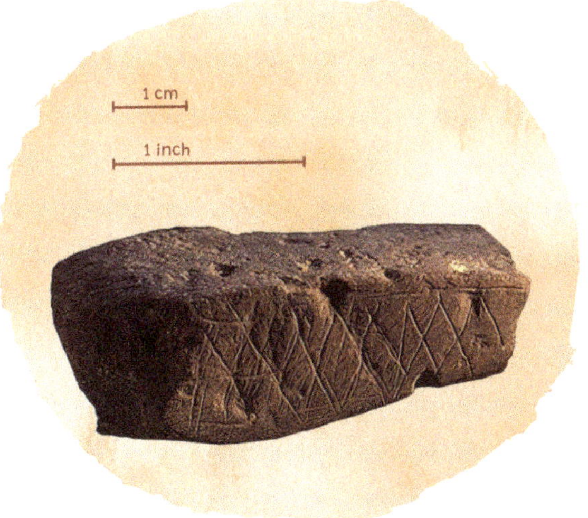

Blombos Cave Art, circa 73,000 BCE

When I was flying over Earth in my spaceship, I saw some amazing drawings on the ground in Peru. These drawings are called the Nazca Lines! They are really huge and can only be seen from high up in the sky.

The largest Nazca Line is about 400 yards long, and the drawings show things like a monkey, a spider, a tree, and a lizard. They are so big that you can't see the whole picture when you stand on the ground. It must have taken a lot of planning and teamwork to make them!

People still don't know why the Nazca Lines were made. One theory is that they were used in special ceremonies to ask gods for rain. It's a mystery that humans are still trying to solve!

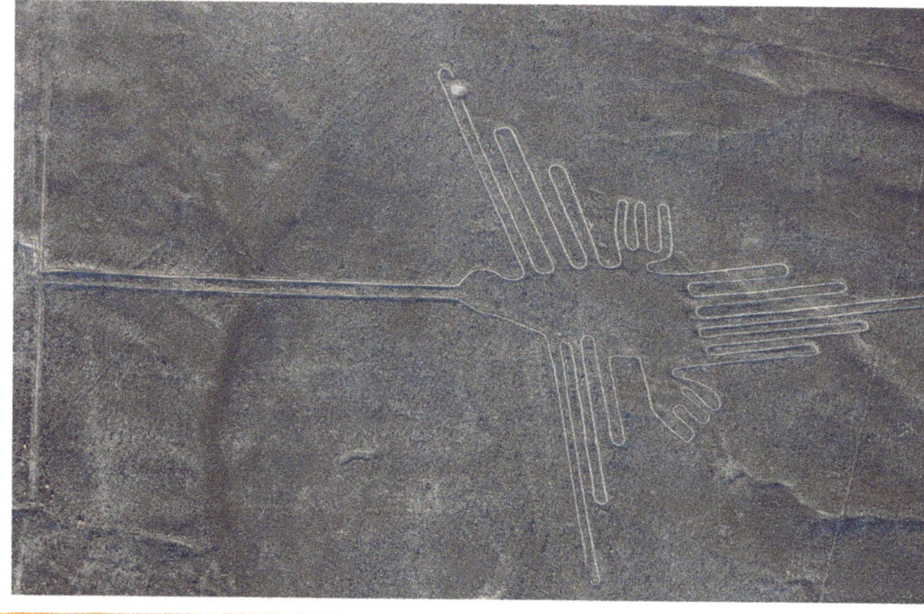

Nazca Lines (Hummingbird), created between 200 BCE and 500 CE

The Nazca civilization was structured between 200 BCE to 600 CE.

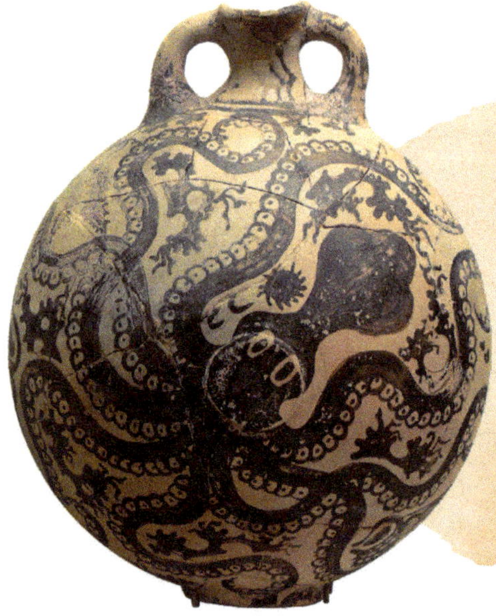

There are so many examples of pottery and sculpture that were produced in prehistoric times, and I wish we could check them all out! Since we have a long road ahead, let me just show you this cool piece of octopus pottery. It was produced around the year 1450 BCE by the Minoan civilization. They lived in what humans today know as Greece.

Clay Flask, circa 1450 BCE

Activity

Hand stencils

There is a place called Cueva de las Manos (or "Cave of the Hands" in English) in Argentina. These images were made over many years and consist of drawings of animals, people, and hands. The hand stencils were created by using a piece of hollow bone to blow natural pigment over hands. The pigment would stick to the cave wall and create an outline of the hands.

How about we create our very own hand stencils?

For this cool activity, you will need the following:

- **Spray bottle**
- **Gouache paint**
- **A large piece of paper**

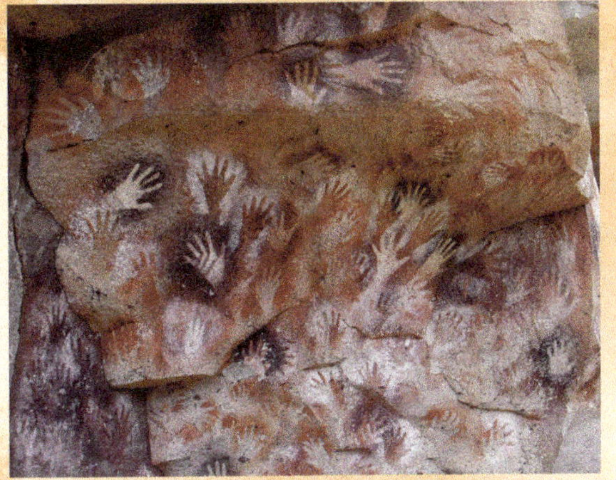

Cave of the Hands, Argentina, 7300 BCE - 700 CE

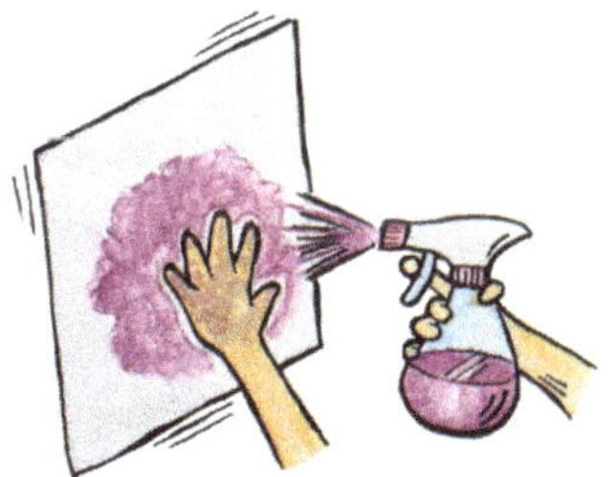

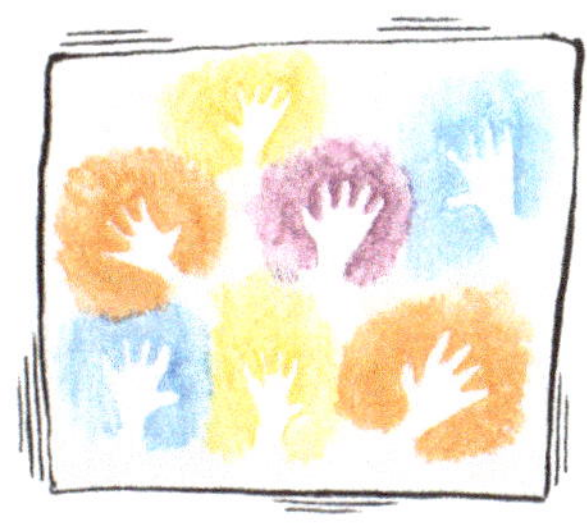

How to do it:

1 First, add water to your spray bottle. Don't fill it up too much! Then, choose a color, add some drops of gouache paint to the bottle, and shake. Add only a few drops so it's still see-through and doesn't clog up the spray.

2 Place your hand on the paper and spray over it to create a stencil effect, just like the Cave of Hands. Create your own composition by placing your hand in different spots. You can even overlap them and use different colors.

3 Make sure your paper is thick enough so the water doesn't damage it.

4 This activity can also be done on a large panel or a wall. Don't forget to ask an adult for help.

Ancient Egypt

Let's take a leap to one of my favorite periods in Earthling history, ancient Egypt. This period went from the year 2649 BCE all the way to 1070 BCE, and they created every kind of art you can imagine! From paintings to sculptures, architecture, textiles, ceramics, and even jewelry – the ancient Egyptians were extremely artistic.

Spirituality and politics were very much aligned in ancient Egypt. Ancient Egyptians even believed that their leaders, called pharaohs, were living gods! That's why a lot of the artwork portrays pharaohs as big and powerful.

Eight different dynasties were in power during this period, and the way art was created was defined by the pharaohs that ruled each dynasty. Each pharaoh had their own rules about how art should be made. Even though the artists had to follow their pharaoh's guidelines, you can still see unique styles in every piece of ancient Egyptian art.

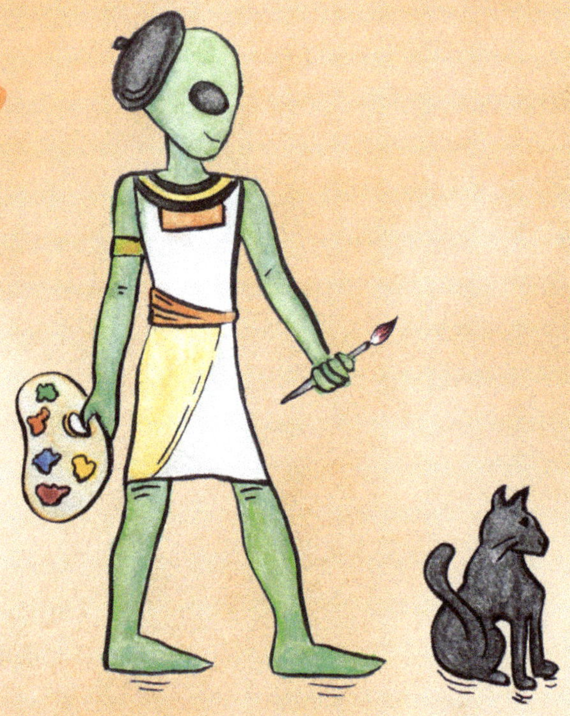

Craftsmen, Tomb of Nebamun and Ipuky, circa 1390–1349 BCE

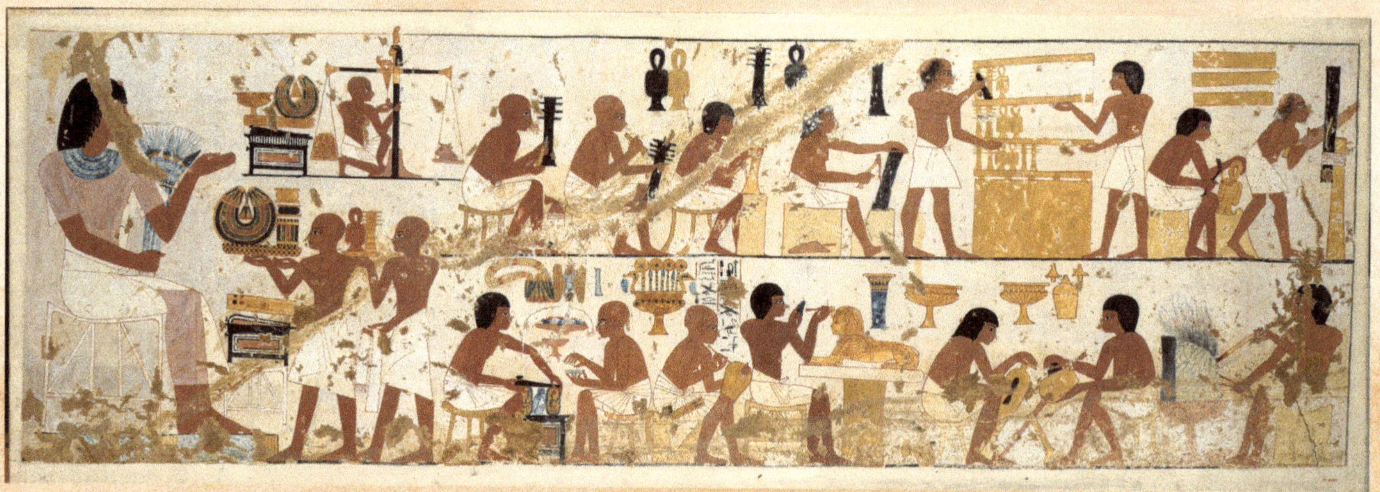

The Egyptians' view on death also influenced the way they made art. They believed in an afterlife in which they would be able to take their earthly possessions. Because of this, the pharaohs were mummified and kept inside the great pyramids after their death. This would ensure less decomposition of the bodies and help, as they believed, with their rebirth.

One of the most beautiful and luxurious pieces I have come across during my adventures has been, without a doubt, the mask of Tutankhamun, which was excavated from his tomb in 1922. The youngest of all pharaohs, Tutankhamun, also known as King Tut, became pharaoh when he was only around 10 years old and passed away when he was just 19.

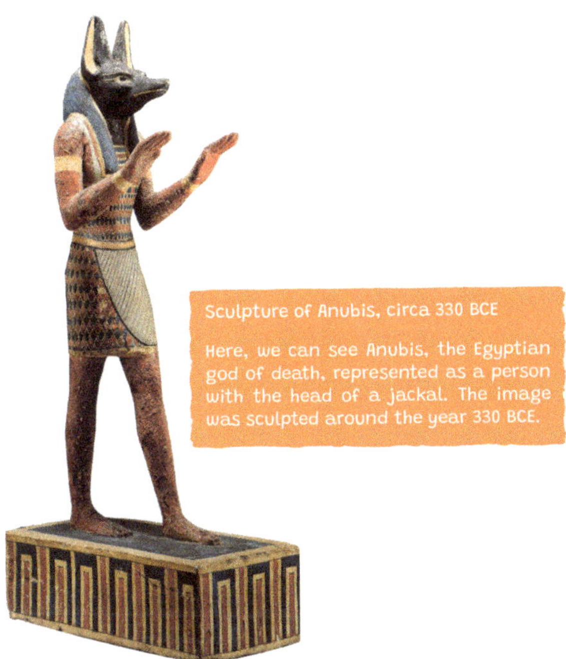

Sculpture of Anubis, circa 330 BCE

Here, we can see Anubis, the Egyptian god of death, represented as a person with the head of a jackal. The image was sculpted around the year 330 BCE.

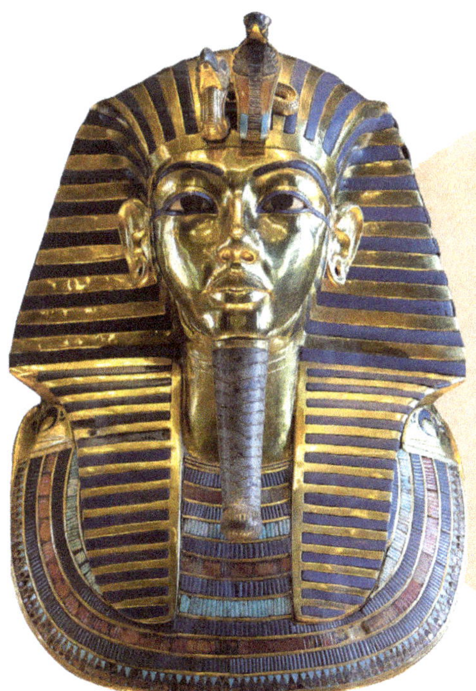

Just like the rest of the coffin, the mask of Tutankhamun was made with gold and other precious gems in 1323 BCE. His head is covered with a striped head cloth called a nemes (pronounced "neh-mehs"). King Tut's nemes features the image of a cobra and a vulture - symbols of power and protection.

The face shows a calm expression and symbolizes Osiris, the Egyptian god of the afterlife, agriculture, and fertility. Egyptian hieroglyphs can be seen on the back of the coffin, near King Tut's shoulders. Hieroglyphs were symbols that were used to write at the time, and ancient Egyptians believed the hieroglyphs on King Tut's tomb protected it.

Tutankhamun's Mask, 1323 BCE

Mesopotamia and Persia

Speaking of ancient art, how about we go to Mesopotamia and see what they were creating around the same time as the ancient Egyptians? Let's explore the ancient civilization of Babylonia, which is modern-day Iraq. Their art dates back to 4000 BCE and was just as sophisticated as that of the ancient Egyptians.

One powerful ruler, named Nebuchadnezzar II, lived there around 605 BCE. He had the city rebuilt and put a huge wall around it. The gates of the wall were covered in pictures of animals like bulls, lions, and an imaginary creature called the mushkhushshu. Artists used a technique called high relief to make pictures stand out from the surface and look really cool, like the one below.

In 539 BCE, Babylon was conquered by Cyrus the Great and became Persian territory. Persians built incredible palaces filled with intricate metal and stone artwork.

High Relief Featuring The Mushhushshu

The Mushkhushshu was a sacred creature in Babylonian mythology creature that is like a mixture of a snake, a lion, a bird, and a dragon.

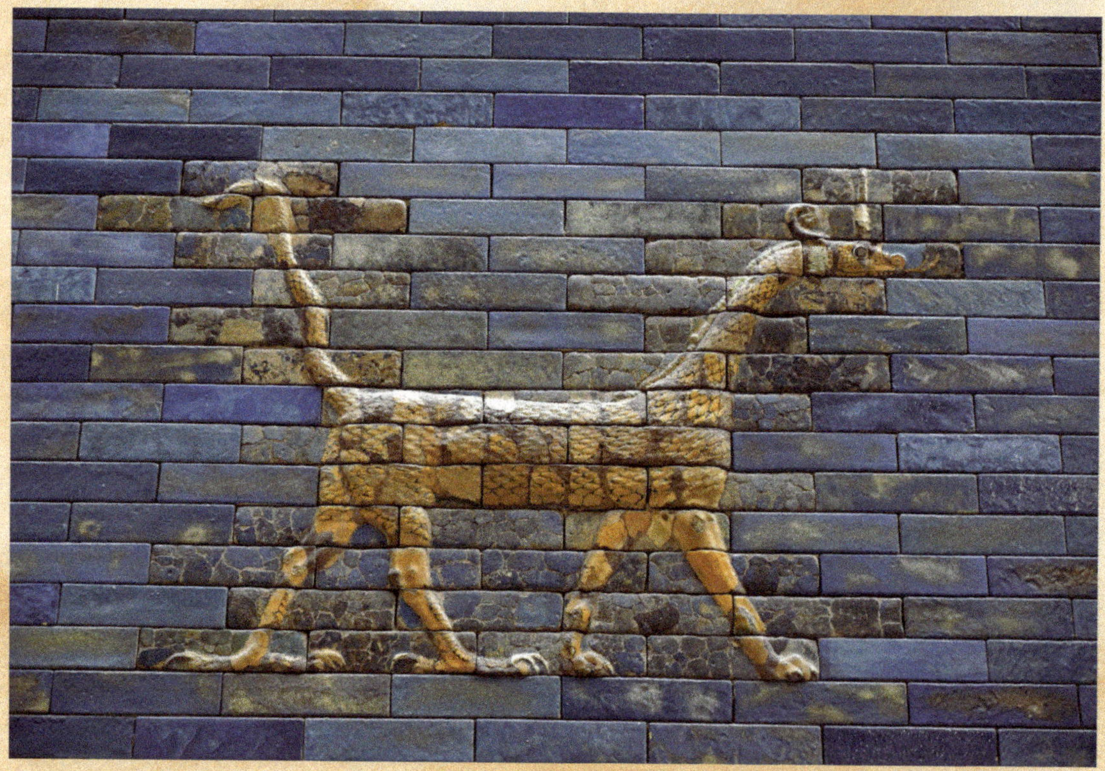

Here is a really cool sculpture of a *lamassu*, which was a mythological creature with the body of a lion, the wings of a bird, and the head of a human. They were placed as statues in front of important buildings in ancient Mesopotamia to guard them. People believed *lamassu* protected them from evil spirits and other dangers.

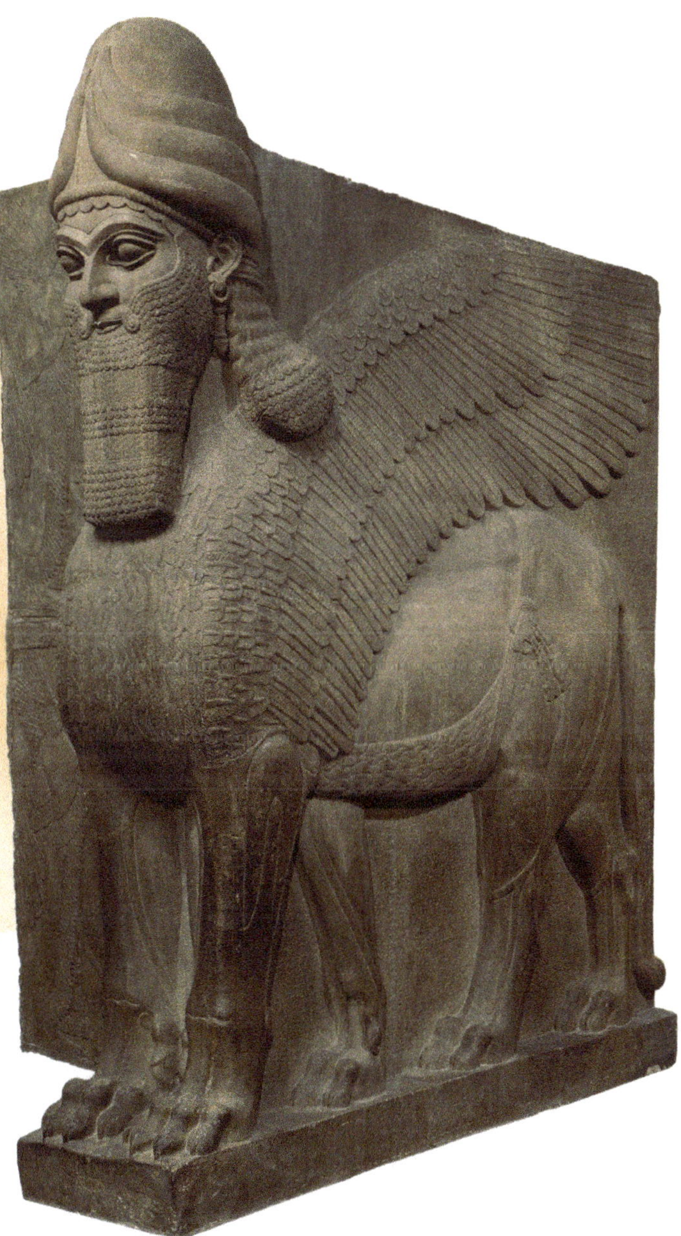

Human-headed winged lion (*lamassu*), Assyrian, circa 883–859 BCE

Ancient Chinese Art – Terracotta Army

Let's make a pit stop in ancient China so I can show you the largest sculpture that has ever been made on Earth, ever. Imagine building an army of life-size soldiers out of clay! That's exactly what the Chinese did over 2000 years ago, and it took them about 40 years to finish what is known as the Terracotta Army.

More than 700,000 workers helped build the Terracotta Army, including the soldiers and tombs they were meant to protect. For centuries, these clay warriors remained hidden underground, untouched and unknown to the world until 1974, when some lucky farmers accidentally found them.

It is believed that the Terracotta Army was created to protect the first emperor of China in his afterlife. The craftsman that made it created a basic shape of each soldier using a mold made out of terracotta clay. The molds were created in sections for the head, arms, legs, and torso. After shaping the form of each soldier, the artists carefully added details like armor and weapons.

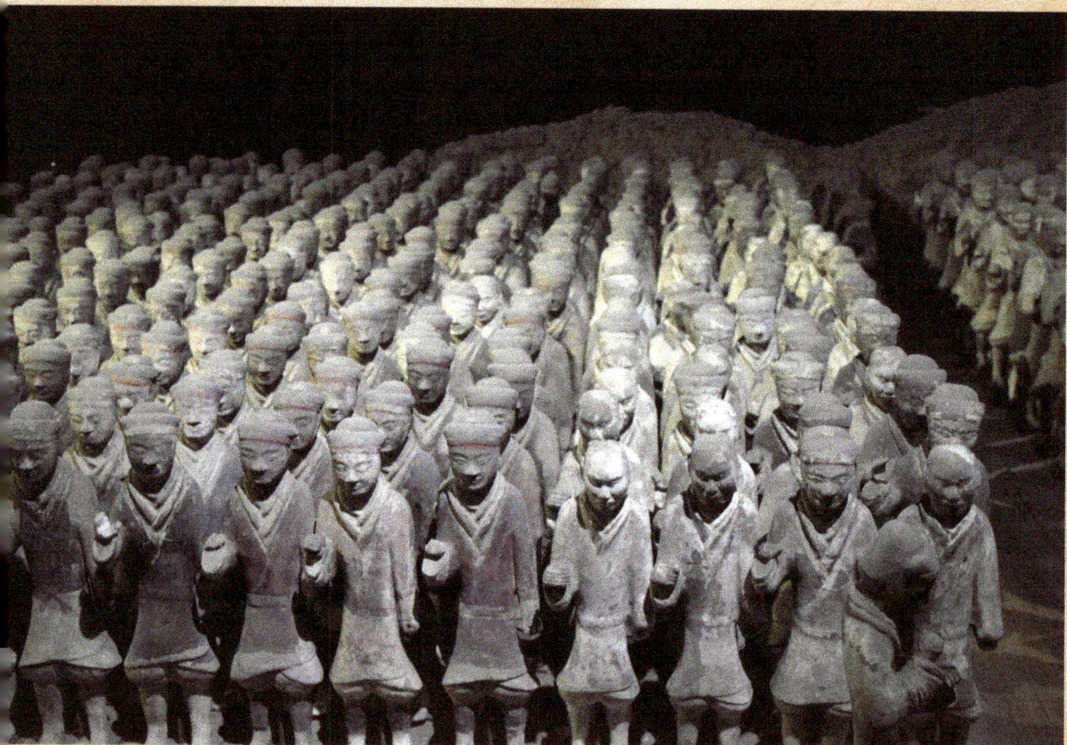

Terracotta Army, circa 248 BCE

What's truly amazing is that each soldier has a different face! The artists used a unique mold for each one.

When the soldiers were completed, they were baked in a huge oven called a kiln, which hardened the clay. Each soldier was placed in a vault based on their rank and position in the army. They also made clay horses and chariots.

Seeing the Terracotta Army is like being transported back to ancient China!

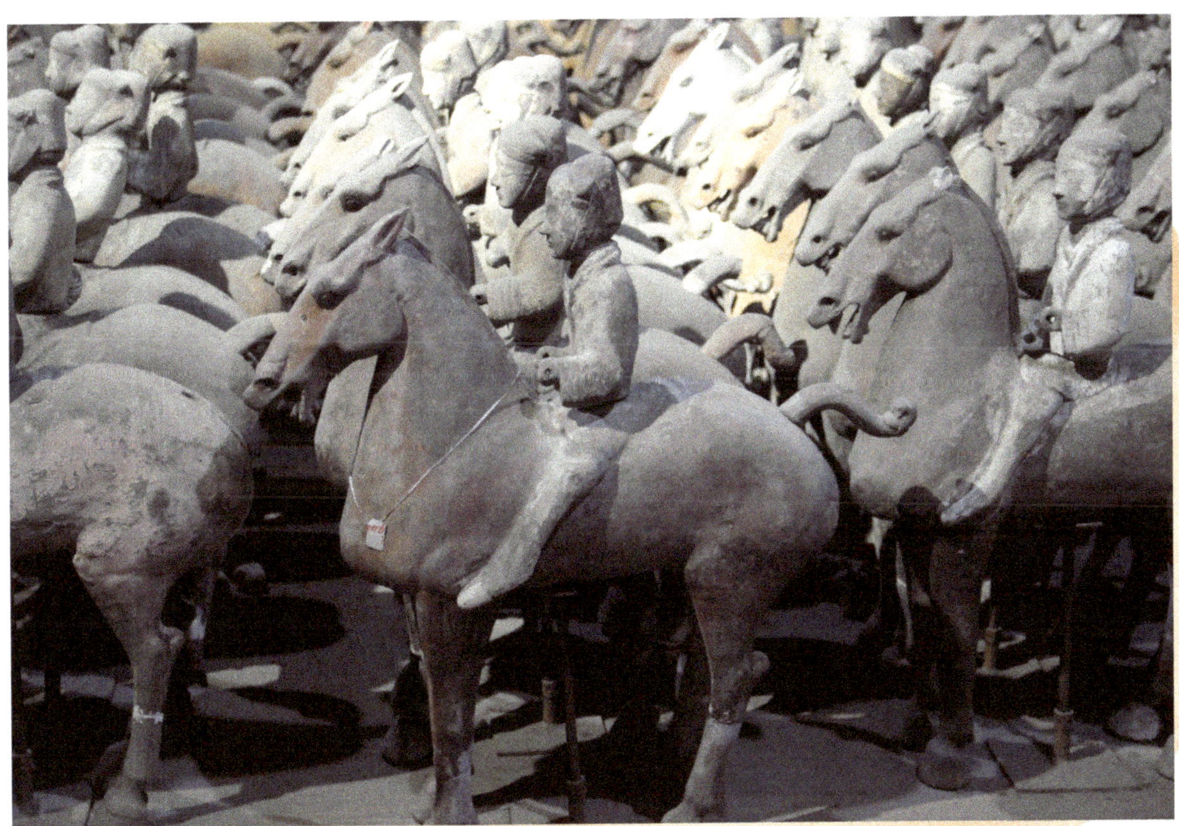

Terracotta Army, circa 248 BCE

Ancient Greek and Roman Art

So now I am going to show you something really cool that changed the course of art history forever.

The ancient Greeks developed studies on art, philosophy, architecture, and math, which had a huge impact on Earth as you know it today.

The Greeks created amazing artwork that celebrated military victories, recognized important people, and honored their gods in temples. Greek mythology was the most prominent theme in their art.

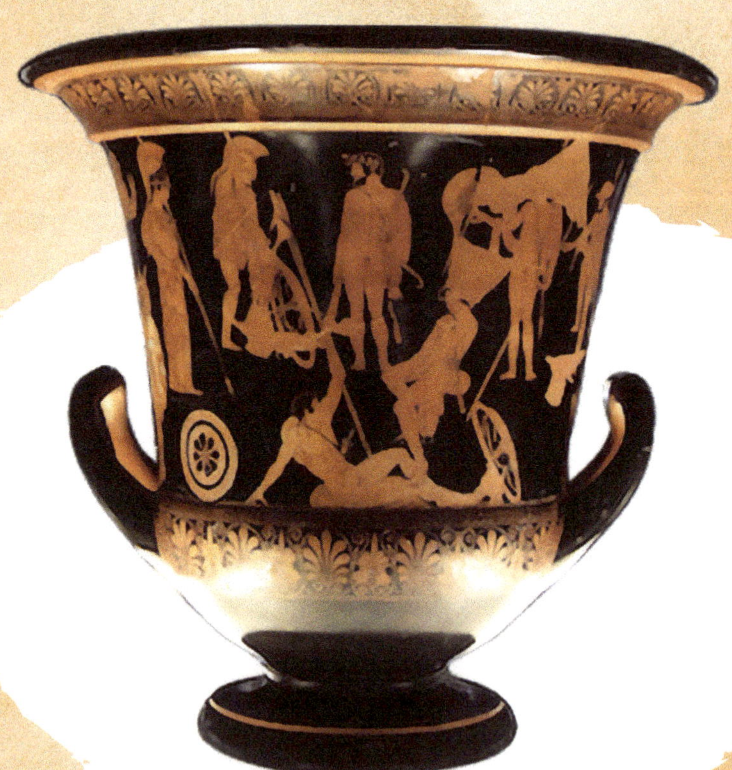

Attic Black-Background Amphora by Exekias, 540 – 530 BCE

This attic black-background amphora was created by Exekias around 540 – 530 BCE. The Greeks painted black figures onto pottery, which resulted in a beautiful contrast between the figures and the background.

Greece experienced a period of prosperity in the 7th and 6th centuries BCE as the middle class rose and democracy was instituted. This gave artists the opportunity to travel to Egypt and near Asia to explore other artistic styles, which inspired new forms of multicultural art.

Artists became focused on creating balanced and harmonious works of art with idealized human figures - in other words, bodies considered perfectly beautiful because of their proportions. Like the ancient Egyptians, Greeks were masters of sculpture as well as architecture and relied on math to make dimensions precise.

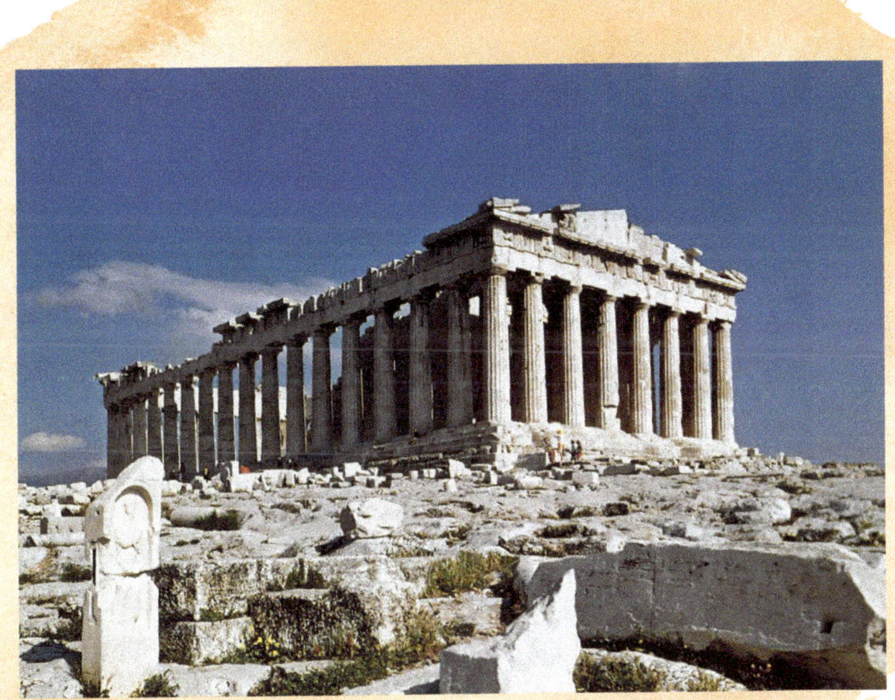

Parthenon

The Parthenon was built between the years 447 BCE and 432 BCE.

In 509 BCE, Rome became a republic, and the Romans conquered so much territory that it's sometimes hard to pinpoint the extent of Roman art. Also, Greek art influenced Roman art so much that it can be hard to tell them apart. Historians use the term Greco-Roman when talking about Greece and Rome because of how connected they were.

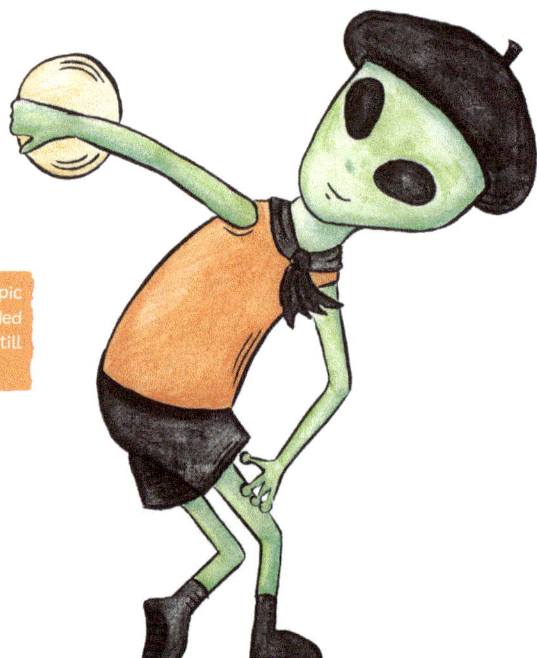

Check it out! Discus was a big part of the Olympic games in ancient Greece. Other sports included wrestling, jumping, running, and javelin. I am still learning, but it's so much fun!

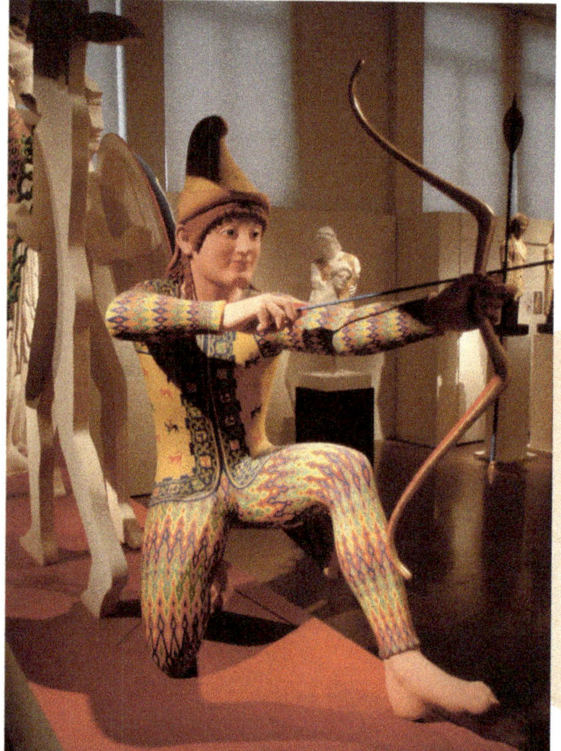

Did you know that most Greek and Roman sculptures were originally painted and were really colorful? The paint wore off with time, and humans didn't discover that Greco-Roman art exploded with color until many centuries later, in the mid-1800s.

Trojan archer from the Temple of Aphaia, Aegina, circa 500 BCE

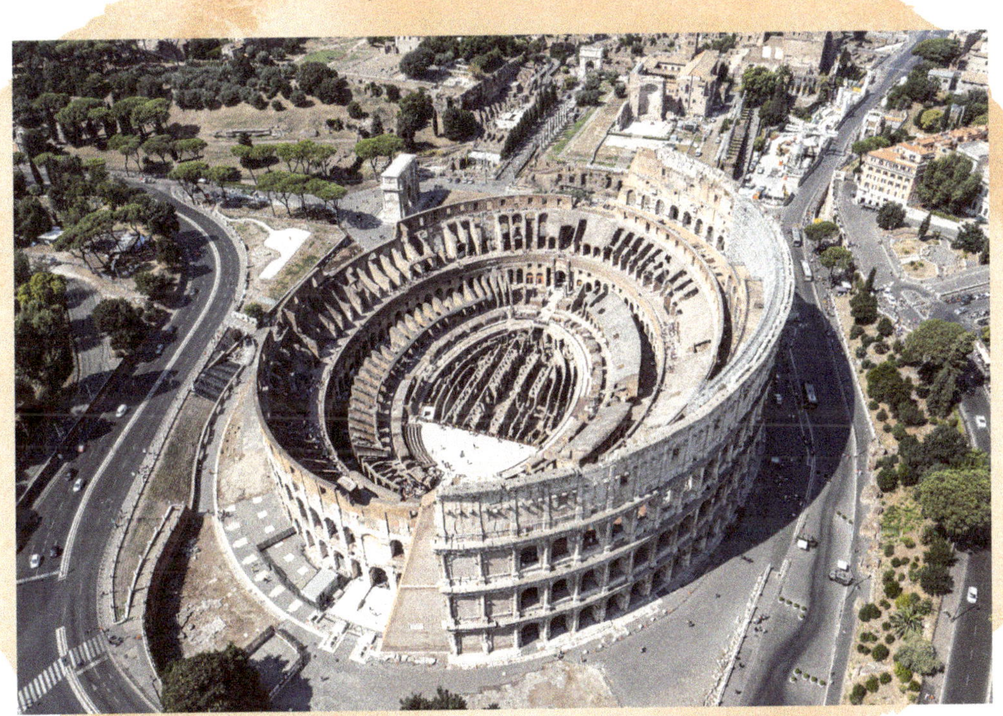

Colosseum, 80 – 70 BCE

Roman architecture was highly innovative, as seen in the famous Colosseum of Rome.

Where on Ea

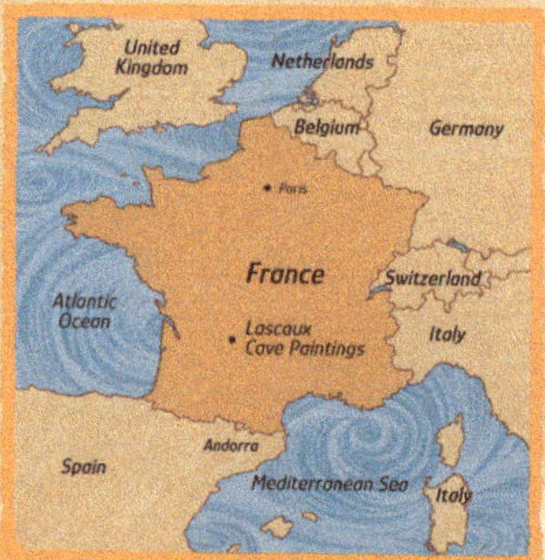

1 Lascaux Cave Paintings, circa 14,000 BCE (page 14)

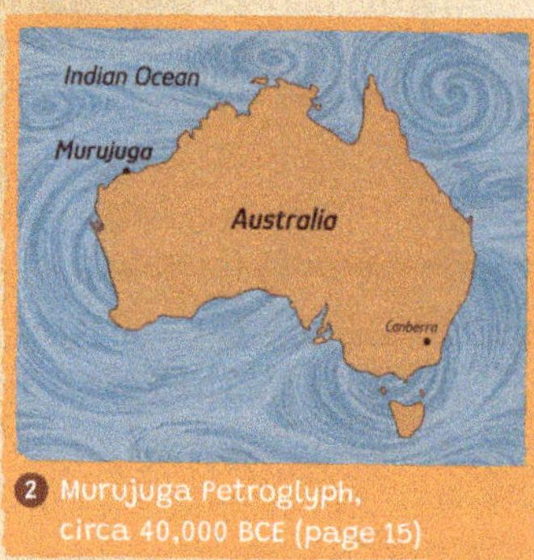

2 Murujuga Petroglyph, circa 40,000 BCE (page 15)

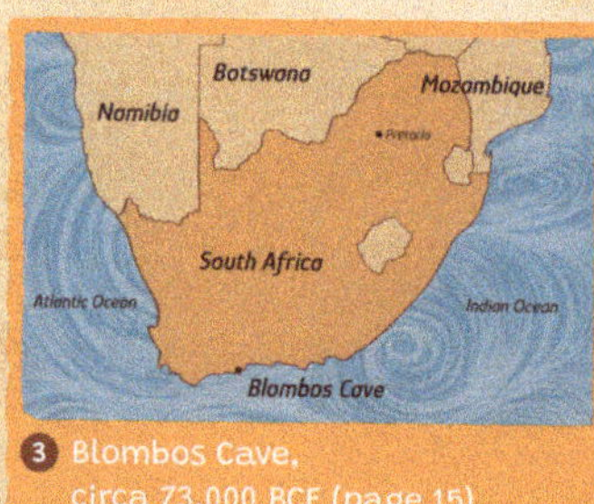

3 Blombos Cave, circa 73,000 BCE (page 15)

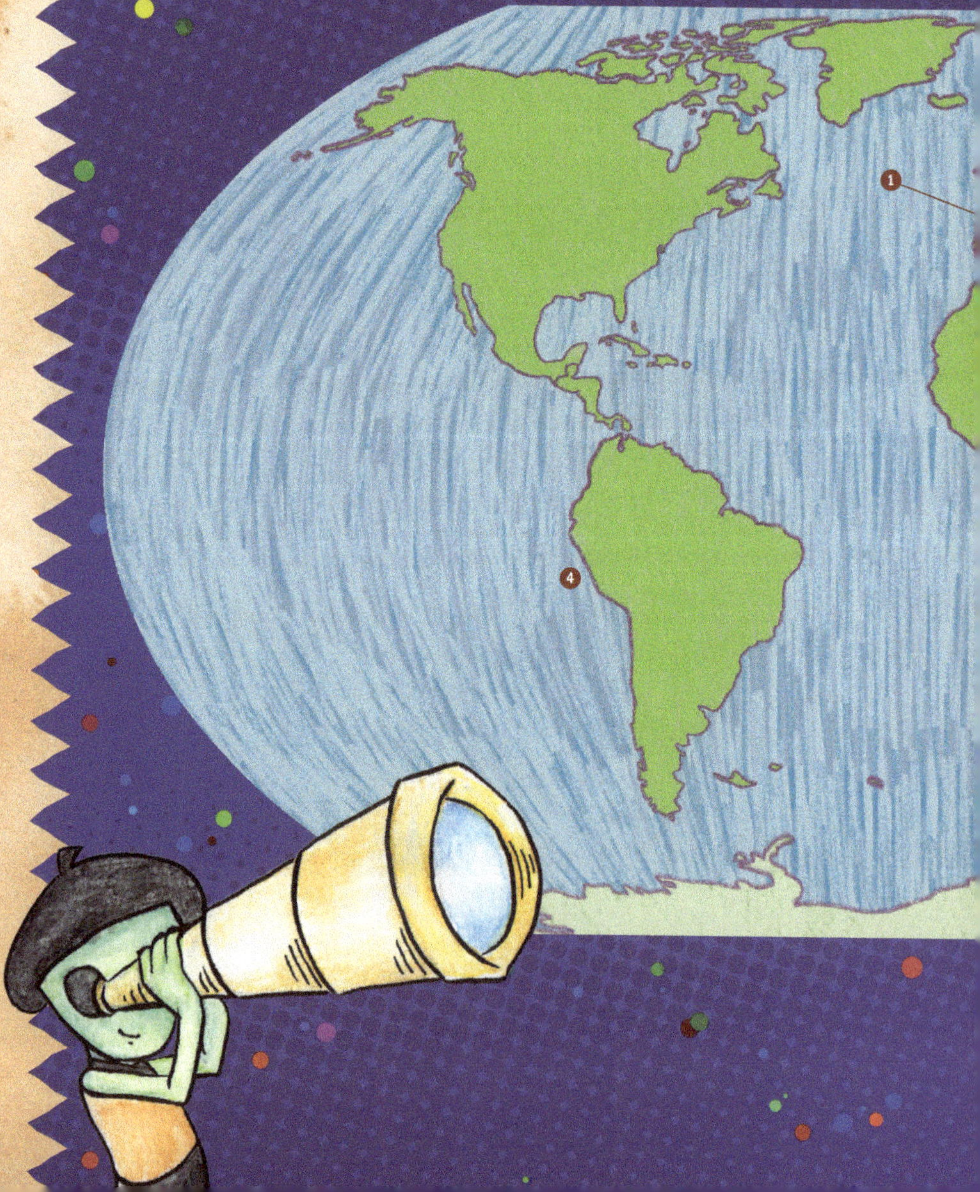

th are We?

Maps: Prehistoric and Ancient Art

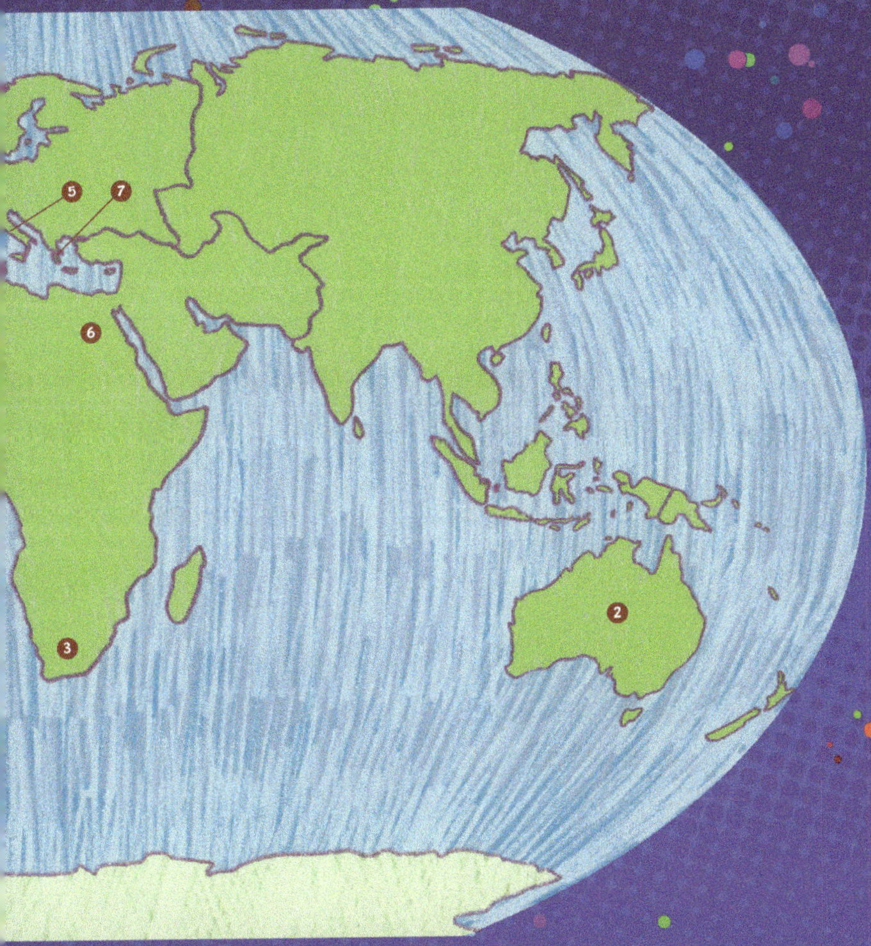

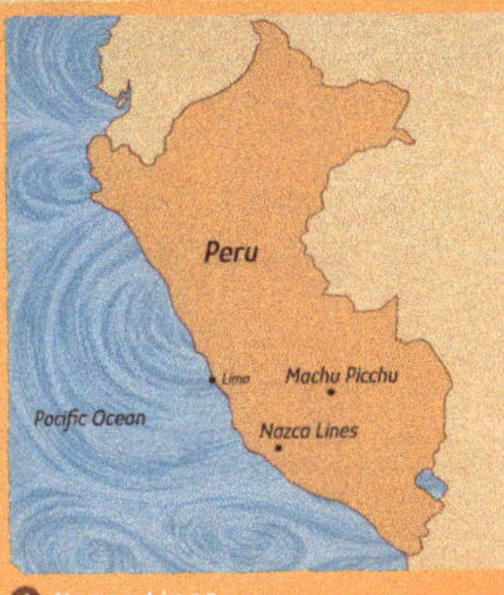

4 Nazca Lines,
circa 200 BCE – 500 CE (page 16)

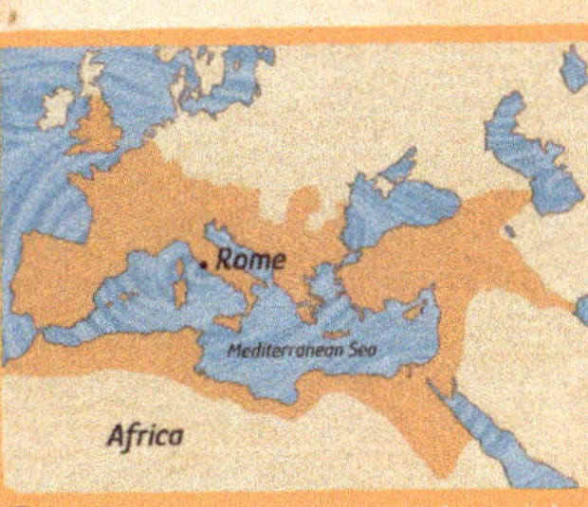

5 Roman Republic, 509 – 27 BCE (page 26)

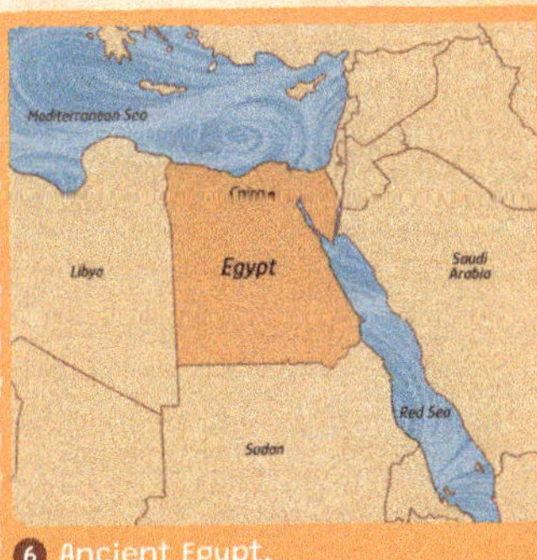

6 Ancient Egypt,
2649 BCE – 1070 BCE (page 18)

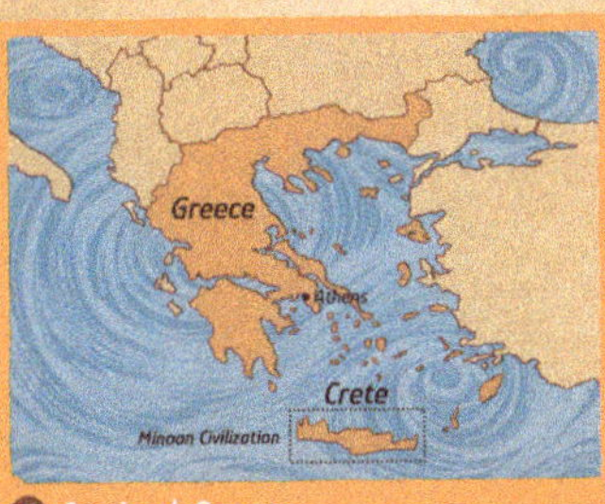

7 Ancient Greece
circa 1100 BCE – 330 CE (page 24)

Art from around 300 - 1500

Byzantine Art

In the year 330 CE, a Roman Emperor named Constantine I, also known as Constantine the Great, made a big decision that would change how art was made in the Roman Empire. Constantine I moved the capital city of the Roman Empire to a place called Byzantium, which was later renamed Constantinople. Since it sat on the only water where ships could pass from the Mediterranean into the Black Sea, Constantinople was a great city for people from different parts of the world to meet and trade.

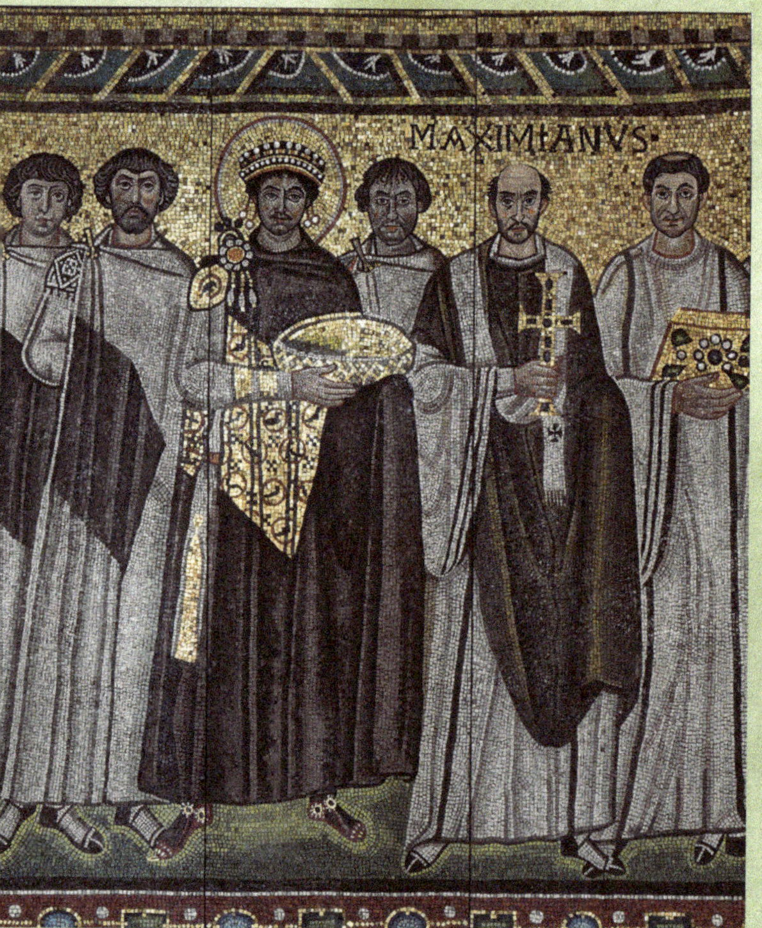

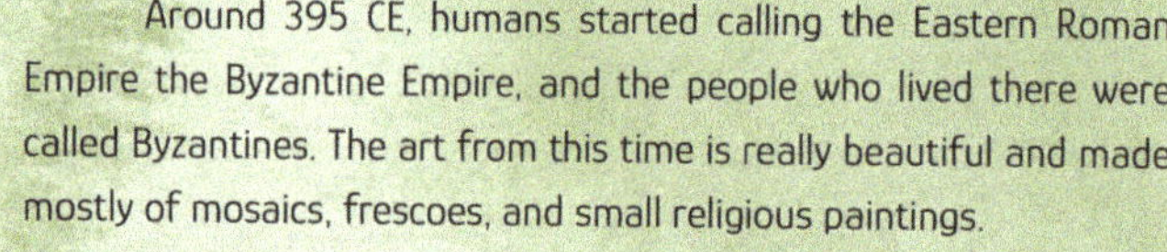

Around 395 CE, humans started calling the Eastern Roman Empire the Byzantine Empire, and the people who lived there were called Byzantines. The art from this time is really beautiful and made mostly of mosaics, frescoes, and small religious paintings.

Byzantine artists used a lot of gold and bright colors, which made artworks look very shiny. They also liked to use symbols and patterns. Some of the artworks tell stories from the Bible or show important people from the Byzantine Empire.

Their sense of spirituality also went hand in hand with a sense of order, and they achieved this by using geometry and math. Even so, their paintings were bidimensional, meaning they hardly had any depth.

Byzantine architecture was astounding! They would calculate how natural light entered a church when designing it and use colors that would be enhanced with the light that shined through, especially earthy tones and gold. By pairing beautiful colors with light, Byzantine architects created a sense of spiritual awe.

Speaking of light, let's see how gold was used in Byzantine art.

Mosaic of Justinian I, 548 CE

Emperor Justinian I was portrayed in this mosaic with a golden halo over his head as a sign of his connection to God. It is currently in the Basilica of San Vitale, Ravenna, Italy.

Byzantine mosaics were created with thousands of small pieces of precious stones, glass, marble, and pearls. They would also coat mosaics with gold and silver.

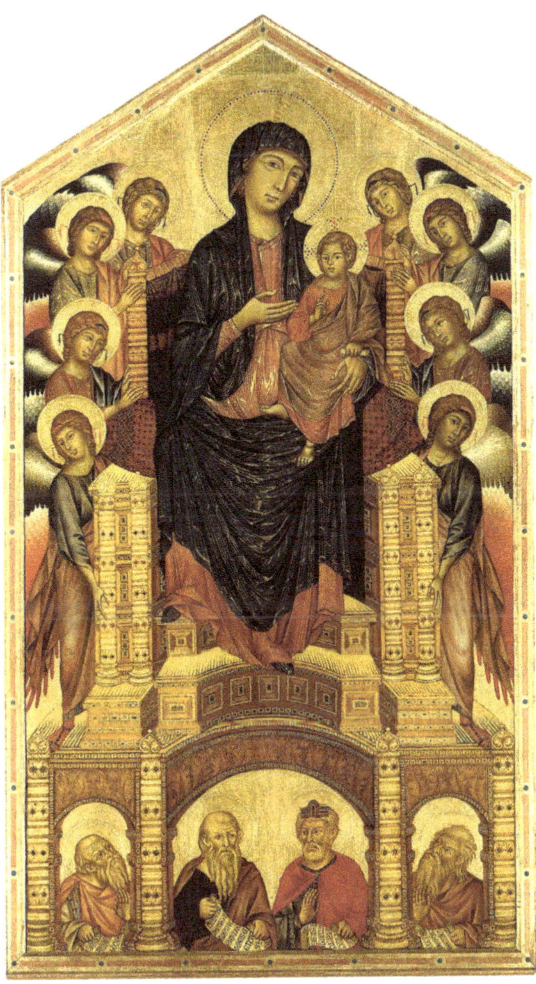

Giovanni Cimabue
Majesty of the Holy Trinity, circa 1280 CE

Christ Pantocrator, 1180 – 1190 CE

Located in modern-day Sicily, Christ Pantocrator is a massive mosaic and a beautiful example of Byzantine art created from 1180 to 1190 CE.

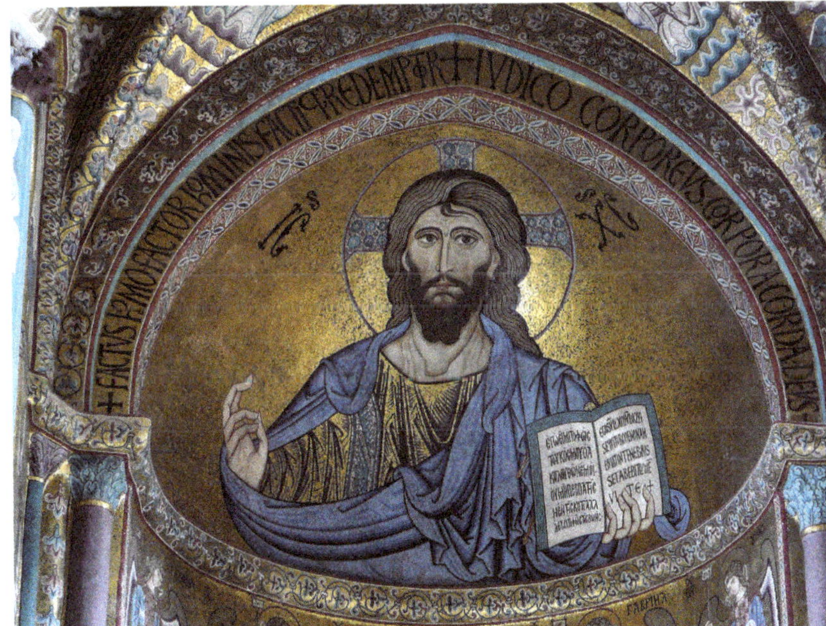

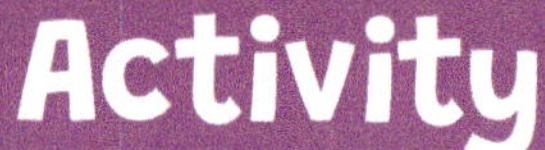

Activity

Create a Paper Mosaic

Byzantine mosaics were created with precious gems and stones, but we can make our own mosaic out of paper. Let's do it together!

What you'll need:

- **Construction paper of various colors**
- **White paper**
- **Pencil**
- **Scissors**
- **Glue**

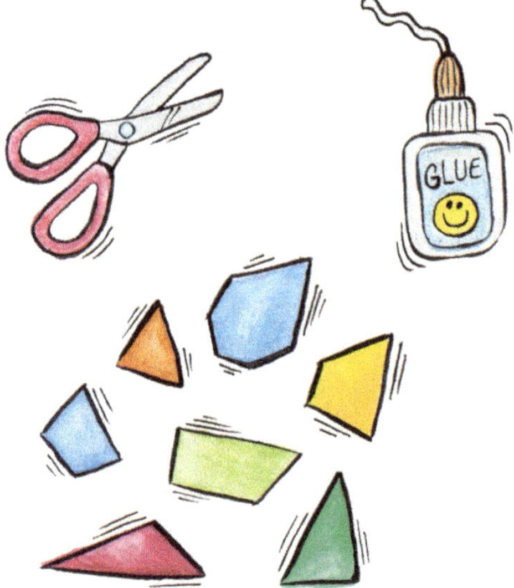

How to create your mosaic:

1 To start this activity, choose what subject you wish to draw. It can be your beloved pet, your friends and family, or even your favorite activity. Create a sketch of it on your white sheet of paper.

2 After completing your sketch, define what colors you will use and pick out the construction paper with these colors. Using your scissors, cut out small irregular shapes of each color. You can cut them randomly as triangles and squares without needing to measure each one.

3 Lastly, glue the pieces of construction paper over your drawing and fill in the entire page.

4 If you feel inspired by Byzantine art and want to give your mosaic extra flare, use metallic or gold paper!

West African Art

Have you ever wondered what was going on in Africa during what you humans call the Middle Ages? Let's blast off to Western Africa and find out!

The first sculpture found on African land was created way back in 500 BCE, many years before the Middle Ages even began when the Nok culture was transitioning from the Stone Age to the Iron Age. Most of their sculptures used ceramic and iron to depict human faces and bodies. Not much is known about why these works of art were created.

Unlike other cultures during the Middle Ages, West African societies usually held women, rather than men, responsible for creating art, such as textiles, pottery, and sculpture. Also, families usually inherited things and artistic talents from the mother's side. This is different from Europe and other places during the Middle Ages, where things would usually be inherited through the father's side.

The city of Ife in what is now South-West Nigeria was quite prosperous from the 11th century until the 15th century. Along with the region's growing agriculture, the production of metal sculptures and glass beads grew.

Nok sculpture,
circa 500 BCE – 200 CE, Nigeria

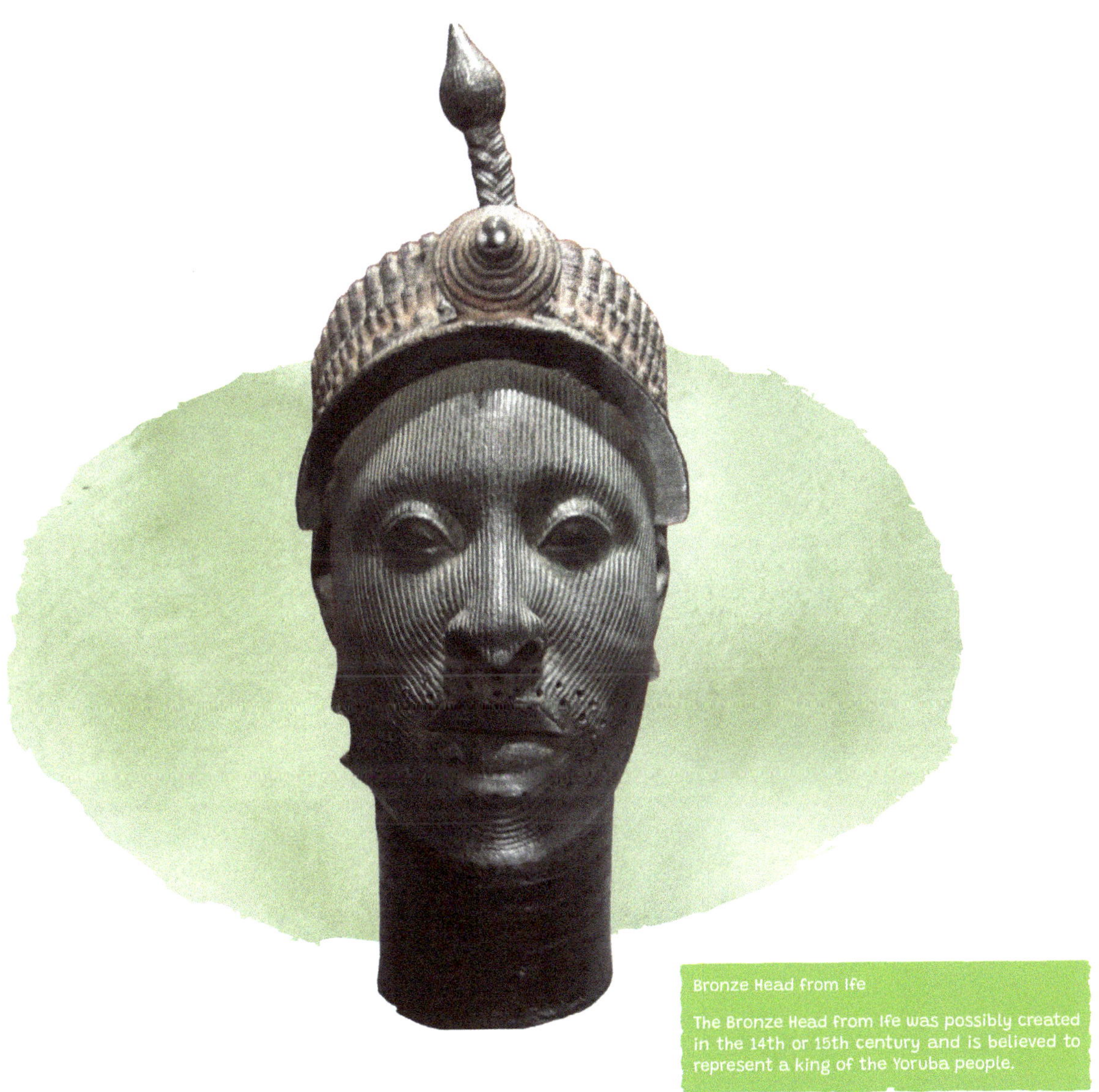

Bronze Head from Ife

The Bronze Head from Ife was possibly created in the 14th or 15th century and is believed to represent a king of the Yoruba people.

Hindu Art

Let us take a quick trip to India and check out what was happening over there!

The Gupta Empire, which existed in India from around 320 CE to 550 CE, is considered the Golden Age of India because it was a time of great cultural and economic prosperity. During this period, India saw big advances in science, math, literature, art and architecture. Like in other cultures, art and religion were closely related, and there were many amazing sculptures of Hindu gods.

Picture of Shiva Nataraja Sculpture, circa 11th century

Created around the 11th century, this bronze sculpture represents Shiva, the god of destruction and reconstruction. Shiva was thought to have many forms, and this sculpture shows him in the form of Nataraja, which means "the Lord of Dance".

Buddhist Art

Buddhist art focuses on the teachings of Buddhism, which began in the 5th century BCE and spread throughout most of Asia.

One of the most important forms of Buddhist art is sculpture. Buddhist sculptures typically depict the Buddha himself along with figures called bodhisattvas, arhats, and deities. These sculptures can be made from stone, bronze, or wood.

Buddhist art also includes paintings, murals and frescoes. These artworks can be found in temples and monasteries, and often portray scenes from the life of the Buddha or other important figures in Buddhism. They also symbolize Buddhist concepts like karma and rebirth.

Mandalas are also important in Buddhist art. They are geometric patterns made with sand, stone, or paper. The act of creating a mandala can be considered a form of meditation. After being carefully created, mandalas are gently destroyed to symbolize that all things are temporary.

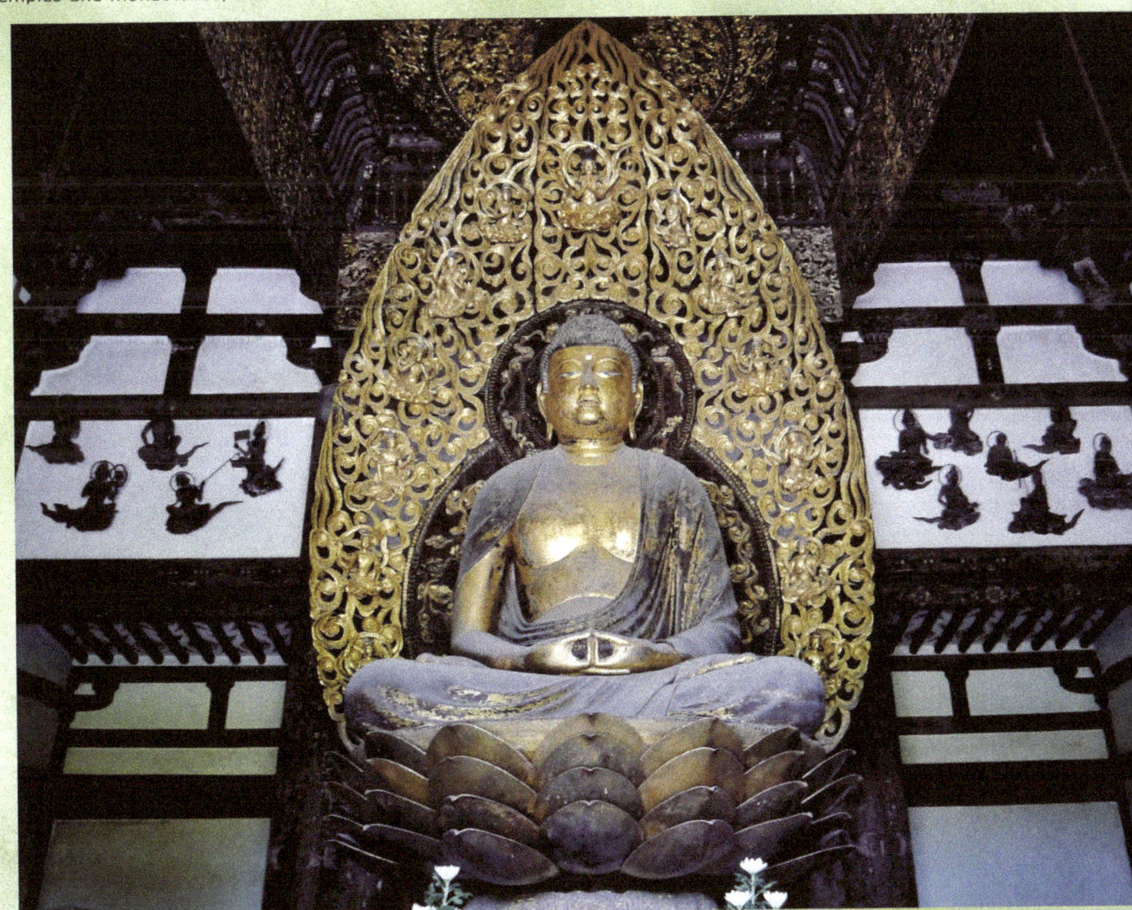

Amitābha in Byōdō-in temple by Jōchō, 1053 CE

Ajanta Caves

The Ajanta Caves are a series of 29 Buddhist cave monuments in India. They were built around 2000 years ago and include a collection of beautiful paintings and sculptures that portray Buddha's life and other important moments in Buddhist history. Today, the Ajanta Caves are recognized as a UNESCO World Heritage site and are an important historical landmark in India.

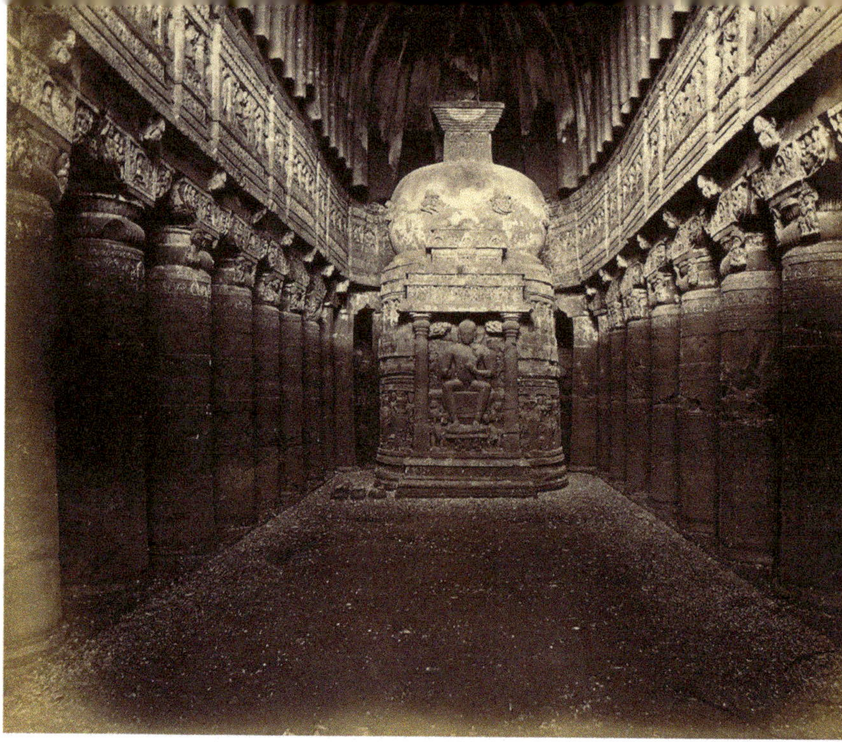

Ajanta Caves, India, circa 200 BCE - 480 CE

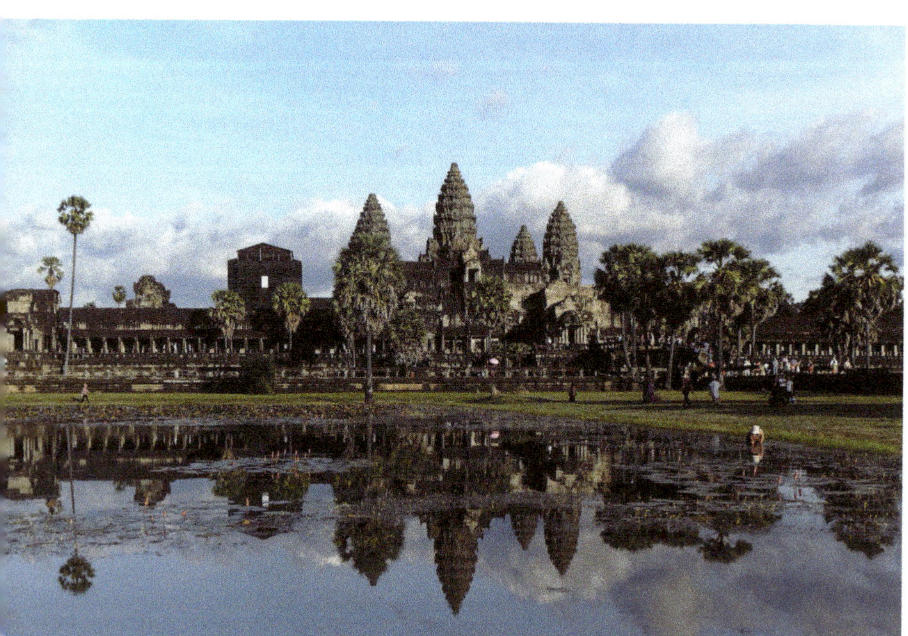

Angkor Wat

Angkor Wat is a temple complex in Cambodia that was originally built as a Hindu temple during the 12th century. Later transformed into a Buddhist temple, Angkor Wat is renowned for its intricate carvings and impressive architecture. Its big towers symbolize Mount Meru, a sacred mountain in Hinduism.

Angkor Wat, Cambodia, circa 1150 CE

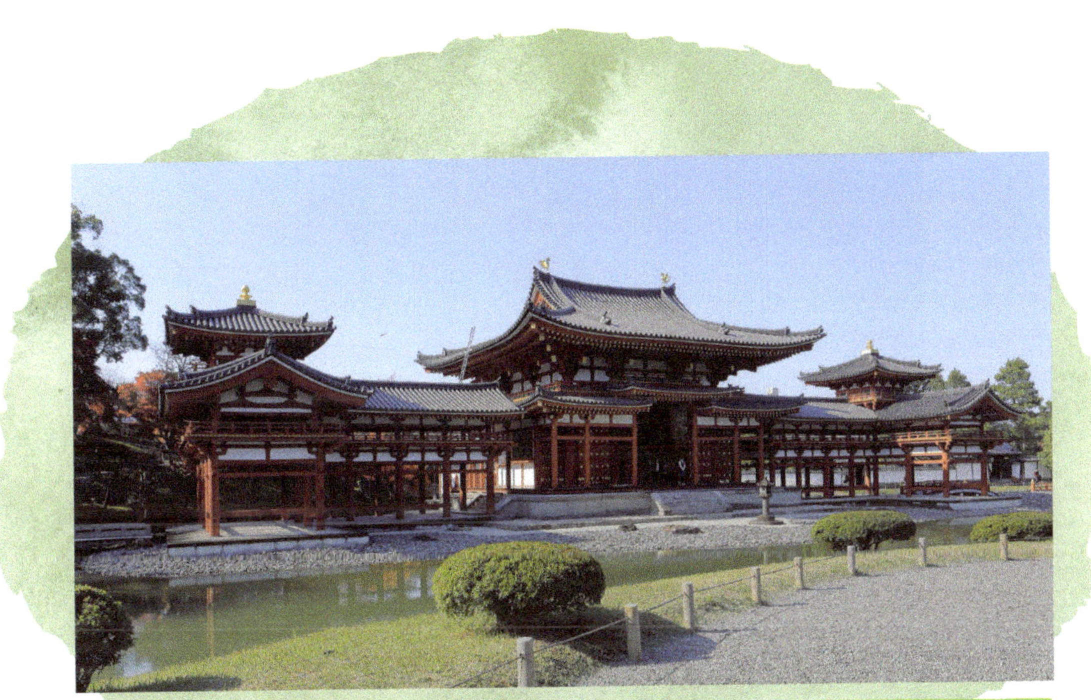

Temple of Equality, 998 - 1052 CE

The Temple of Equality in Uji, Japan, is an impressive example of both Buddhist symbolism and traditional Japanese architecture. Its most iconic structure, the Phoenix Hall, is beautifully simple, symmetrical, and elegant.

Islamic Art

MUSLIM artists and craftsmen were driven by their faith and culture to create art. Islamic art is renowned for its patterns, shapes, vibrant colors, and use of precious gems.

Islamic art is also known for calligraphy, or beautiful handwriting. Calligraphy was used to decorate books, manuscripts, pottery and textiles. Well-known calligraphers were Ibn Muqla, Ibn al Bawwab, and Yaqut al Musta'simi.

Islamic architecture embraced domes, arches, and intricate patterns. Some great examples include the Alhambra in Spain and the Great Mosque of Damascus in Syria.

Interior of the Great Mosque of Damascus, Syria, circa 715 CE

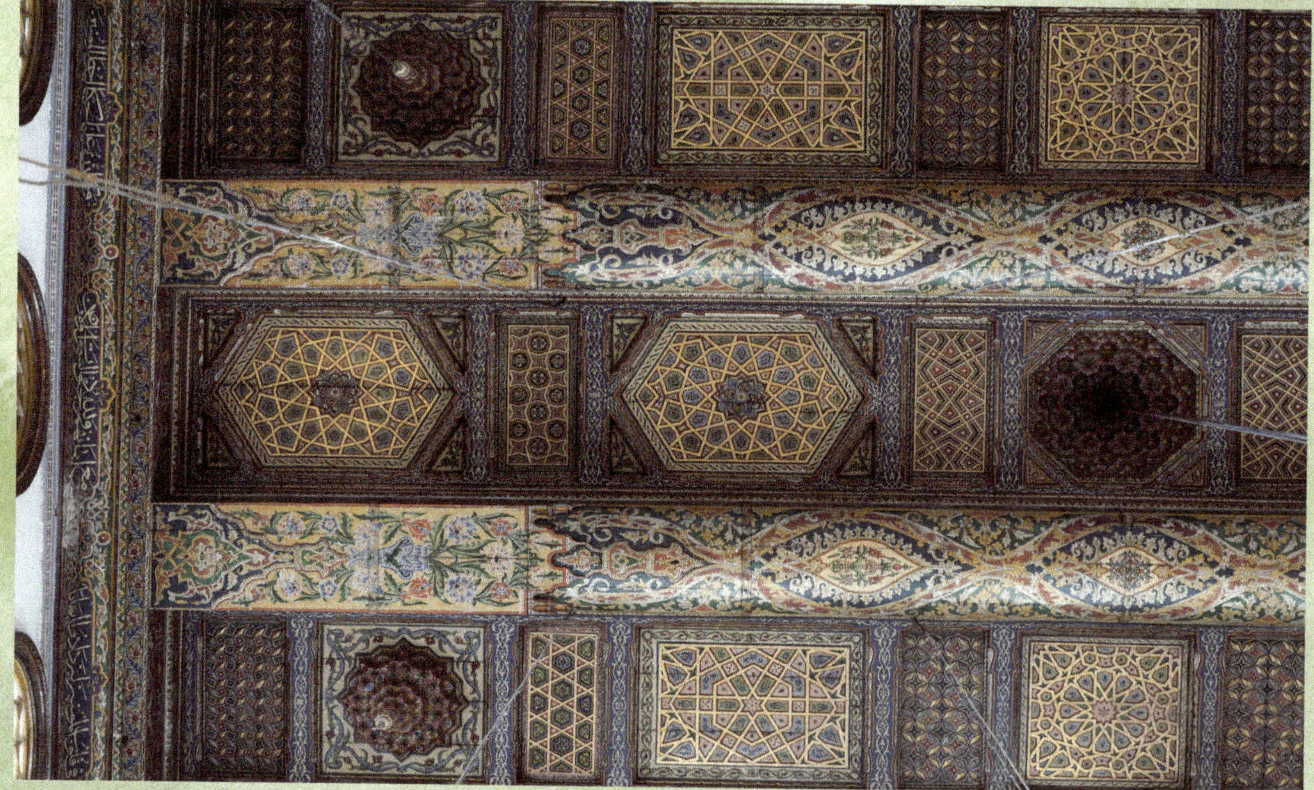

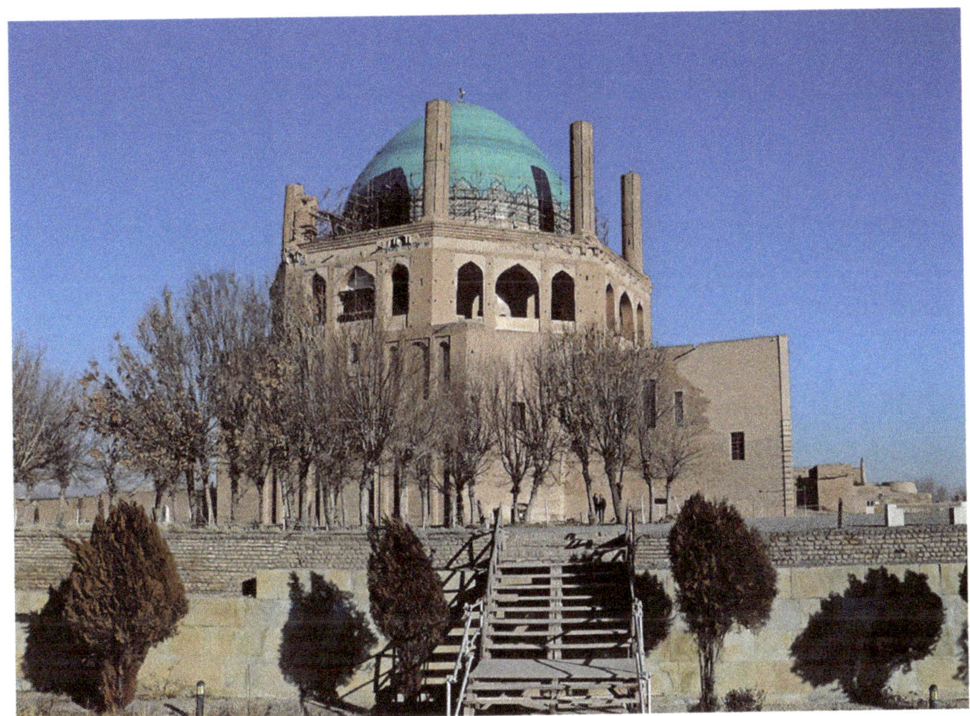

Dome of Soltaniyeh in Soltaniyeh city, Iran, 1302 – 1312 CE

Hagia Sophia

The Hagia Sophia is another great example. It was originally built as a church by the Byzantine Emperor Justinian I in 537 CE in Turkey. When the Ottoman Empire conquered it in 1453, they turned it into a mosque. Renowned for its size, huge dome, mosaics, and calligraphy, the Hagia Sophia is a wonderful symbol of Islamic architecture.

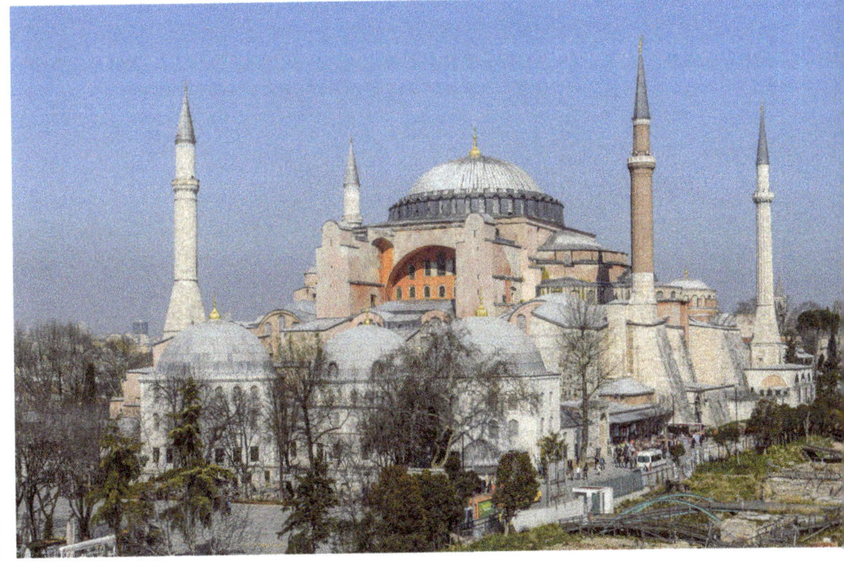

Hagia Sophia, 537 CE

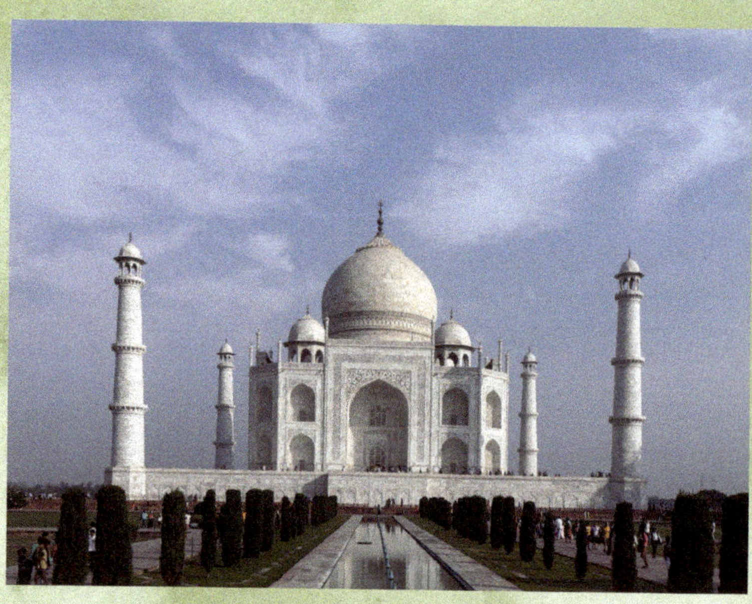

Taj Mahal

The Taj Mahal was built by the Mughal Emperor, Shah Jahan. He intended it to be a tomb for his wife, Mumtaz Mahal, after she passed away. Construction began in 1632 and involved around 20,000 artisans!

Amazingly, the Taj Mahal changes its appearance depending on the weather and time of day. At dawn it has a shade of pink, and in the evening it glows gently like the setting sun. At night, countless lamps and candles light up its interior, creating a warm glow from within.

Crafted entirely from marble, the Taj Mahal has a dome that stands over 70 feet tall! The Taj Mahal is well known for pietra dura, a technique that involves cutting and fitting together precious stones to make beautiful patterns. Pietra dura was used to create the floral designs and calligraphy you can find throughout the monument.

Symmetry and balance play an important role in the architecture of the Taj Mahal. Each side of the building mirrors the other, and its reflection in the surrounding water creates a sense of balance and harmony.

Today, the Taj Mahal is regarded as an architectural wonder around the world and attracts millions of visitors every year!

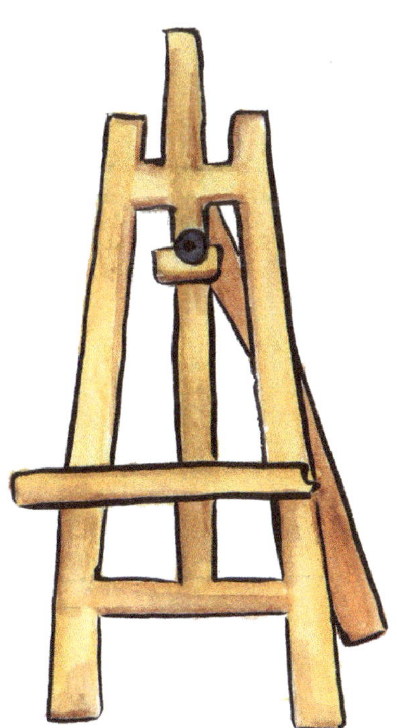

Pre-Columbian Art

I would love to show you the Americas and what kind of art they made by the year 1200 CE. Come on, my fellow human friends, let's go!

I bet you know who that Christopher Columbus fellow was, right? And how he traveled to America while looking for India in 1492? Well, the Pre-Columbian period was before he came along, when many civilizations flourished in North, South, and Central America.

Some of Earth's most magnificent civilizations existed during this time, like the Inca Empire located in modern-day Peru and the Aztecs from Mexico.

Aztec Sun Stone, circa 1500

The Sun Stone was created around the year 1500 and was probably used for rituals.

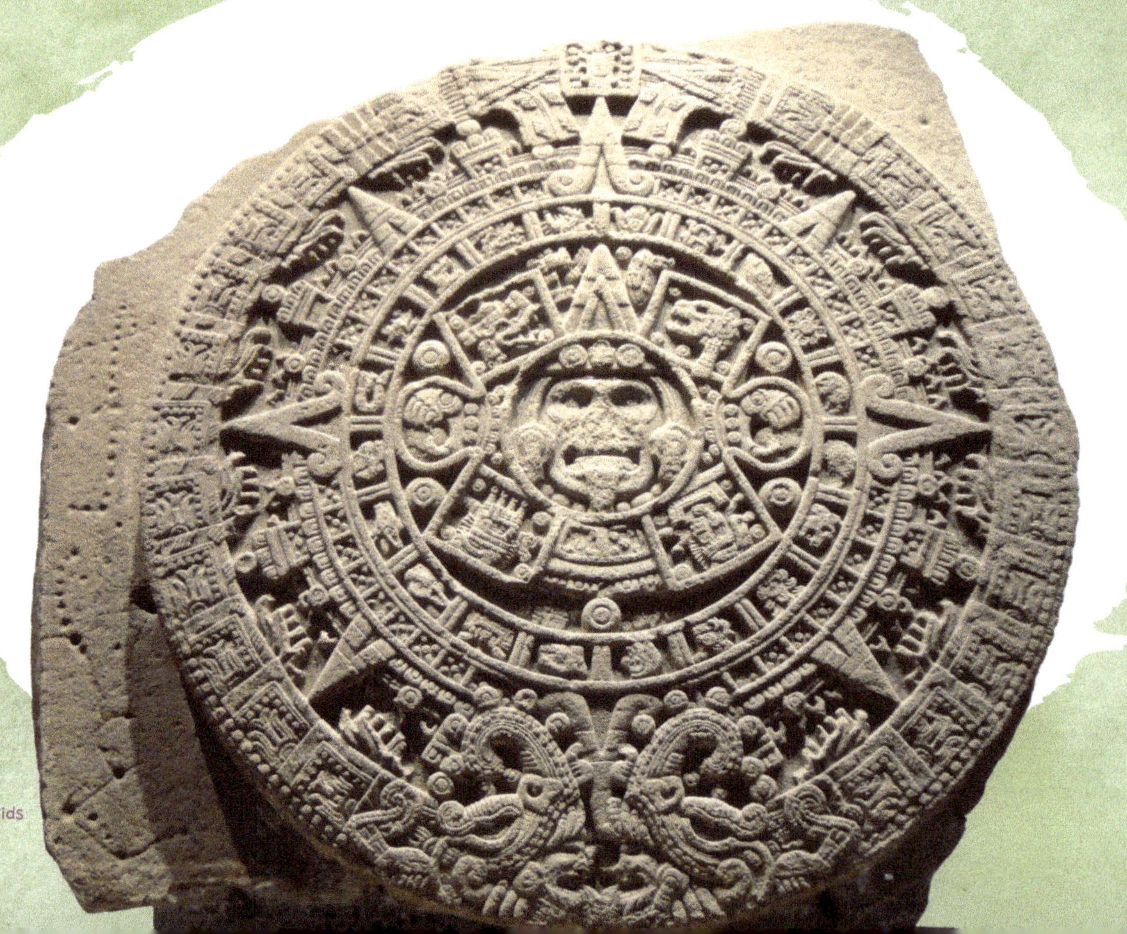

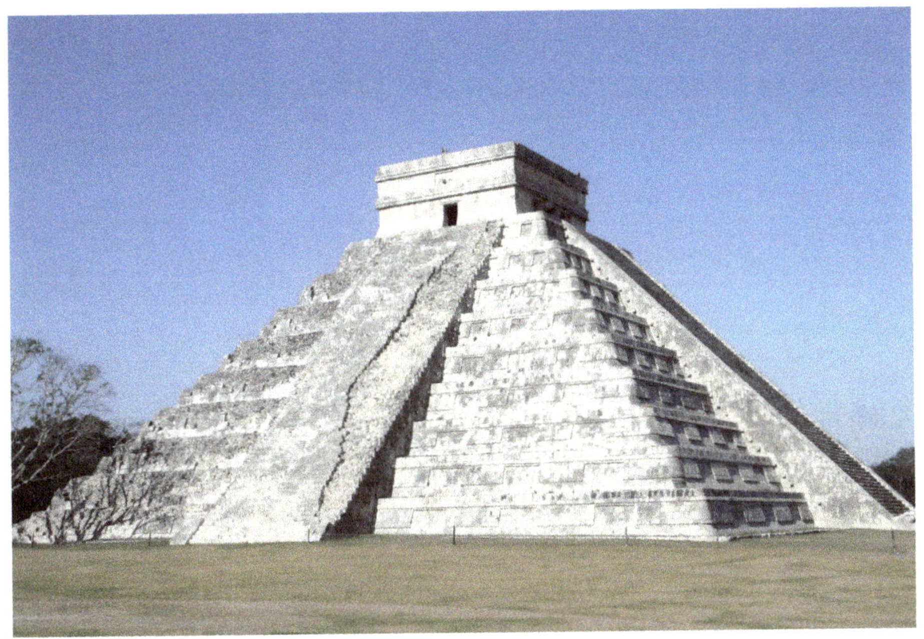

Temple of Kukulcán,
circa 6th – 12th century

Temple of Kukulcán, or El Templo de Kukulcán in Spanish, is a pyramid found in the archeological site called Chichen Itza, in Yucatán, a Mexican state.

Let's talk a bit about the Aztecs, who were made up of many ethnic groups and developed an incredibly unique culture. They created monuments like the pyramids found in Teopanzolco. Aztecs worked with ceramics, sculpture, mosaics, and painting. There were also many elaborate pieces created with feathers and gold.

Aztec art had a lot of religious symbols, and they created interesting calendars that often represented the seasons of the year. The Aztecs believed that the passing of the seasons and certain dates were guided by their gods.

This ceramic, made around 1100 - 1400, is a water vessel.

Activity

Natural prints in clay

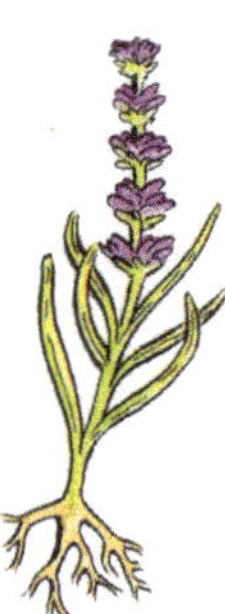

Humans have created works of art with clay ever since ancient times and continue to create things with it to this day. Let's make some clay stamps with natural materials!

What you'll need:

- Polymer clay (or any other non-toxic clay)
- Paper
- Brown paper to cover the table
- Paper towels for cleaning
- Rolling pin
- Natural elements found outside
- A plastic knife

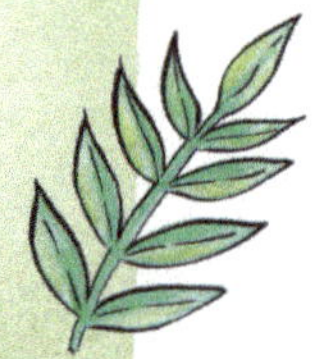

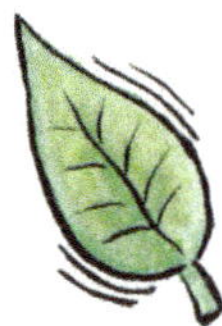

Choose your natural item.

Next, use a rolling pin to gently press your item onto the clay.

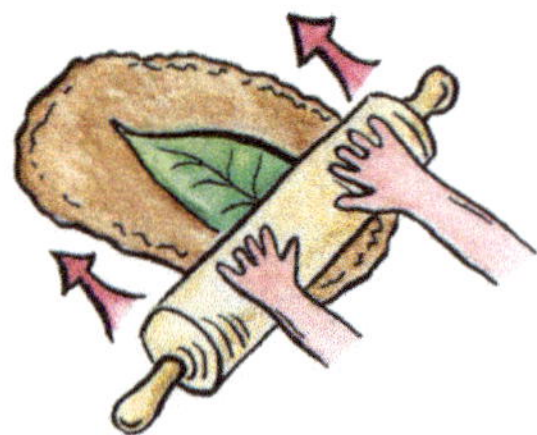

Cut out any uneven edges from your clay print.

How to create your clay print:

1 To start this activity, you'll need to go outside. Find a park or somewhere with plenty of grass and trees. Look around and gather leaves, sticks, pebbles and other natural things you find.

2 Collect a range of items from nature and pay attention to their texture and shape. After you've gathered the items, start working with the clay by squeezing and molding it. This will help soften the clay while removing any air bubbles or pebbles that may be inside.

3 Next, flatten the clay on a table using a pin. Arrange the items you collected on top of the clay and cover them with a piece of paper. Use the pin to press them into the clay.

4 Carefully remove the leaves and twigs from your clay masterpiece. See the results! If needed, remove any excess clay with a plastic knife and help from an adult.

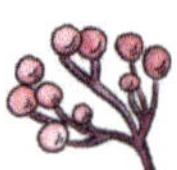

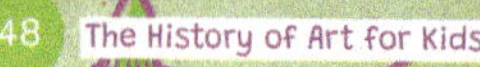

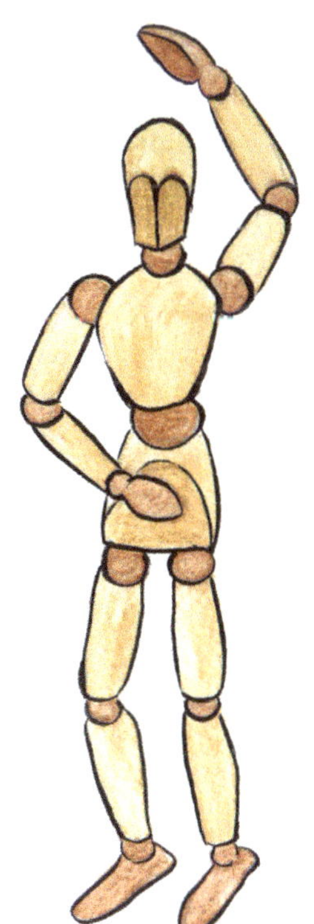

Italian Gothic and International Gothic

WHILE we're still in the Middle Ages, let's stop by Europe again and see what was happening by the 12th century. Let's go, Earthling friends!

From the mid-12th century until the late-14th century, Europe went through what is known as the Gothic period. It was an era filled with creativity and innovation as humans pushed their limits and made breathtaking buildings. Magnificent cathedrals and churches were built with beautiful carvings, sculptures and stained glass windows.

At the beginning of the Italian Gothic period, religious art was still mostly financed by the Catholic Church, which supported artists who made paintings about Christianity. Compared to earlier Byzantine art, Gothic paintings were more detailed and lifelike.

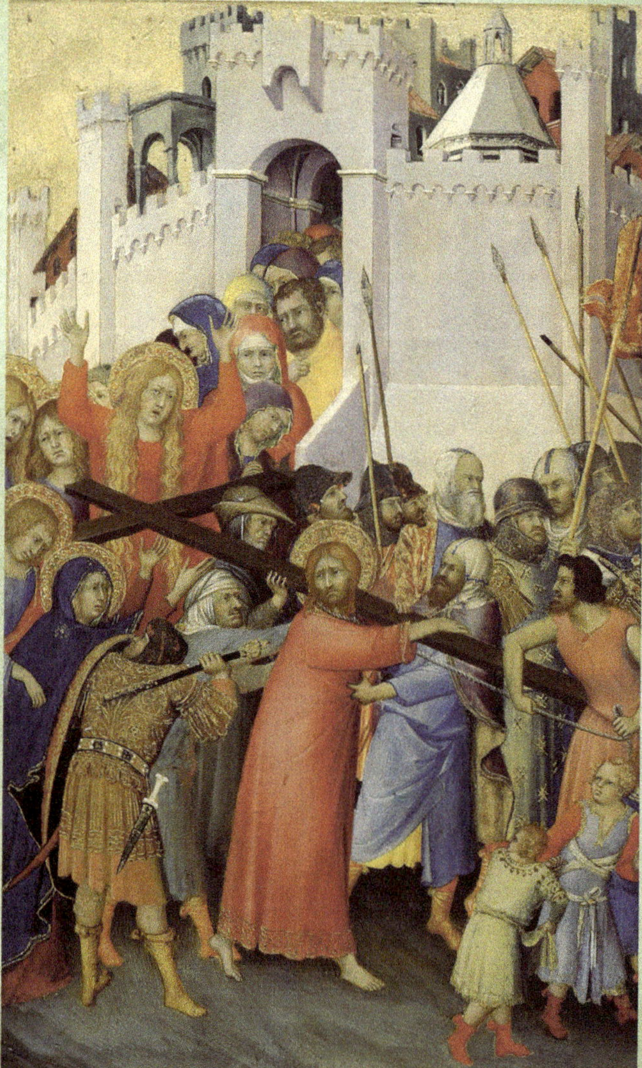

Simone Martini
The Carrying of the Cross, 1335
Tempera on wood

By the end of the 14th century, the Gothic style spread through Europe and became even more detailed and sophisticated. Artists in Italy, France, Austria, and England all produced beautiful Gothic art, which was often ornamented with gold and bright colors.

Gentile da Fabriano
The Adoration of the Magi, 1423
Tempera on panel

The altarpiece *The Adoration of the Magi* was painted by Gentile da Fabriano in 1423 and is a beautiful example of how storytelling was represented in Gothic painting.

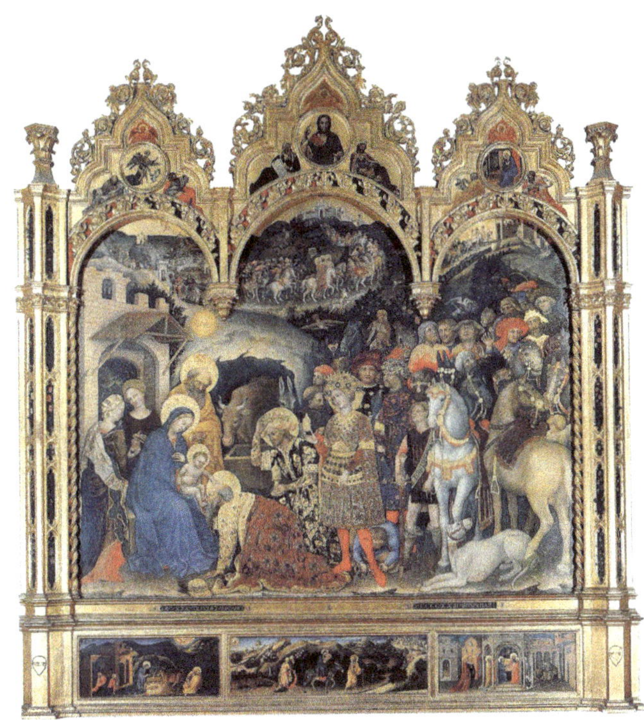

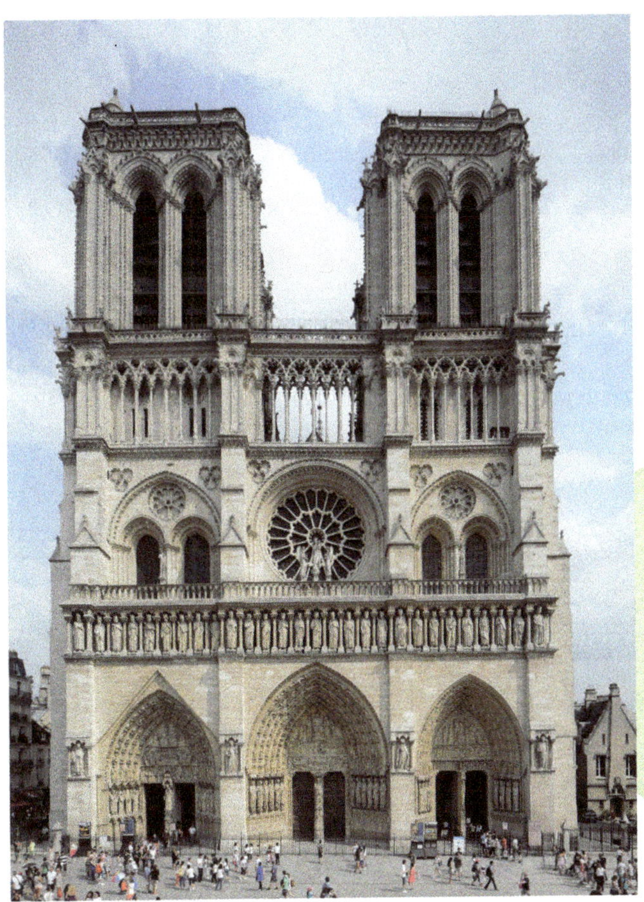

One of the most fantastic parts of Gothic art was the architecture. Gothic churches featured pointed arches, beautiful stained glass windows, and a lot of elaborate details.

Notre-Dame de Paris, 1163

The Notre-Dame de Paris is an amazing example of a church with Gothic elements. Sadly, a fire destroyed part of its roof in 2019.

Chinese Art: Ming Dynasty

Do you know what Chinese artists were creating while European artists were creating Gothic art? Let's check it out!

The Ming Dynasty was a prosperous period for China, as their troops defeated the Yuan Dynasty in 1368, ending Mongol control over their land. Many palaces, temples, and tombs were built during the Ming Dynasty.

Classic painting techniques were taken to a new level during the Ming Dynasty. Paintings began to use more color and calligraphy.

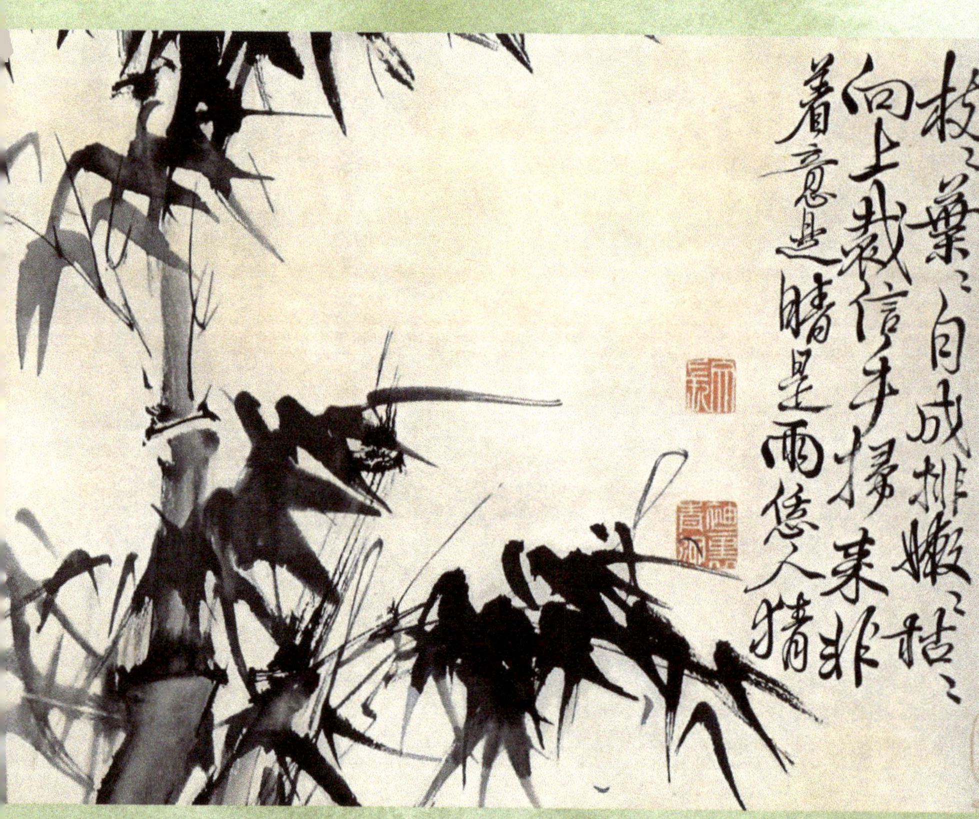

Xu Wei
Bamboo, circa 1540
Ink on panel

The painting *Bamboo* was painted with ink on paper around 1540 by Xu Wei. His use of loose brushstrokes beautifully combines the natural elements with the calligraphy in this piece.

China was famous for porcelain, which is a ceramic material made of white clay and other mixtures that hardens into a fine glass-type material when heated. Porcelain was upgraded considerably during this period, and it was one of the main products China traded with other countries.

In fact, China was so famous for porcelain that people started calling it "china" in English! So, if you hear someone say "china" or "fine china", they might be talking about porcelain from China.

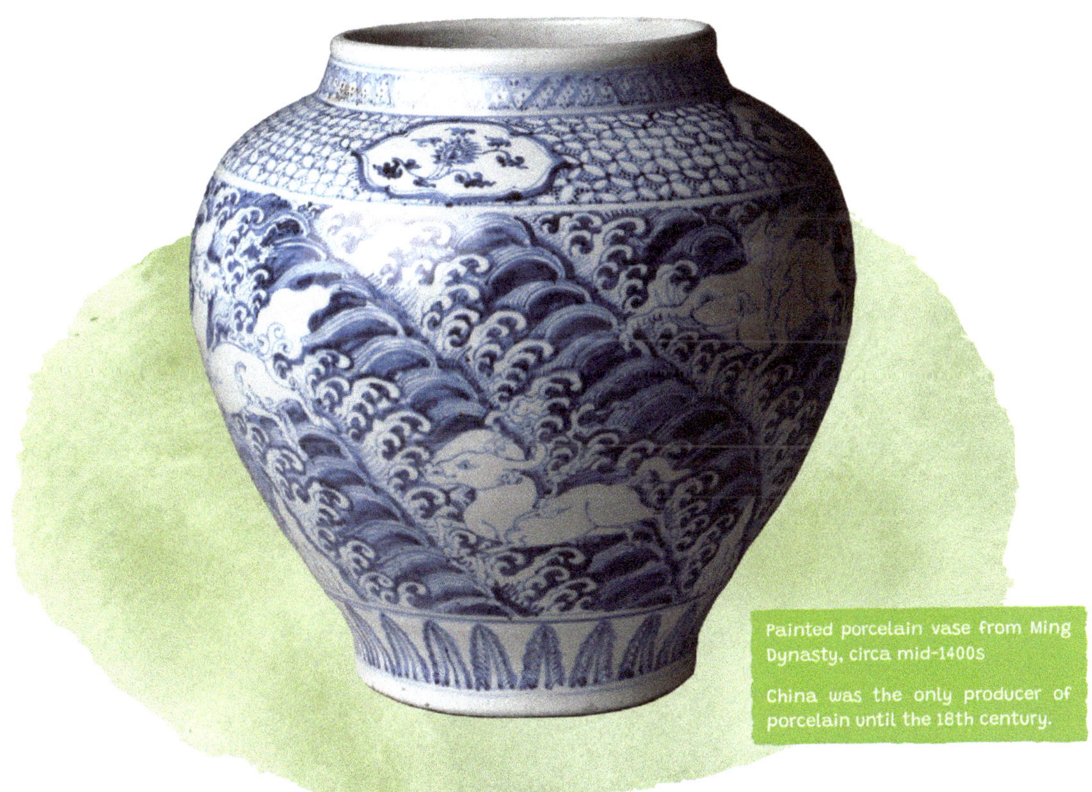

Painted porcelain vase from Ming Dynasty, circa mid-1400s

China was the only producer of porcelain until the 18th century.

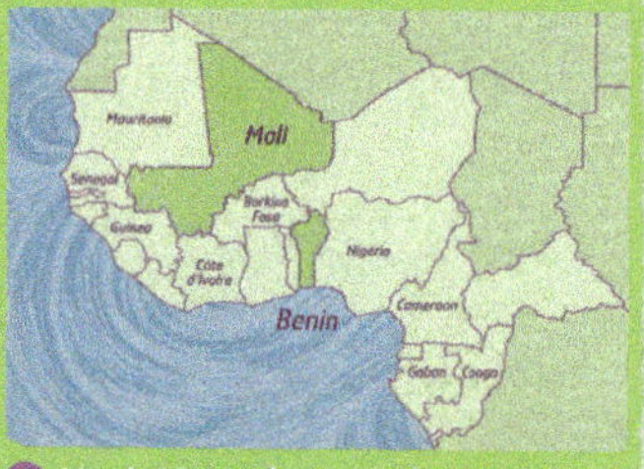

1 West Africa (page 36)

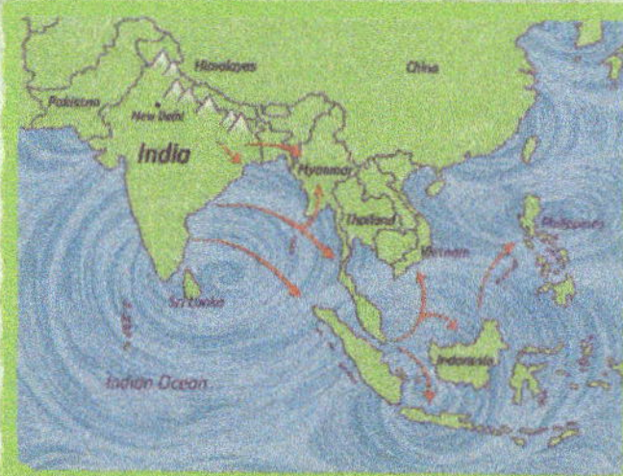

2 Spread of Hinduism (page 38)

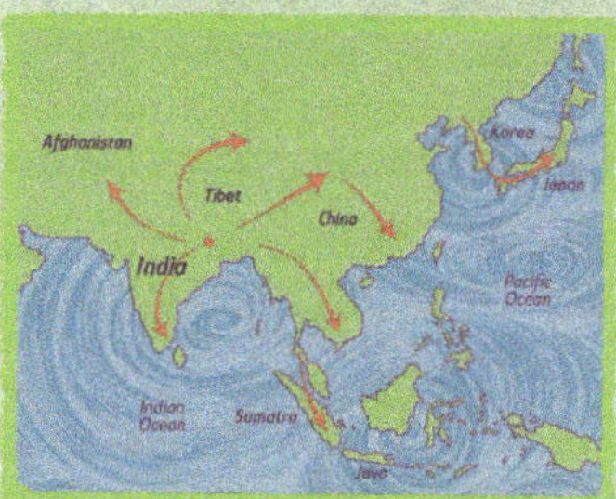

3 Spread of Buddhism (page 39)

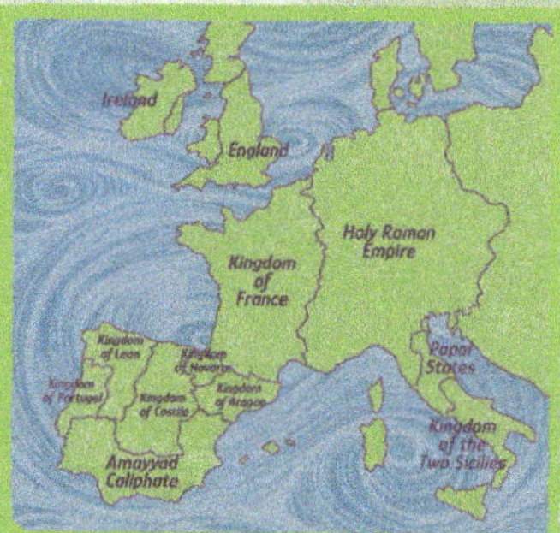

4 Gothic Europe, 1200s CE (page 50)

Where on Ea

th are We?

Maps: Art from around 300 –1500

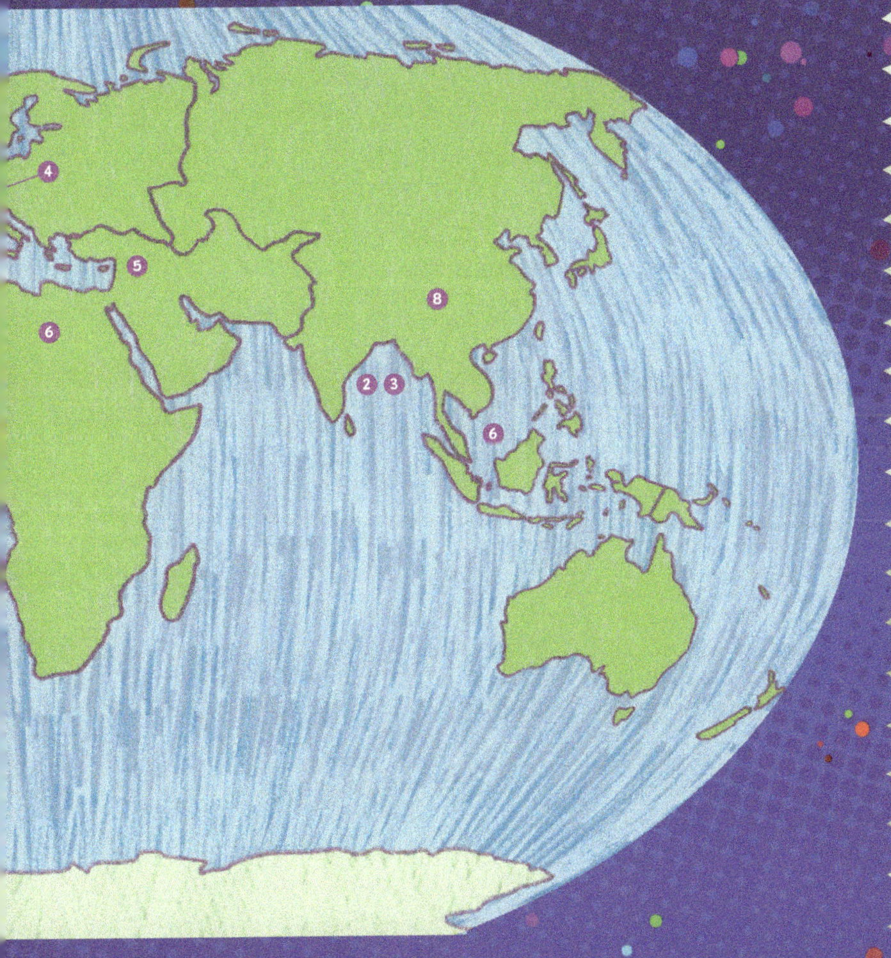

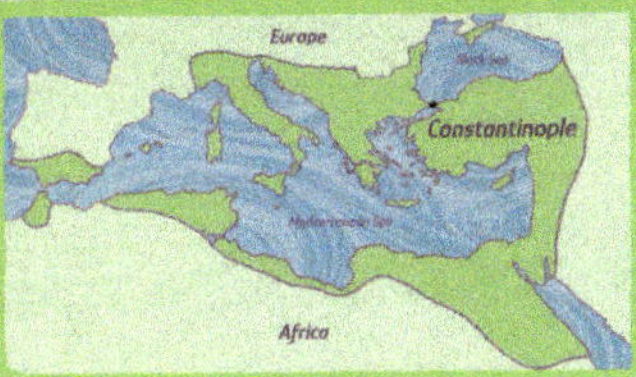

5 Byzantine Empire, 500s CE (page 32)

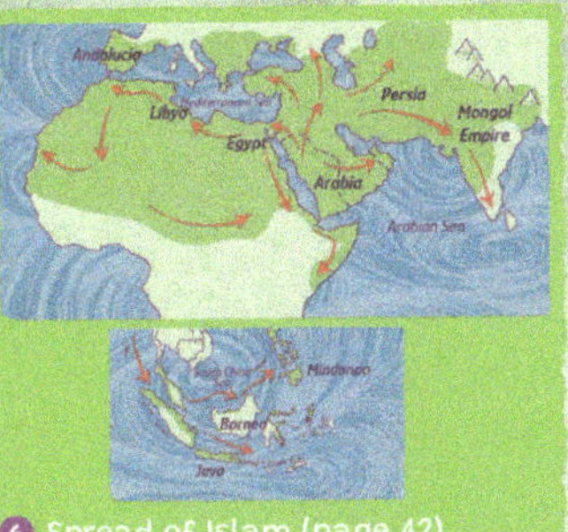

6 Spread of Islam (page 42)

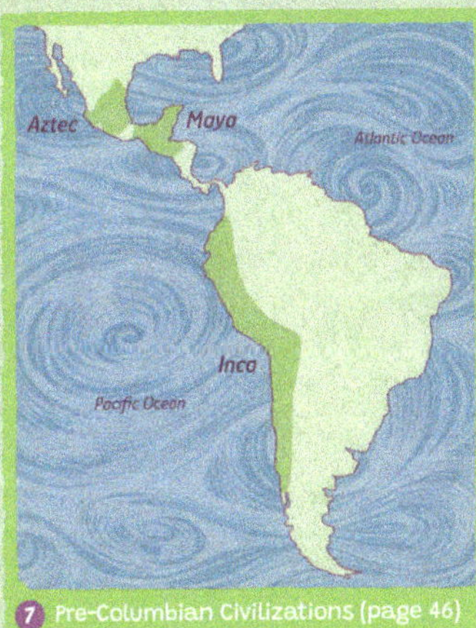

7 Pre-Columbian Civilizations (page 46)

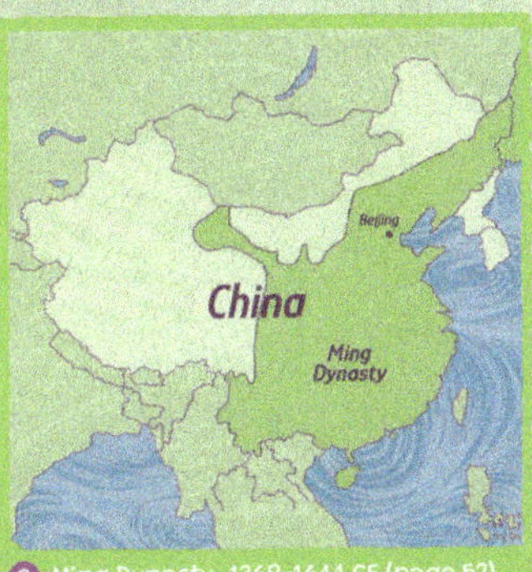

8 Ming Dynasty, 1368–1644 CE (page 52)

Art from around 1400 - 1600

Flemish Gothic

Let's leap from the Medieval period to the 15th century, when Flemish Gothic architecture first emerged in Flanders, which is located in parts of modern-day Belgium and Luxembourg.

During this period, also known as late Gothic, artists from across Europe flocked to Flanders, attracted by the lively art scene in the region. Late Gothic artists did not want to continue the elegant and ornate style of International Gothic art. Instead, they focused on more realistic styles. Although both movements have similar names - International Gothic and Flemish Gothic - they were pretty different movements.

Flemish art was heavily influenced by the Renaissance (page 60), which was taking place in Italy during the same time period. However, unlike the Italians, Flemish artists did not rely on math to compose their paintings or create the illusion of depth. Instead, they just used their instincts.

Clergy and nobility weren't the only ones who purchased art - religious guilds and fraternities did as well.

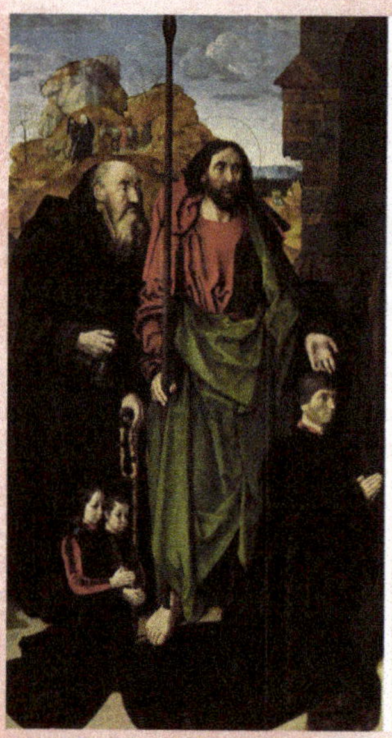
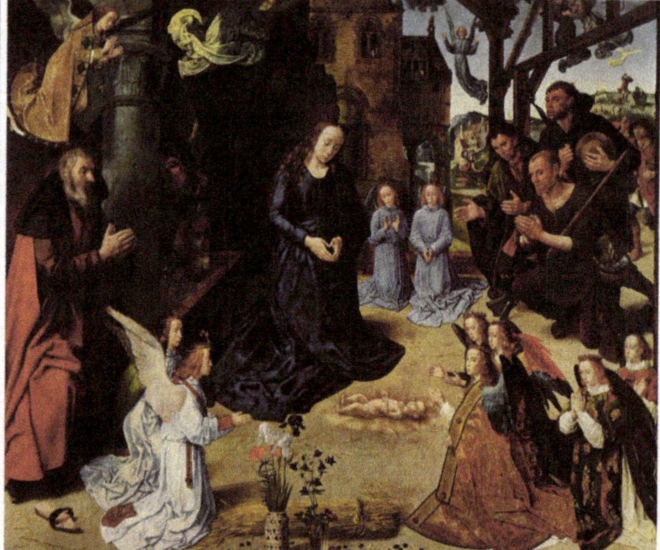
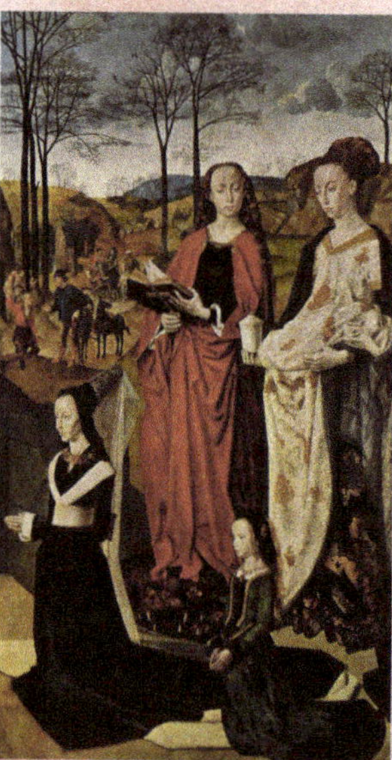

Did you know that a triptych is a painting made of three parts? This format became popular among religious artworks because it worked very well as altarpieces in churches and was a great way to tell a story. Traditional triptych artworks will often feature a main painting in the middle with two other paintings on each side. The two side paintings measure about half of the central painting, allowing them to close evenly like closet doors.

Hugo Van Der Goes
The Portinari Triptych, 1475 – 1478
Oil on wood

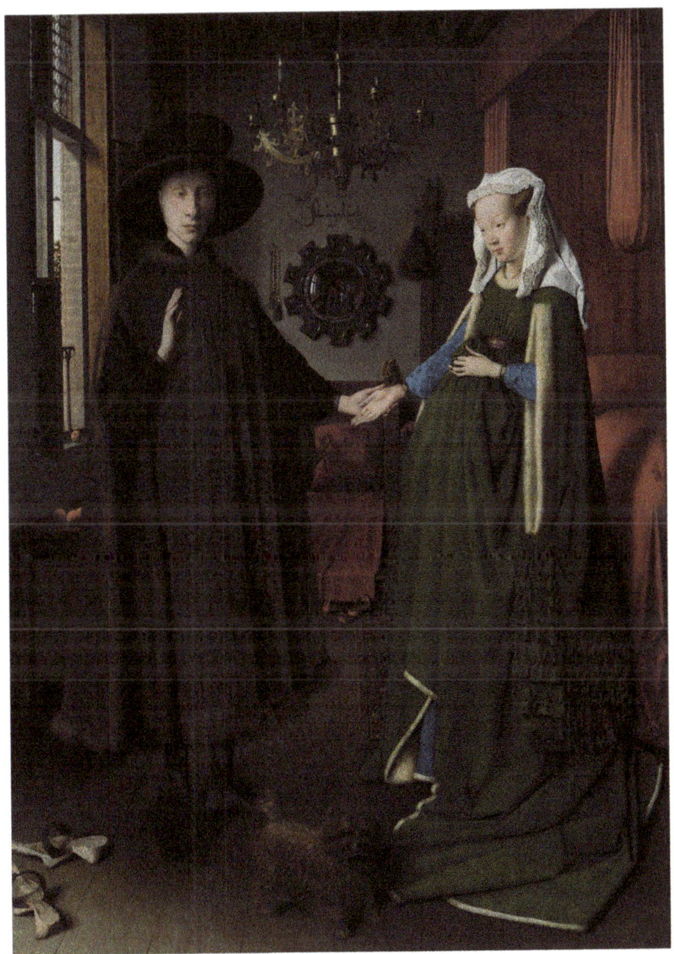

Jan van Eyck is considered the first master of oil painting. His iconic work *Arnolfini Portrait* depicts a married couple and is rich with hidden meanings and symbolism. For example, the chandelier has seven candles, which symbolize the seven sacraments of the Catholic Church, and the oranges, which were expensive to import at the time, represent wealth and prosperity. The mirror in the background perfectly reflects the scene, including the artist, suggesting that the painting itself is proof that people witnessed the marriage ceremony.

Jan Van Eyck
Arnolfini Portrait, 1434
oil on oak panel

Can you guess what the dog in the picture is often thought to symbolize? The answer is written upside down below!

Answer: the dog is often thought to symbolize loyalty and trustworthiness in their marriage.

Renaissance

THE Renaissance began in Italy in the 1300s. It gradually spread from Italy to other parts of Europe including France, Spain, and the Netherlands.

The term "Renaissance" means "rebirth" in French. It marked a period of revived interest in classical art and literature after a period of cultural decline in the Middle Ages. Throughout the Renaissance, artists often used oil paints and explored ideas from ancient Greek philosophy and mythology.

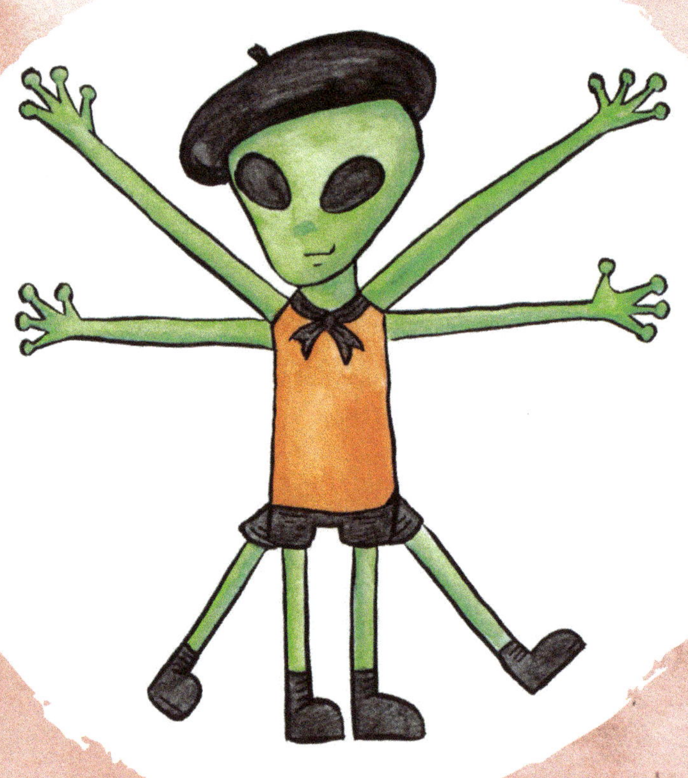

Around 1490, Leonardo da Vinci (page 64) drew the *Vitruvian Man*, which became one of the most iconic images of Western civilization! Da Vinci represented a man with perfect anatomical proportions, according to what people considered ideal proportions at the time. His body fits into a square and circle, symbolizing art, science, and math combined into a single drawing. I wanted to give it a try – who knew an alien could have perfect human proportions?

The Medici family also played a big part in the Renaissance. The Medicis were a very wealthy and powerful Italian family. They loved collecting art and also gave money to the best artists of the time. This gave artists the resources to paint, sculpt and create countless beautiful works of art. The Medicis were incredibly influential, so much so that without them, the Renaissance might not have even happened!

Raphael
Portrait of Lorenzo di Medic, 1518
oil on canvas

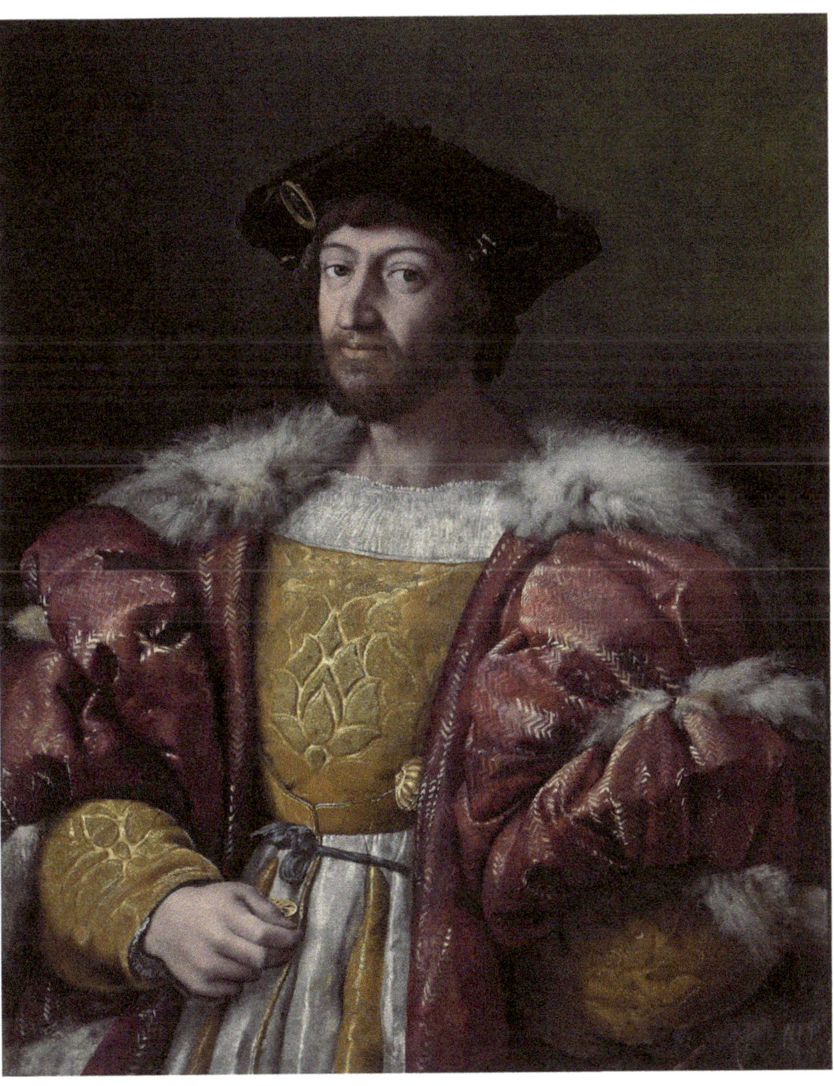

Early Renaissance

This was the first time in history that artists were able to use math to create a three-dimensional space on a flat surface perfectly! Imagine seeing that for the first time during the Early Renaissance.

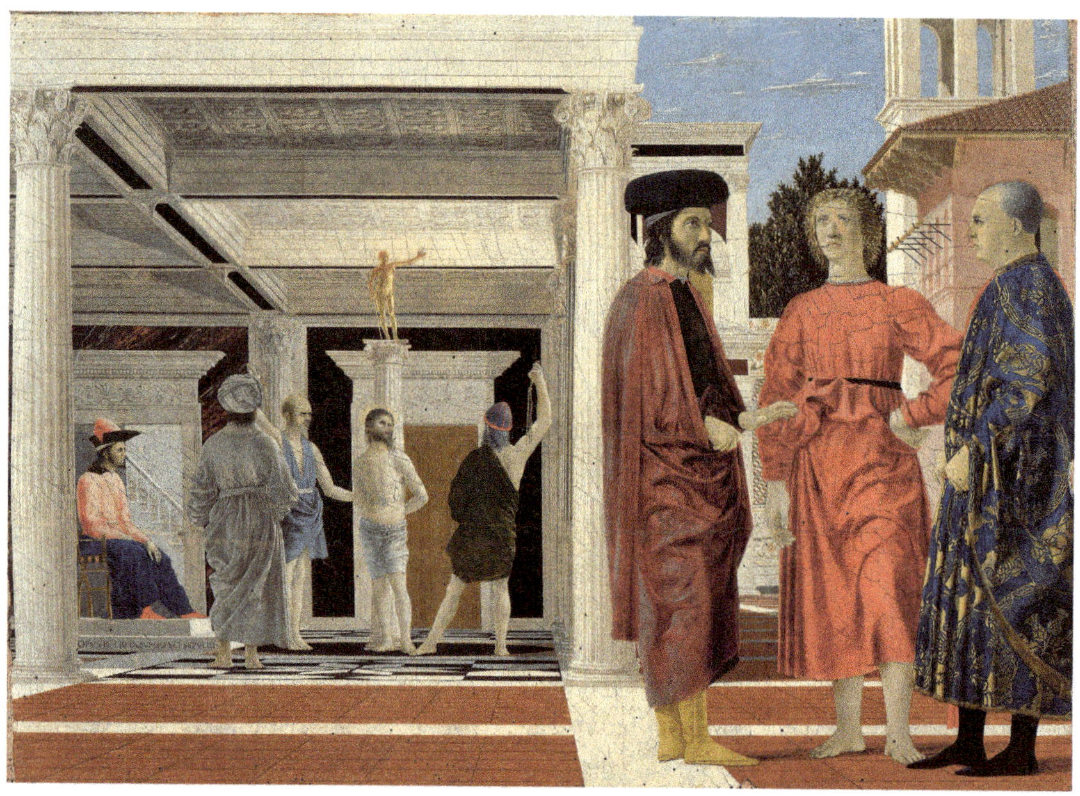

Piero della Francesca
The Flagellation, circa 1468 – 1470
Oil on canvas

Here is a really cool example of a painting created using a one-point perspective. On the left, you can see the original artwork, and on the right, I have added lines to show you how the perspective was built to create this image. Notice how all of these lines come from one point on the horizon, called a vanishing point. An artist can add several vanishing points to an artwork, making the perspective even more elaborate.

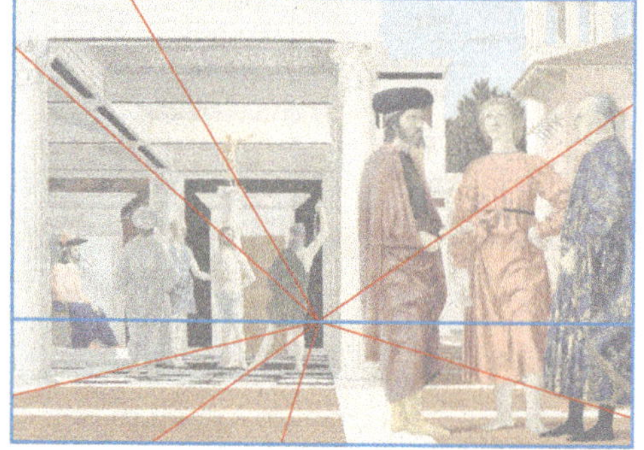

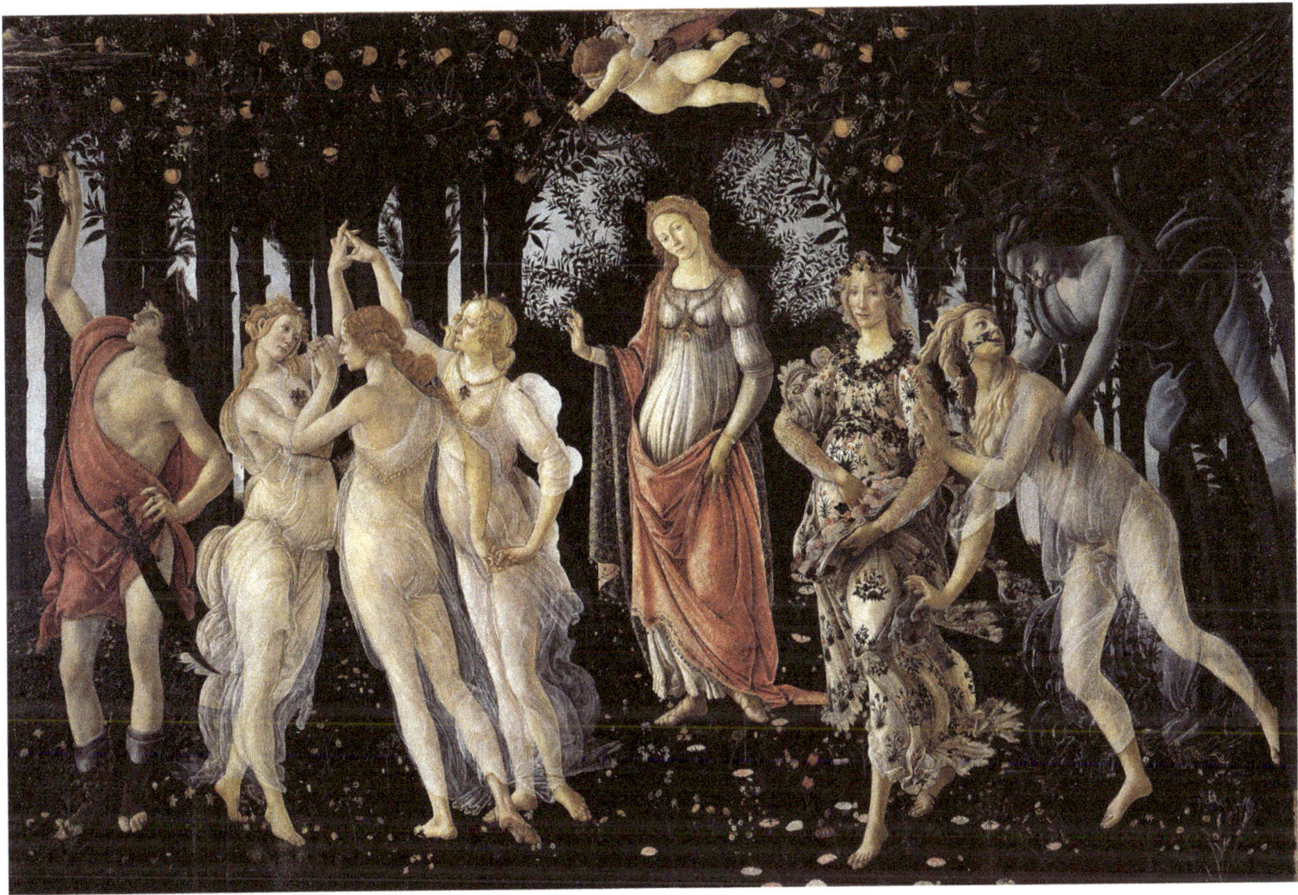

Donatello was an artist who explored the ruins of Rome around 1407 and became one of the most famous sculptors of the Early Renaissance. He was known for his sculptures, which were very realistic and lifelike.

Another famous artist during the Early Renaissance was Sandro Botticelli, who was known for his beautiful paintings. He painted many subjects, like myths and religious stories, but always added his own personal touch. His paintings were big and grand, and he was able to tell stories within them. People still admire his art today, and even in the 19th century, other artists were inspired by his work and called themselves Pre-Raphaelites (page 103).

Botticelli
Spring, 1477 – 1482
Tempera on panel

Figures from classic mythology, like Venus and Mercury, can be seen in this masterpiece. Each section of the painting shows the viewer a different part of the story.

Did you know that during this period, many artists still used a paint called tempera, which was usually created with eggs and pigment?

High Renaissance

The High Renaissance was a time in the late 15th and early 16th century when some of the most famous and beautiful art in history was made. Something was popularized among High Renaissance artists that changed the art world forever... Can you guess what it was?

Oil paint!

It's a no-brainer: oil paints give better results and are easier to work with when compared to tempera made with egg yolks. So you can imagine the giant leap painters took with this new material at hand.

Oil paint was first popularized by Flemish artists, as Flemish Gothic and the Renaissance were happening at the same time (page 58).

The three most famous artists during the High Renaissance are still famous today, and I bet you have heard of them before.

Leonardo da Vinci
The Mona Lisa, 1503
Oil on panel

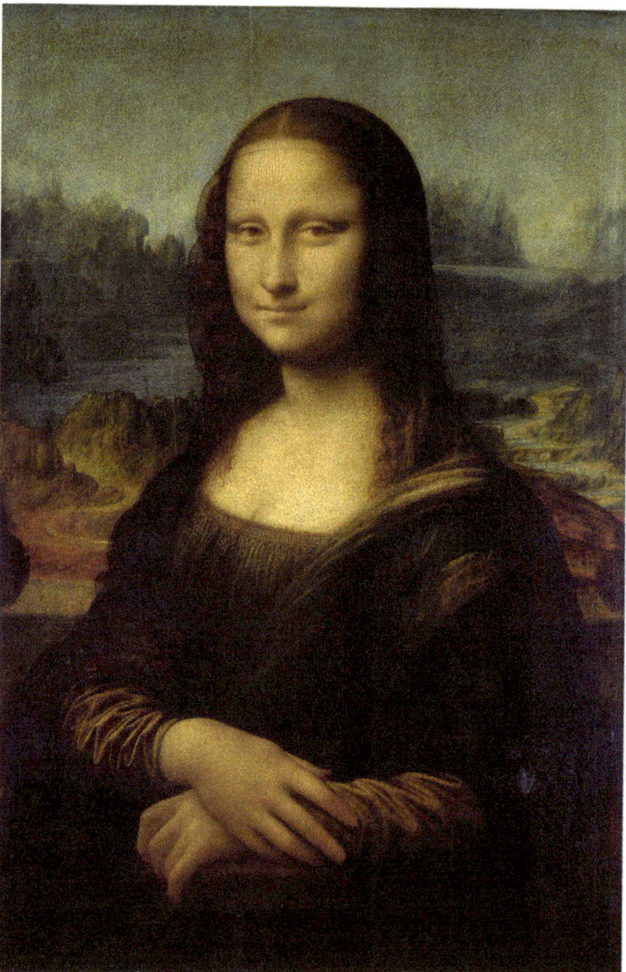

Leonardo da Vinci

Leonardo Da Vinci was a multifaceted artist, scientist, engineer, and inventor. He was born in Anchiano, Italy, in 1452. Da Vinci is, without a doubt, the most notable artist of the Renaissance because of his vast array of talents. He was left-handed and often wrote his notes in reverse!

In painting, he perfected the sfumato technique, which is when the painting has a smoky effect in between colors. A great example of this style of painting can be seen in his most famous painting, *The Mona Lisa*. If you look closely at the shadows, especially on her face, you can see how smoothly it goes from light to dark. This can also be seen in the colors of the background.

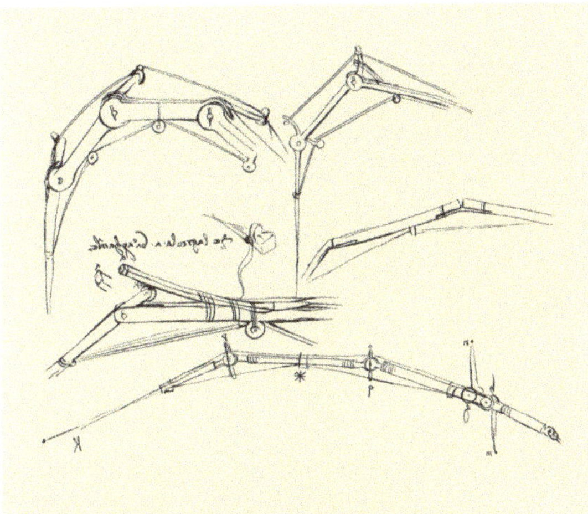

Da Vinci's Diagram of a proposed flying machine

Way ahead of his time, Da Vinci drew potential models of flying machines hundreds of years before the airplane was invented!

Michelangelo

Michelangelo is mostly known for painting the ceiling of the Vatican's Sistine Chapel, in which he included many hidden symbols. He was born in Rome, Italy, in 1475 and was also a magnificent sculptor. His most notable sculpture measures over 17 feet and portrays the biblical figure, David. Michelangelo excelled in creating religious images and produced artwork for nine Catholic Popes during his career.

Michelangelo
Sistine Chapel's ceiling, 1508 – 1512
Fresco

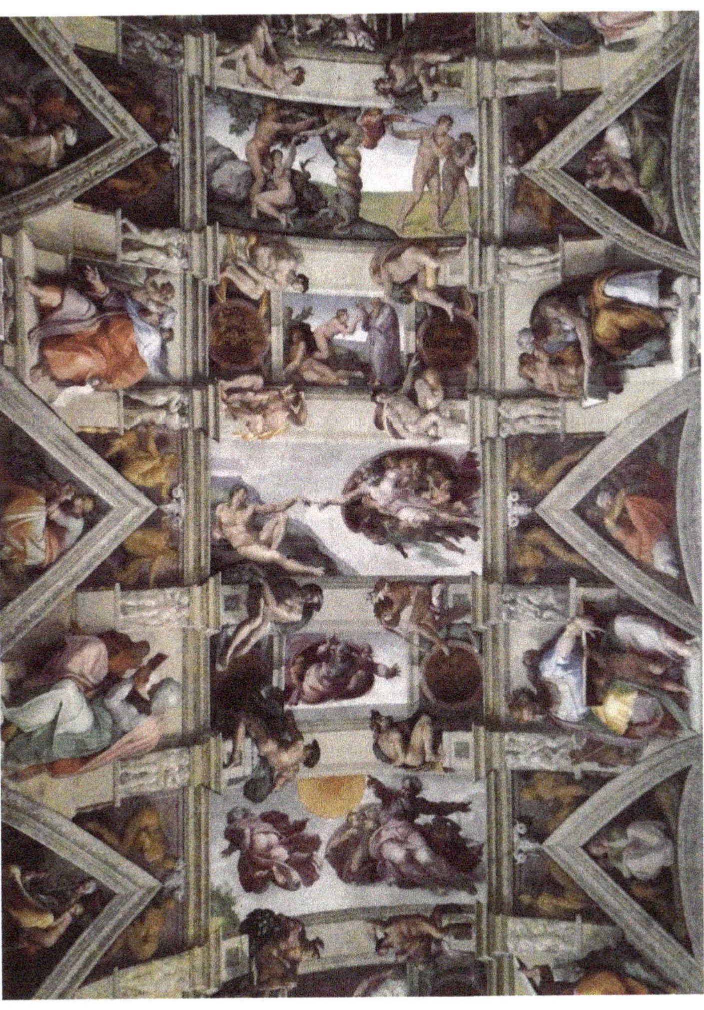

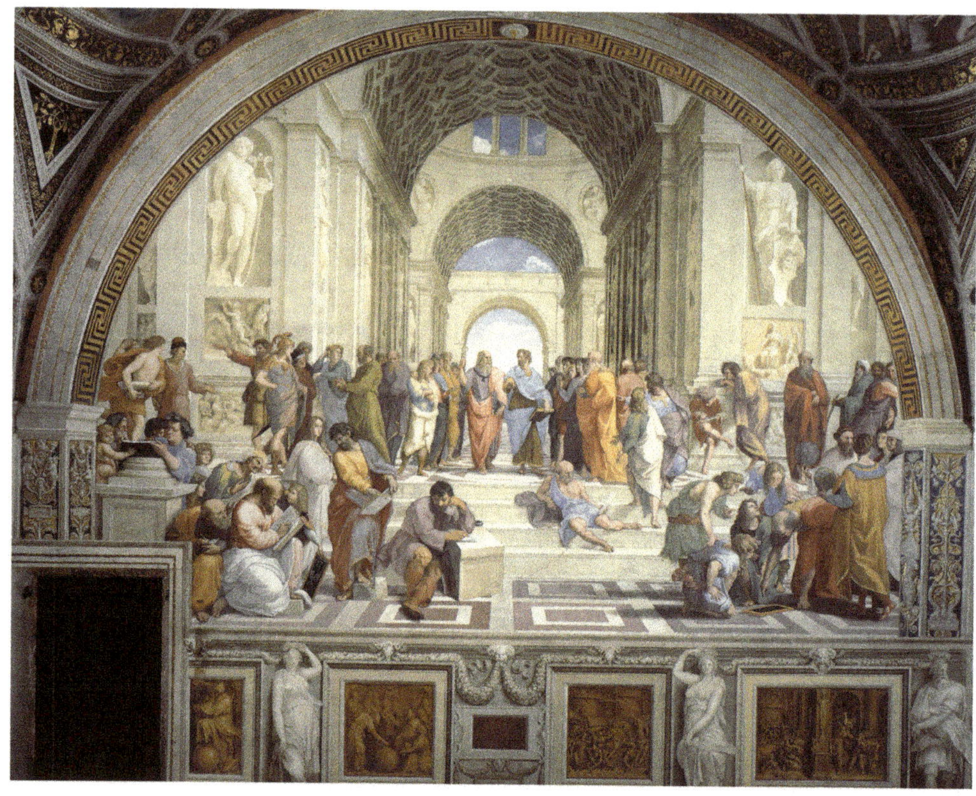

Raphael
School of Athens, 1509 – 1511
Fresco

Raphael

Raphael was the youngest of the three but excelled in painting and architecture. Born in Urbino, Italy, in 1483, he was a master of creating fluid compositions and precise perspectives in his work. After becoming a successful artist, Raphael counted on the help of 50 assistants he trained to complete his masterpieces.

Activity

Making Egg Tempera

Let's recreate a process similar to making tempera and paint with egg yolks!

What you will need:

- One egg per color used
- Disposable Gloves
- Vinegar
- Water
- Paper towels for cleaning
- Non-toxic powder pigment or concentrated watercolor pigment
- Plastic cups or any other containers to mix the paint
- Paint brushed
- Watercolor paper

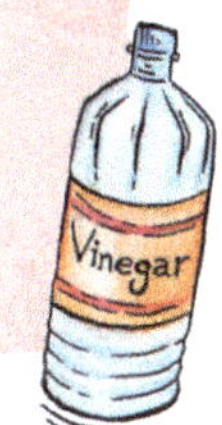

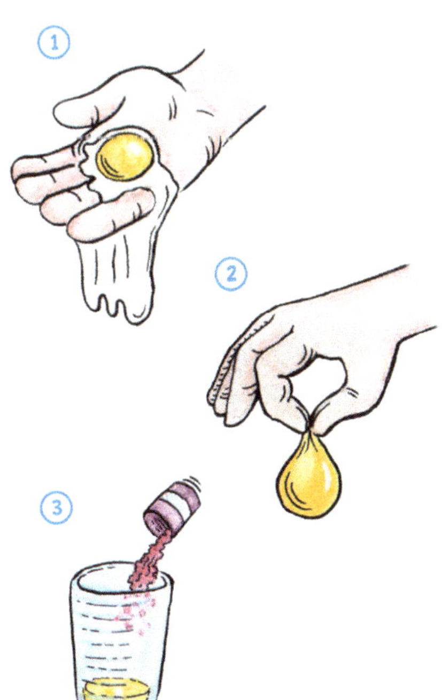

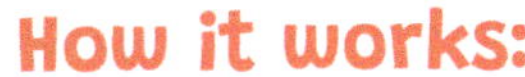

How it works:

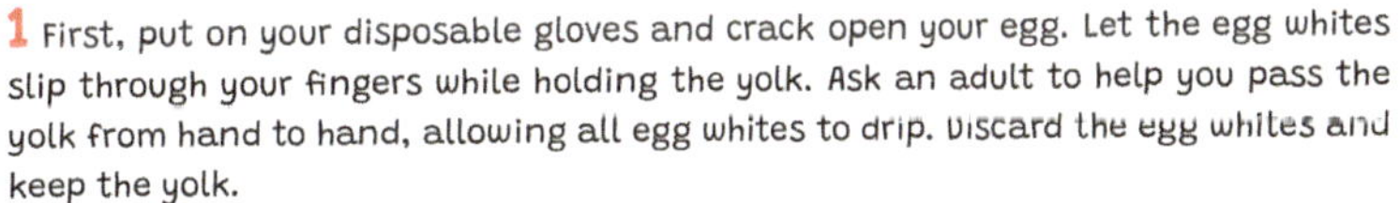

1 First, put on your disposable gloves and crack open your egg. Let the egg whites slip through your fingers while holding the yolk. Ask an adult to help you pass the yolk from hand to hand, allowing all egg whites to drip. Discard the egg whites and keep the yolk.

2 Then, delicately pinch your egg yolk and pull. You'll need a steady hand for this part! Pull on the sack and drain the yolk into a cup.

3 Add 2 to 3 drops of vinegar and mix. Gradually add your pigment to see how much you need to achieve your desired color. Different kinds of pigment use different measurements, so start with small amounts until you get to the point you want.

4 Add a little bit of water if needed. The consistency of your paint should be similar to gravy. Be careful not to make it too watery!

5 Repeat this process for every color you wish to make.

6 When your colors are done, use your tempera like you would any other paint. You can use water to dilute it more and create a beautiful painting on your watercolor paper. After you are done painting, do not keep your leftover paint; discard it.

7 Have fun!

Mannerism

THERE is something quite curious that I have observed about Earth's art history, especially in Western civilization: the idea of Classical art - which began in ancient Greece and Rome - almost always comes up throughout the rest of human history. Sometimes it comes up as an inspiration and a reference to the artists, while at other times, it comes up because the artists want to break free from the Classical norms into something new.

As the Renaissance period was near its end, there was a transition to what Earthlings call Mannerism. This period was a break from the norms of the Renaissance and was not well received by most art critics of the time.

Mannerist artists were known for making people and things in their paintings look a little different, with long arms and legs. They did this to make the painting feel more exciting and they mostly painted religious pictures.

The colors they used were brighter and more intense than what was typical during the Renaissance. Artists would also often create an intense contrast by pairing these bright colors with black shadows, as seen in Jacopo Tintoretto's version of *The Last Supper*.

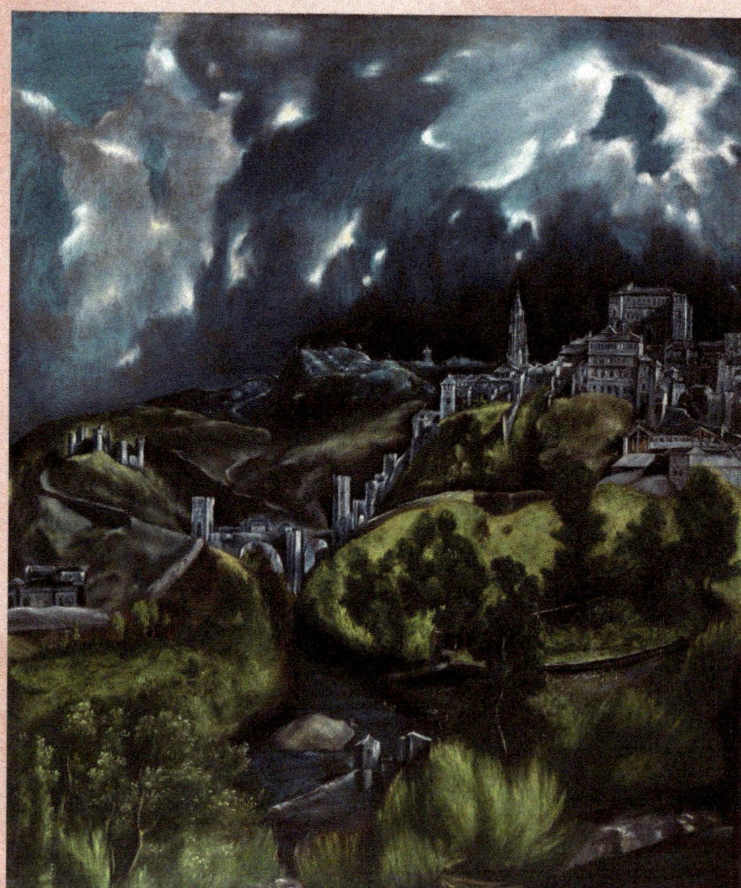

El Greco
View of Toledo, circa 1596 – 1600
Oil on canvas

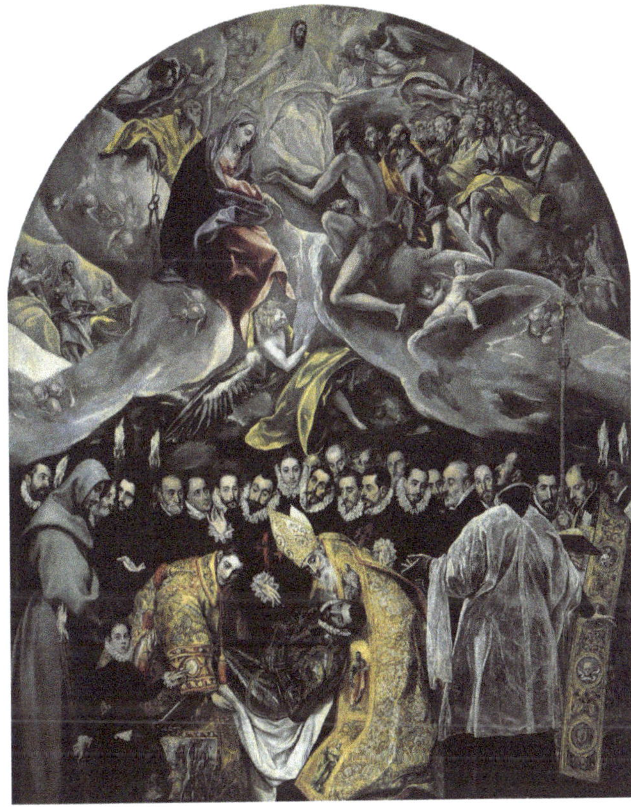

El Greco
The Burial of the Count of Orgaz, 1586 – 1588
Oil on canvas

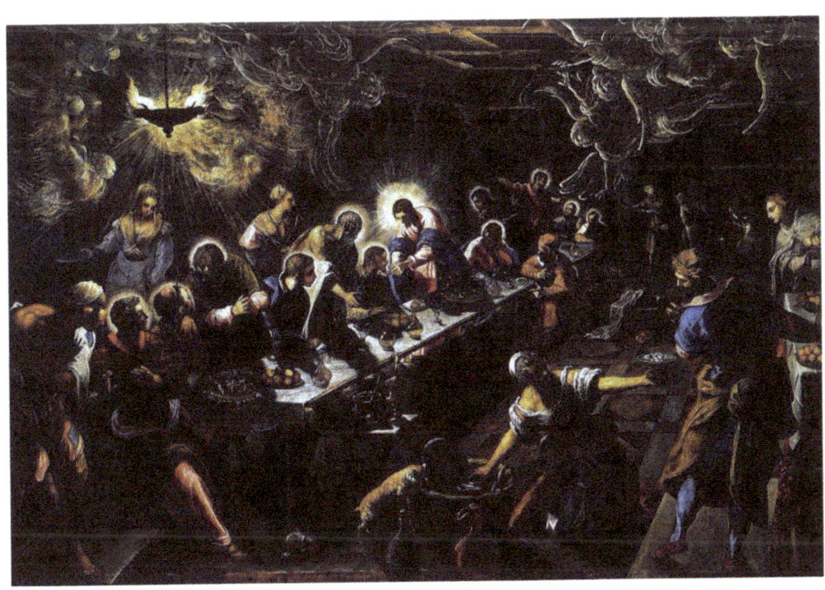

Tintoretto
The Last Supper, 1592 – 1594
Oil on canvas

Activity

Fruit Portrait

Giuseppe Arcimboldo was a very unique Italian Mannerist painter. He created a series of portraits of fruits, vegetables, flowers, and different plants! The painting *Vertumnus* is a great example of his creativity.

Today, you are going to create a portrait made out of your favorite food. It can be a self-portrait (aka, a portrait of yourself) or of someone else.

All you need is a white plate or a clean surface and a selection of fruits you enjoy! Try to pick fruits you will eat so that no food goes to waste.

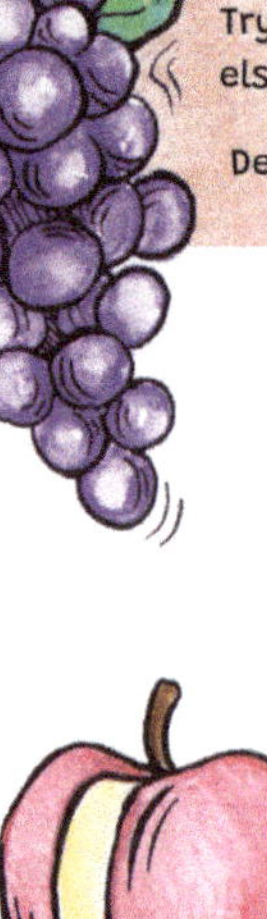

Observe the colors, shapes, and textures of the fruits. See if they have a different color on the inside or the outside. If you need to cut some of the fruit, ask an adult for help.

Try to assemble the fruit so that it looks like a portrait of you or of someone else, and when you are done, take a picture. Then, you can eat your portrait.

Delicious!

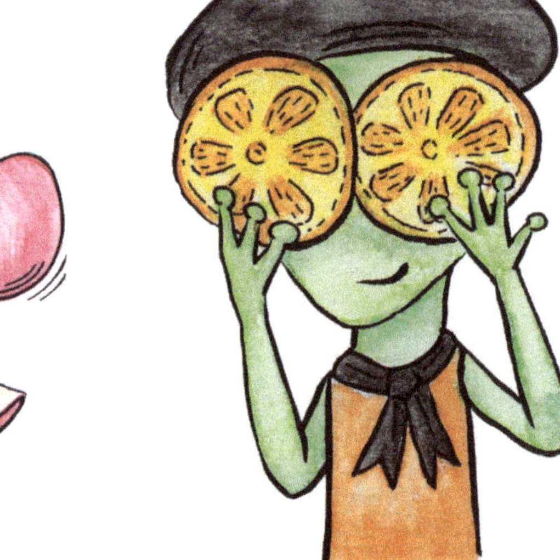

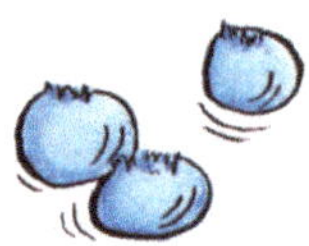

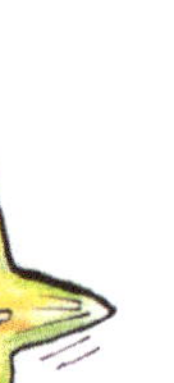

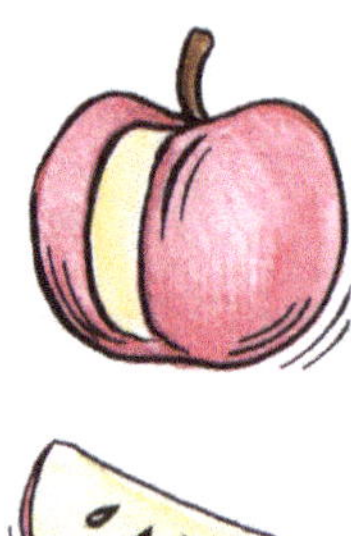

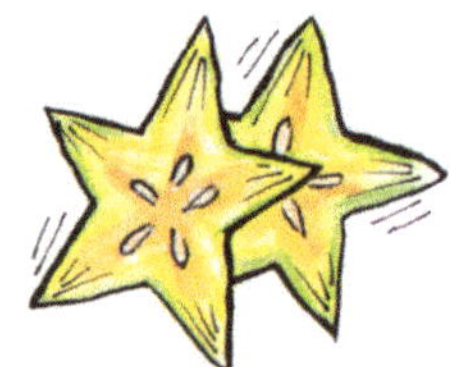

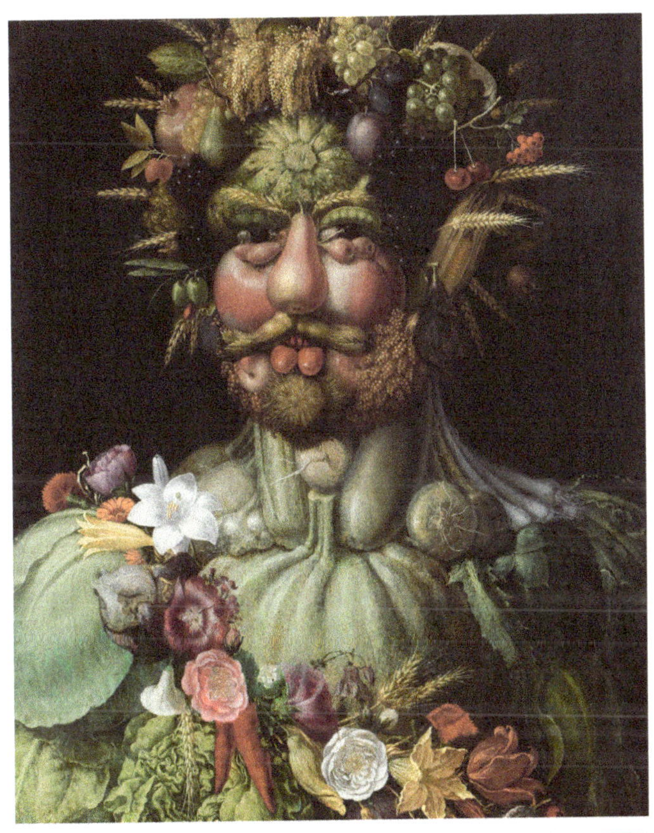

Giuseppe Arcimboldo
Vertumnus, 1561
Oil on canvas

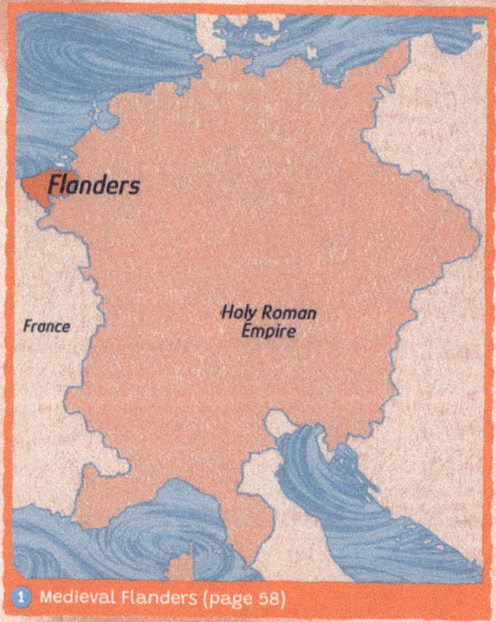

1 Medieval Flanders (page 58)

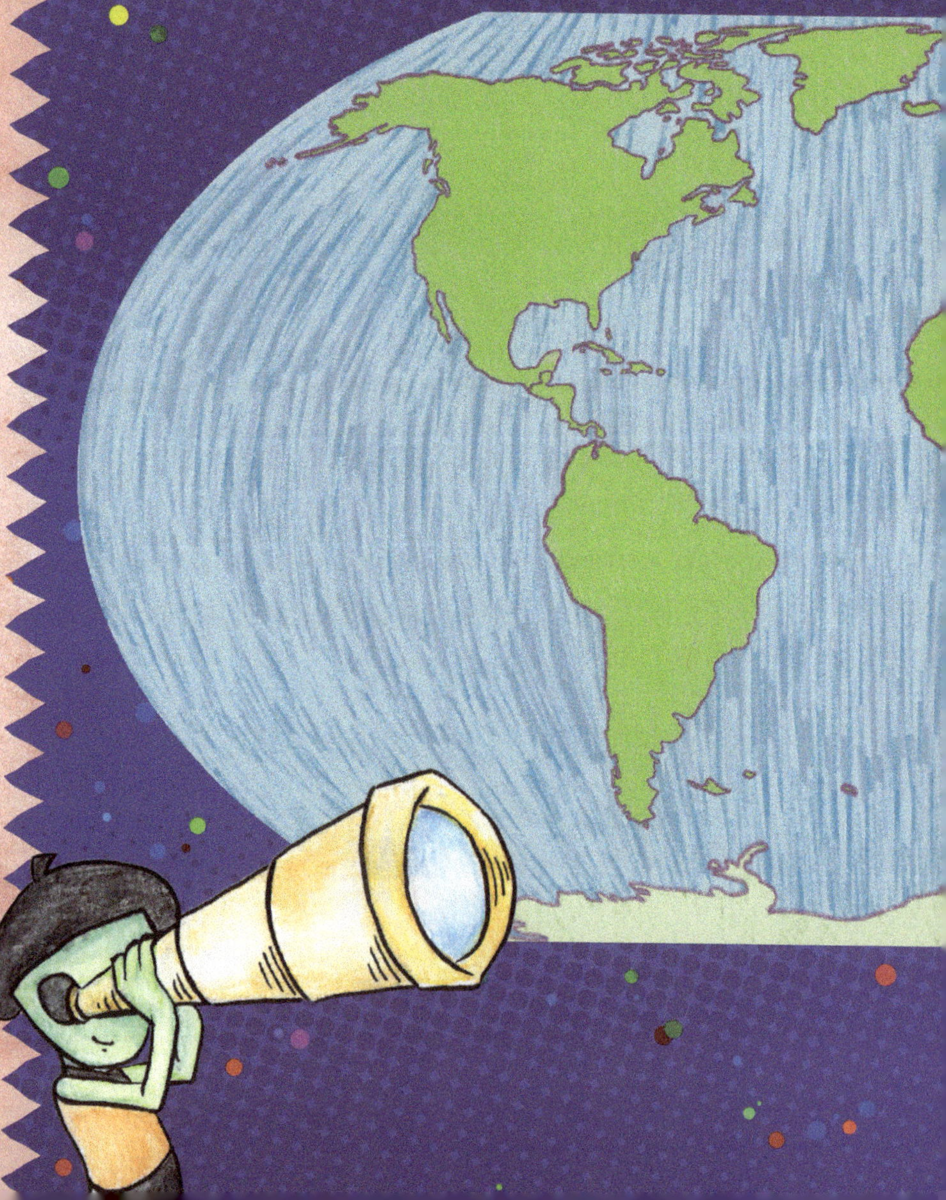

Where on Ea

th are We?

Maps: Art from around 1400 - 1600

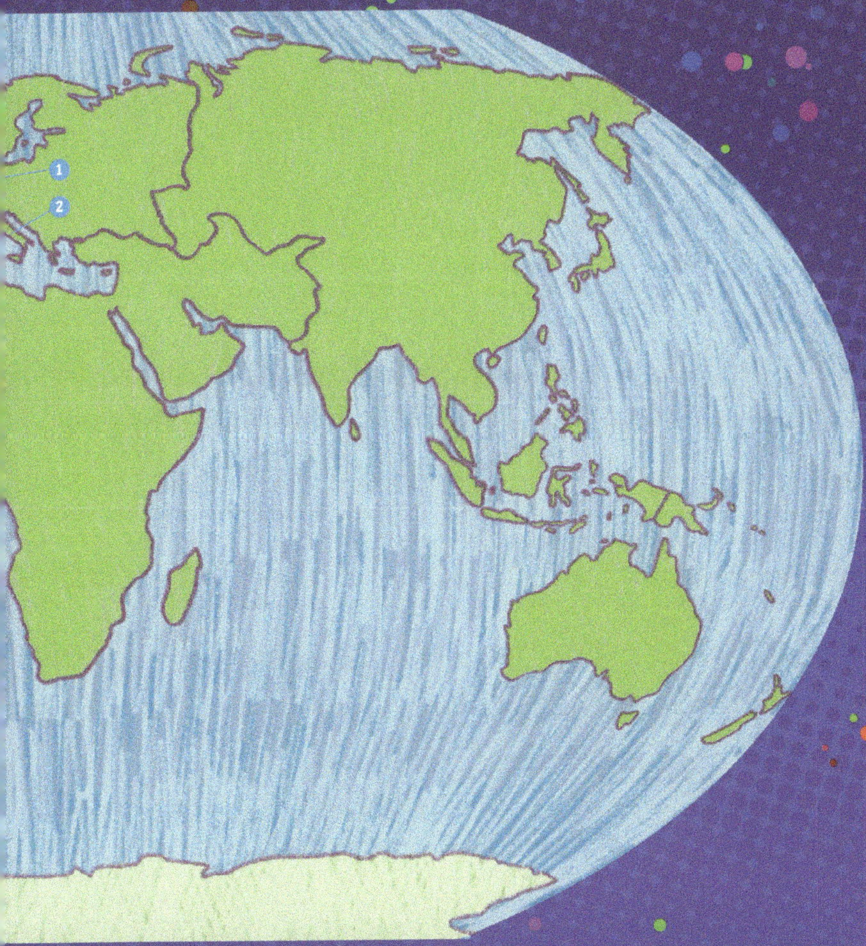

1

2

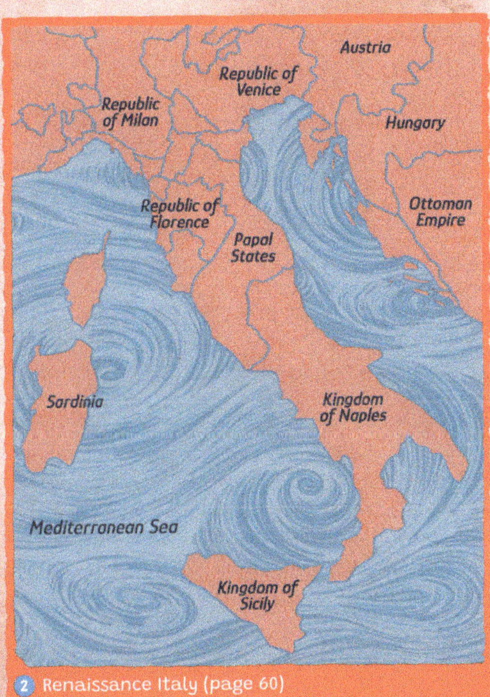

2 Renaissance Italy (page 60)

Art from around 1600 - 1800

Baroque and the Dutch Golden Age

How do you like our adventure so far? It's pretty cool to see how much art and civilizations have changed throughout the years.

The 17th century was wild, especially in Europe. A lot of things were happening and many things were changing, which affected the way people made art.

In the past, the Catholic Church held a lot of power, but over time, people began to question its authority. This gave rise to a new group of Christians known as Protestants. Protestants held different beliefs from the Catholic Church, leading to a major division known as the Protestant Reformation.

To regain its influence, the Catholic Church embarked on what is called the Counter Reformation. As part of this effort, they sought to revive faith through art.

Gian Lorenzo Bernini, a famous Italian artist, gained fame for his sculptures and architectural works. He is particularly renowned for pioneering Baroque sculpture. Remarkably talented from a young age, he unveiled his first statue at only 12 years old. His sculptures were mostly of religious and mythological figures.

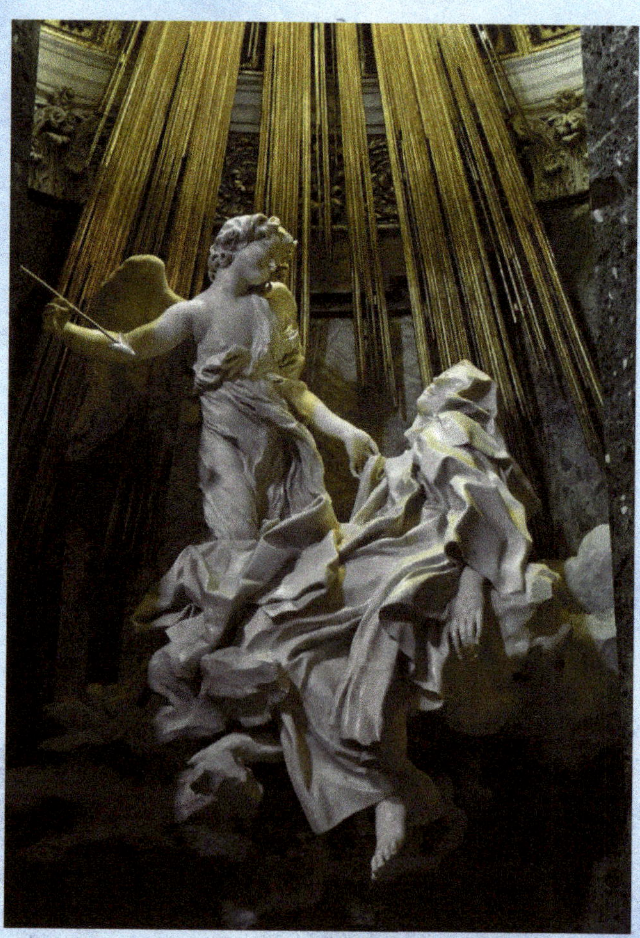

Bernini
Ecstasy of Saint Teresa, 1647 – 1652
Marble

The *Ecstasy of Saint Teresa*, created by Bernini between 1647 and 1652, is a beautiful example of Baroque art. Take a moment to appreciate how Bernini skillfully sculpted flowing fabric from marble, infusing this scene with movement and drama.

Baroque art captured biblical stories through paintings and sculptures. It created a sense of being right in the action. The artists behind these creations used vibrant colors and bold lines to make images powerful. They skillfully used light and shadow.

Among the Baroque masters, Caravaggio stands out for his use of chiaroscuro, a technique that relies on the difference between light and dark. He enchanted audiences with his use of lighting, showing biblical scenes in fresh imaginative ways. One notable example is *Conversion on the Way to Damascus*.

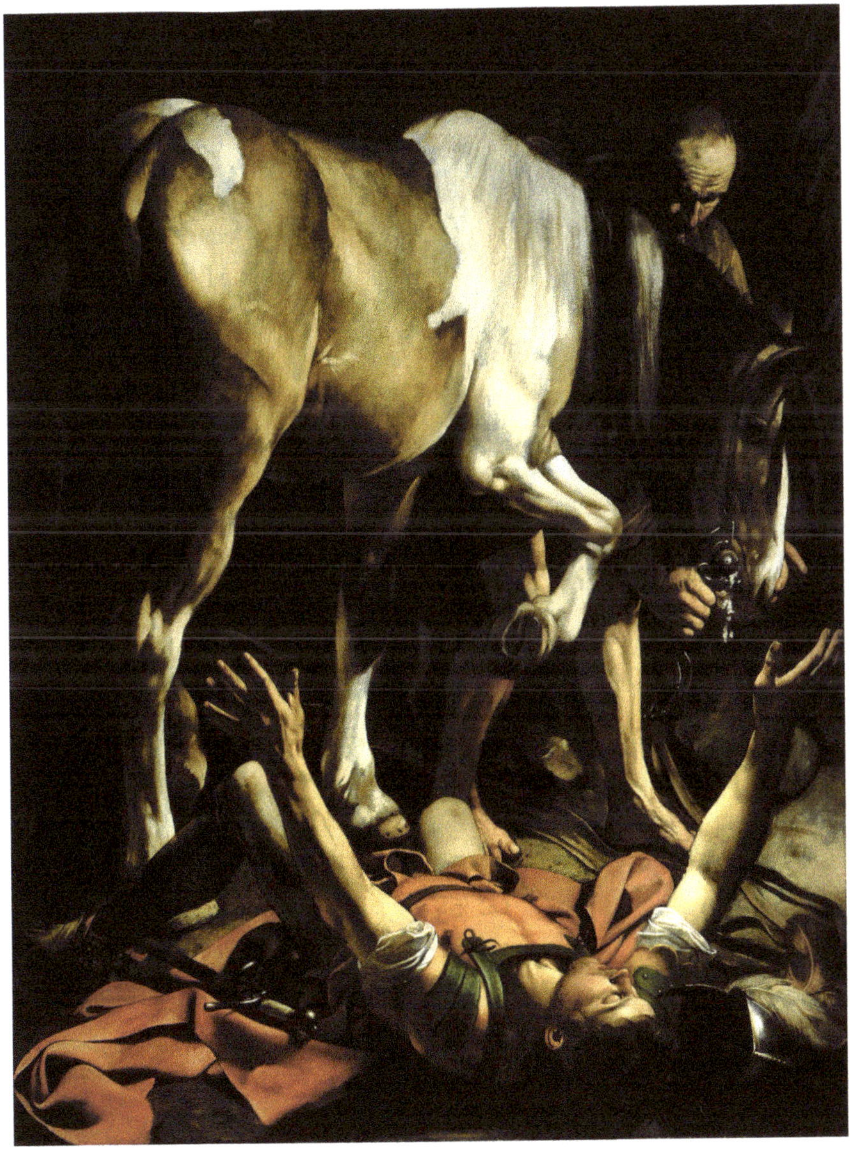

Caravaggio
Conversion on the Way to Damascus, 1601
Oil on canvas

This painting shows the moment in which Saul, who went against the Christian faith at the time, fell from his horse after seeing a bright light and hearing the voice of Jesus. The horse is also startled but does not harm Saul, creating a dynamic scene. The divine light shines on Saul, who raises his arms to the sky.

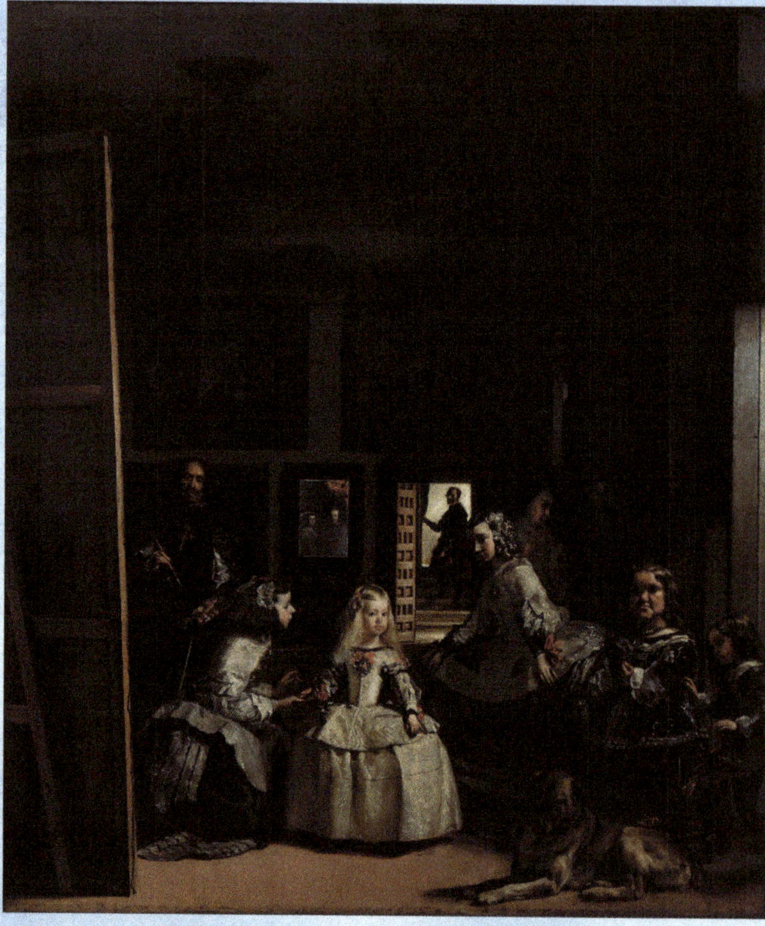

Velazquez
Las Meninas, 1656
Oil on canvas

Another artist worth mentioning is Diego Velazquez, who was the court painter of King Philip IV from Spain.

Las Meninas by Velazquez is considered one of the most important works in all of Western art history. The title is Spanish and means "The Maids of Honor", referring to the ladies in the painting who are assisting Princess Margaret Theresa, the central figure. You can see the artist, Velazquez, on the left. He's looking straight at us!

Las Meninas may make you feel like royalty. If you look closely, you can see the reflection of the king and queen in a mirror in the background, but it's painted as if the reflection is also of you or whoever is viewing the painting. It's like Velazquez wanted us to know what it felt like to be a king or queen and have him paint a special portrait of us!

Dutch Golden Age

In Holland, the Baroque period was known as the Dutch Golden Age. They were also creating bold and dramatic paintings, but instead of focusing on stories from the Bible, they focused on stories about everyday life.

Johannes Vermeer is most known for his intimate interior scenes of people doing ordinary tasks, like reading a letter. His most famous painting, *Girl With the Pearl Earring*, is considered the Dutch *Mona Lisa*.

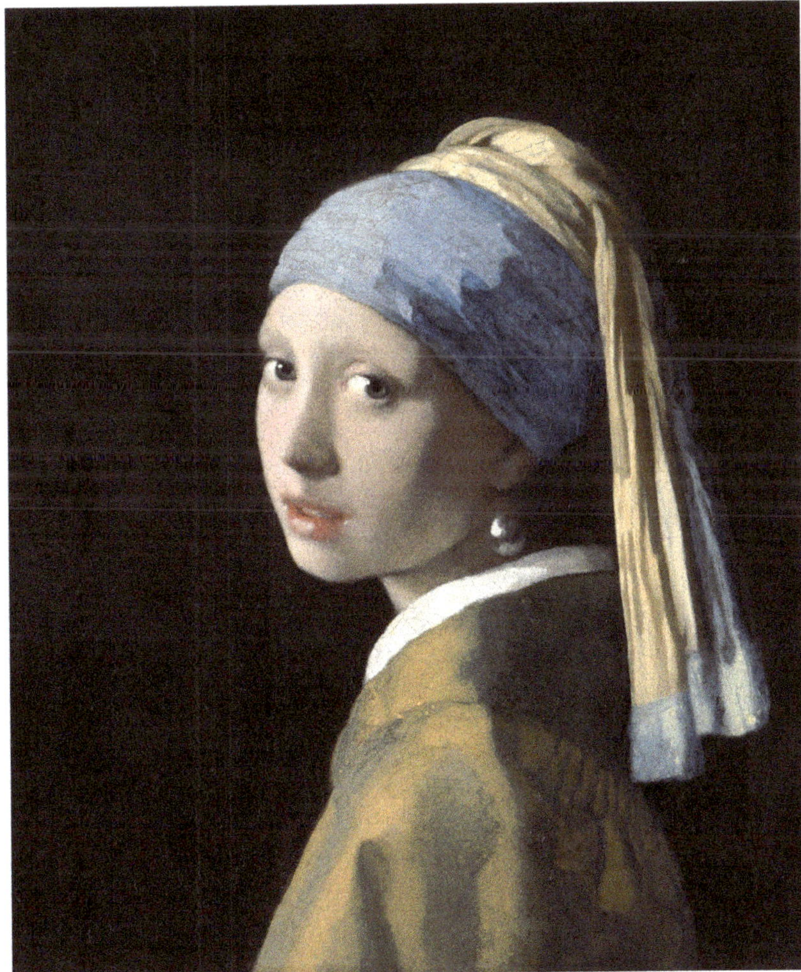

Johannes Vermeer
Girl with the Pearl Earring, (circa 1665)
Oil on canvas

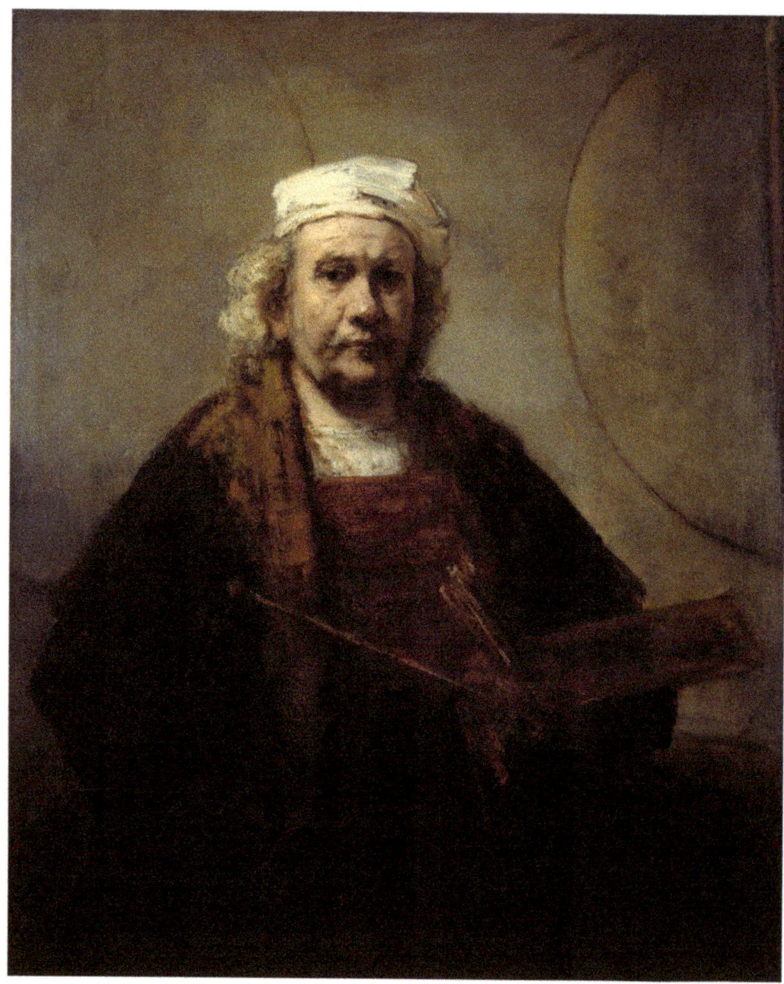

Rembrandt Harmenszoon van Rijn, a famous artist from the Netherlands during the 1600s, gained fame for his extraordinary paintings that captured the emotions and personalities of his subjects. Known for his mastery of light and shadow, Rembrandt's paintings create a warm and radiant aura. His portfolio includes many portraits, including self-portraits, as well as biblical scenes and landscapes.

Amongst his most famous masterpieces is *The Night Watch*, which depicts a group of soldiers seemingly brought to life. Another notable piece is *Self Portrait with Two Circles*, which uses light and shadow to create depth and realism.

Rembrandt
Self-Portrait with Two Circles, circa 1665 – 1669
Oil on canvas

Do you know what a still life is? They were popular during the Dutch Golden Age, and are pictures of things that are not alive, like fruits, vases, and books. Artists who paint still lifes are really good at making things look like they are real, so real that you can almost reach out and touch them! There were no cameras back then, so still lifes were the next best thing.

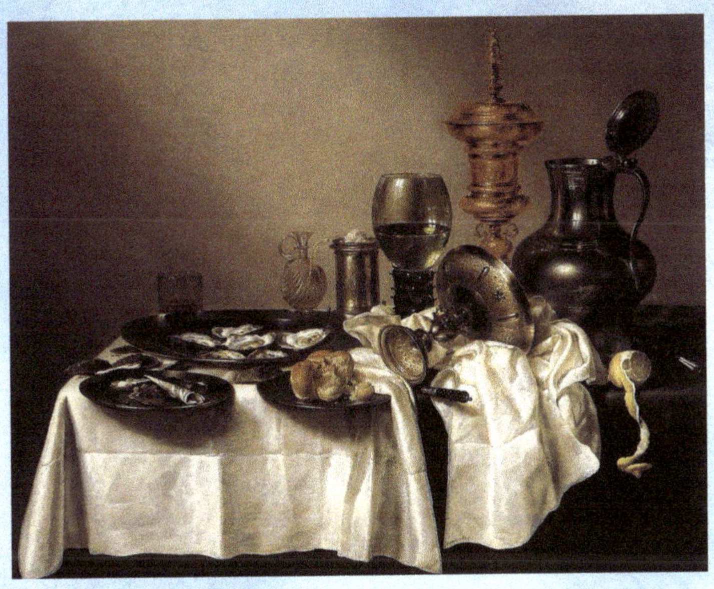

Willem Claesz Heda
Still Life with a Gilt Cup, 1635
Oil on canvas

Still lifes still exist to this day and not all artists create realistic still lifes. Modern (page 95) and contemporary artists (page 139) have created stylized and even abstract still lifes, which are very different from ones created by Baroque artists.

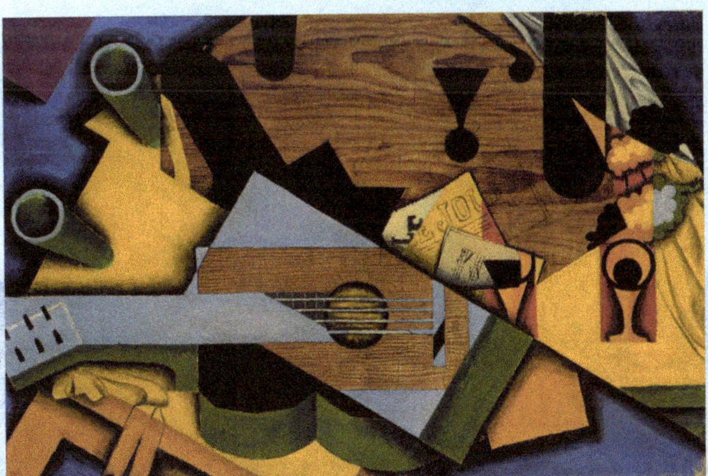

Juan Gris
Still Life with a Guitar, 1913
Oil on canvas

Activity

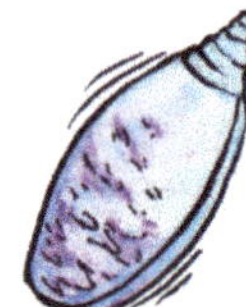

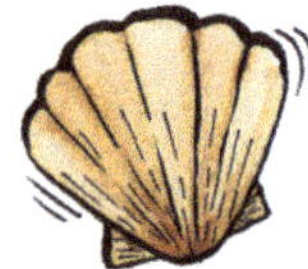

Creating a Still Life

Now it's your turn to make your own still life!

Here's what you'll need:

- Fruit, flowers, and other objects of your choice
- A lamp or any other light source
- Watercolor paper
- Pencil
- Eraser
- Paintbrushes
- Gouache paint (magenta, yellow, blue, black, and white)
- Containers for water and mixing paint
- Paper towels for cleaning

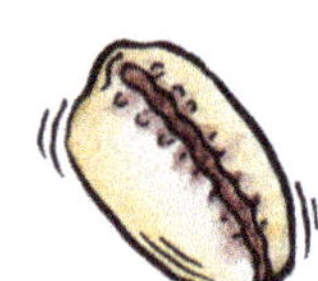

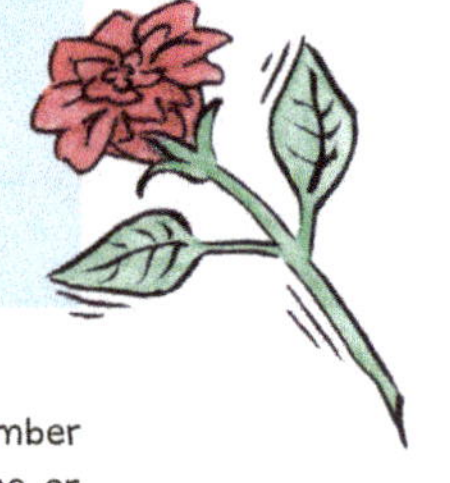

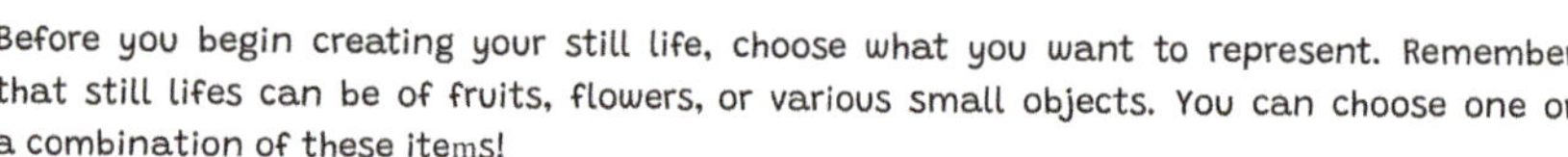

Before you begin creating your still life, choose what you want to represent. Remember that still lifes can be of fruits, flowers, or various small objects. You can choose one or a combination of these items!

Quick tip: Don't add too much to your still life. Start with only 3 or 4 items for each painting. The more items you add to your still life, the harder it becomes to paint.

For example: you can choose 3 pieces of fruit; or you can have 2 pieces of fruit and 1 flower; or 1 object, 1 fruit, and 1 flower. Use your imagination!

After you have chosen your items, it's time to set them up!

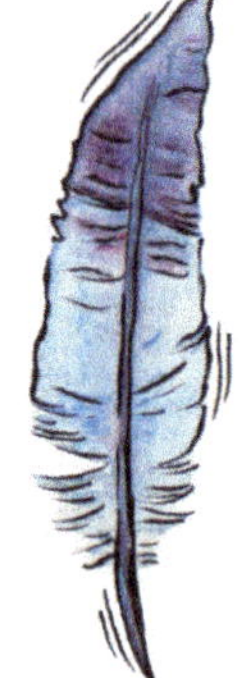

Take the fruit, flowers, and/or objects and display them however you'd like on a table. Make sure they are near each other and can even be placed in front of one another.

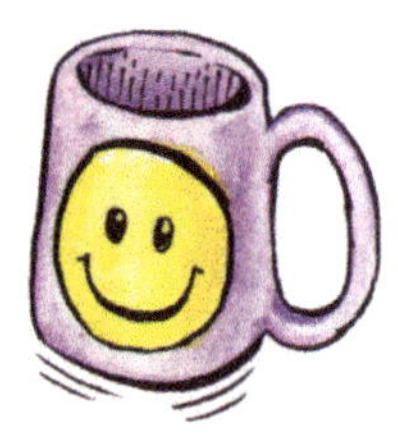

When you are happy with how the items are placed on the table, take your lamp or other light source and place it near the objects. Ask for an adult's help when setting up any electronic device. Observe how the light shines on the items you displayed and where the shadows hit. You can experiment with the position of the light as you please.

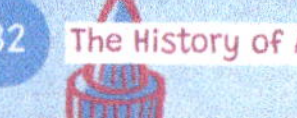

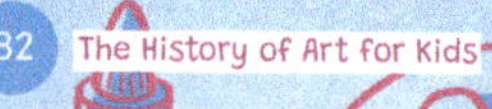

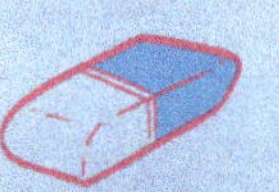

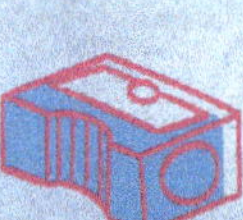

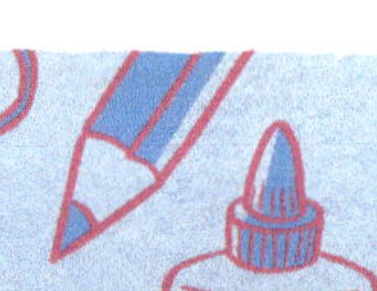

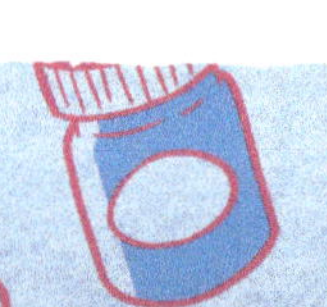

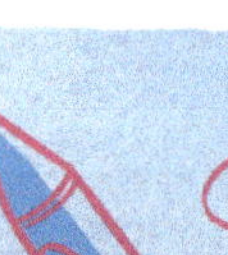

Need inspiration? Scan this QR code and see more still lifes!

With a pencil, softly draw the overall shapes of your still life on a piece of watercolor paper. Make sure not to press hard, so the pencil doesn't damage the paper. Don't worry about drawing minor details because you will be covering the drawing with paint.

With the help of an adult, add the colors you wish to use to your tray and feel free to mix them to make different colors. You can check out the color wheel on page 114 for guidance on how to mix different colors. Paint your still life using your paintbrushes. Pay attention to the colors you see and how the light hits the elements.

When you are done, add the title of your painting, your name, and the date on the back of the paper. When you're done using the paint brushes, wash them right away so the paint on them doesn't dry.

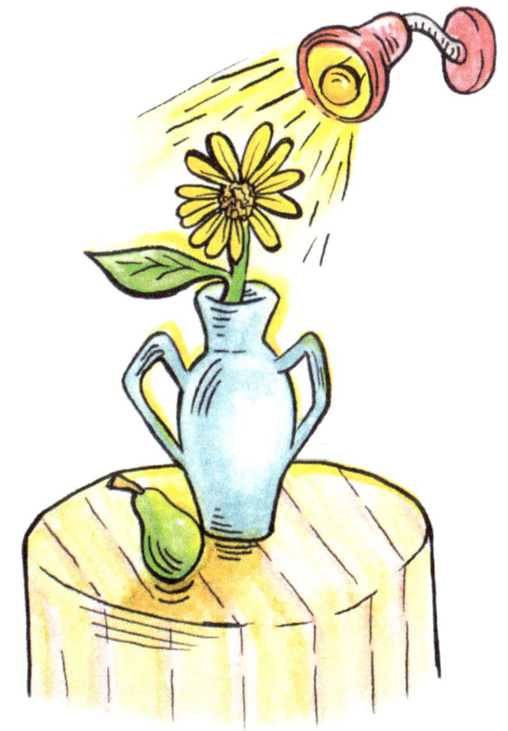

Rococo

Rococo is a fancy style of art that was popular in Europe in the 1700s. It is known for its delicate and detailed designs, often involving curved lines and pastel colors. The name "rococo" comes from a French word that means rock or shell decorations.

Rococo artists wanted to create a style that was different from Baroque. While Baroque art is dense and dark, Rococo art is light, fun, and highly decorative. In Rococo paintings, people wore fancy clothes that looked like costumes, and the paintings often showed beautiful gardens and parks. Although many countries were influenced by Rococo, the most famous artists were in France. They often painted or sculpted about love.

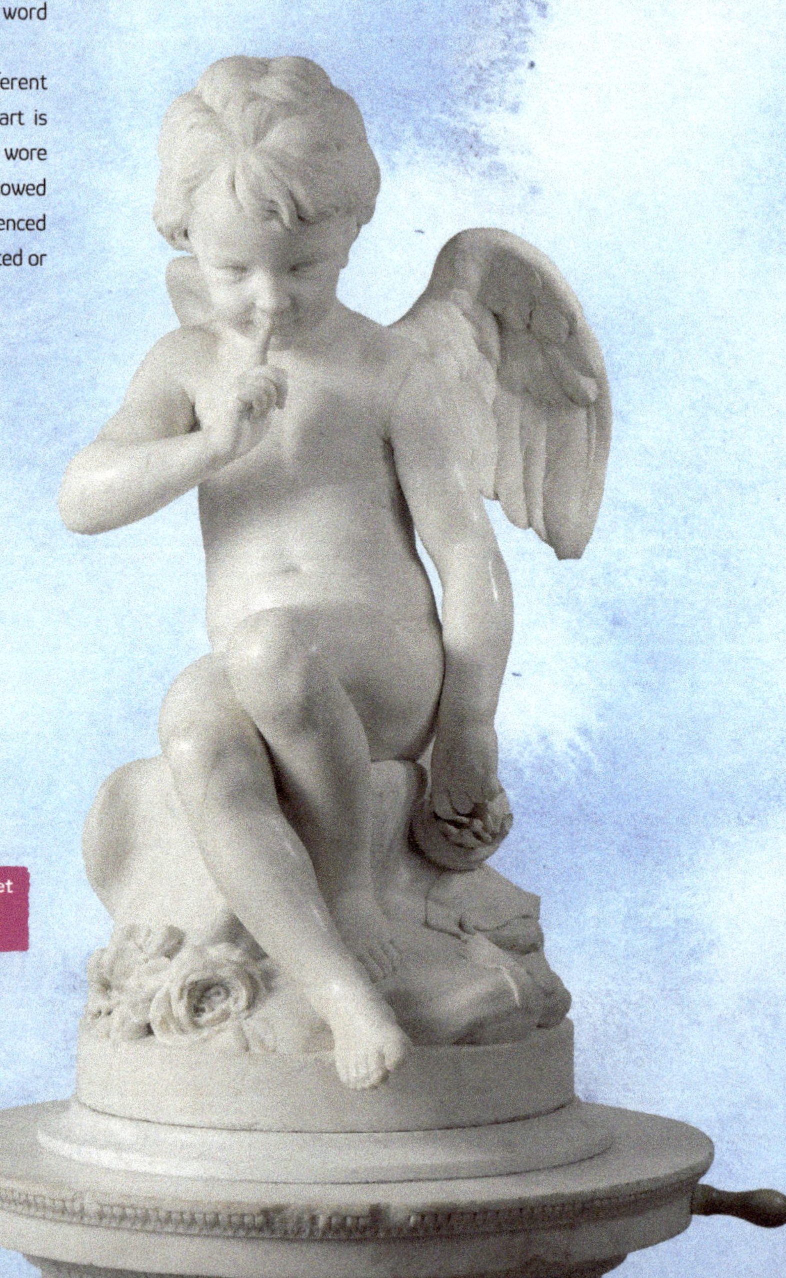

Etienne-Maurice Falconet
Cupid, 1757
marble sculpture

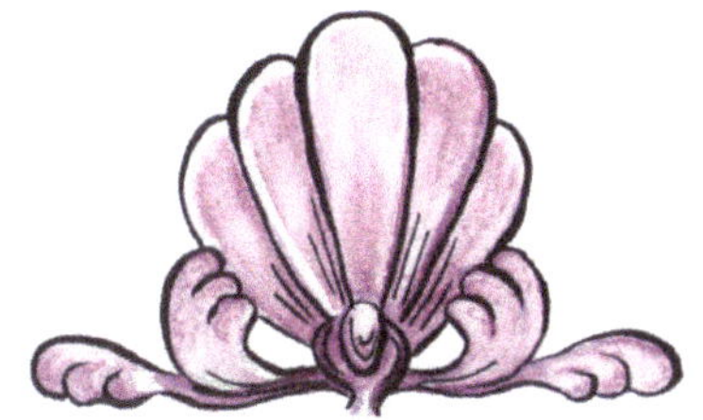

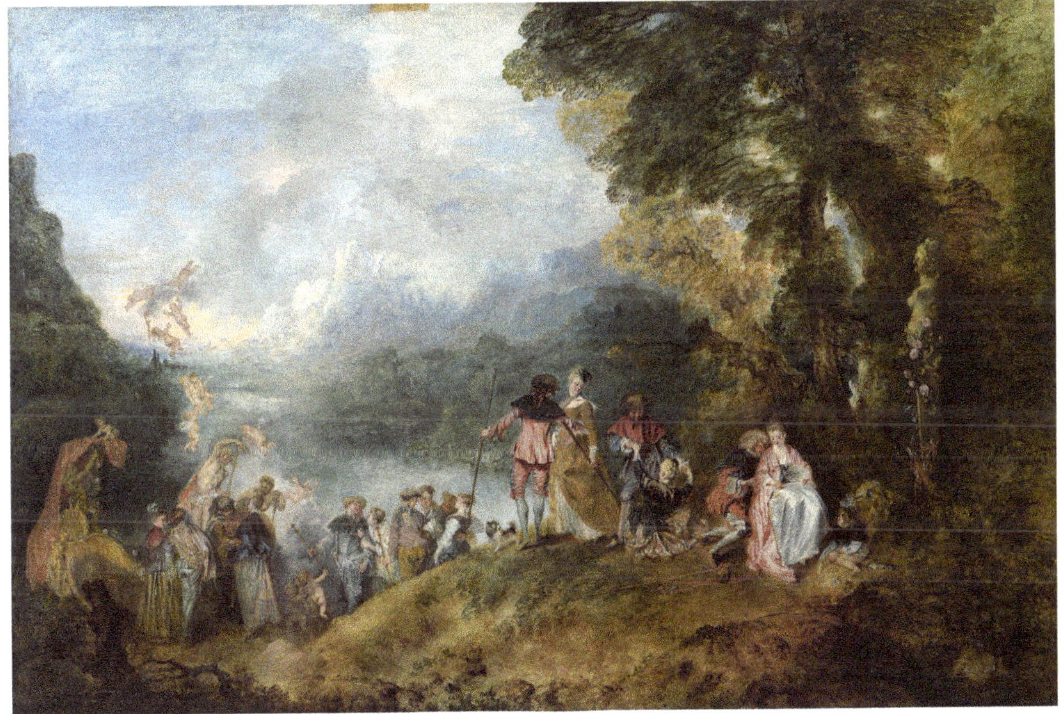

Jean-Antoine Watteau
The Embarkation for Cythera, 1717
Oil on canvas

Neoclassical

As time went on, some people began to dislike Rococo art. They thought it was too fancy and not serious enough. Instead, they wanted to go back to even older styles, like the ones from ancient Greece and Rome. This led to a new style of art called Neoclassicism, which was simpler and more serious than Rococo. By 1770, more and more people preferred Neoclassical art over Rococo art.

Let's break down the word Neoclassical: "Neo" means new, and "Classical" refers to the art and culture of ancient Greece and Rome.

Neoclassicism's main inspirations were Greek and Roman narratives, especially those involving heroic figures. The movement's first masterpiece shows this very clearly! Check out "Oath of Horatii" painted by Jacques-Louis David in 1784.

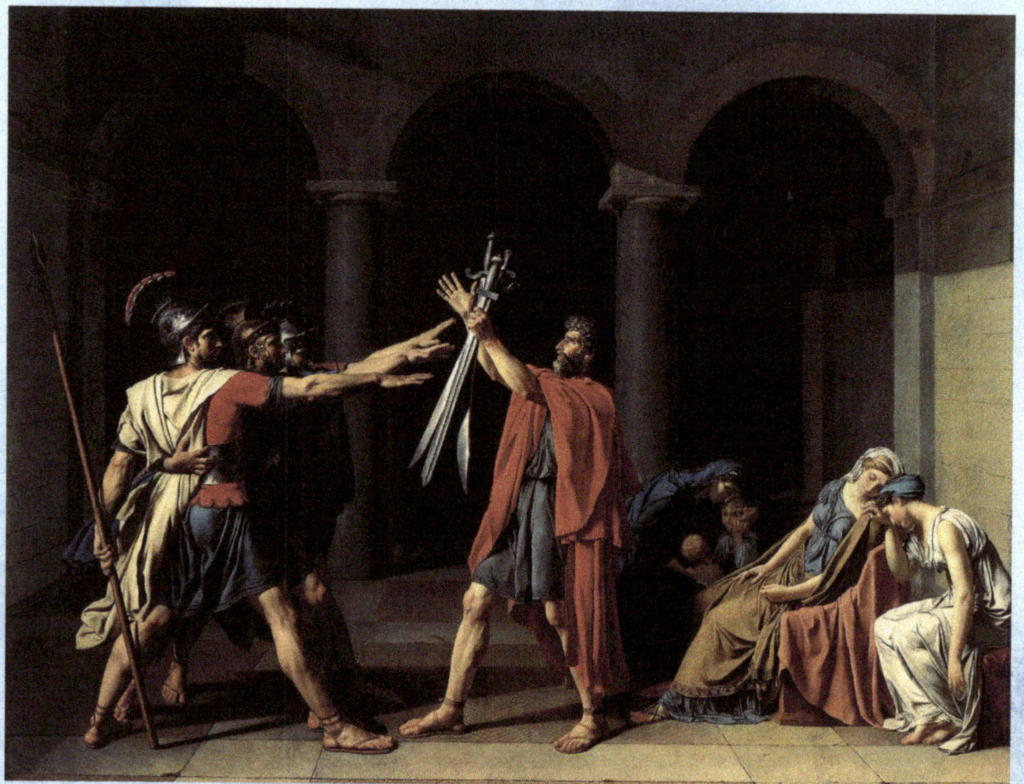

David
Oath of Horatii, 1784
Oil on canvas

This is a great example of how the ideals of ancient Rome were represented in Neoclassical painting. It shows three patriotic brothers before a battle for Rome.

Another artist worth mentioning is Jean-Auguste-Dominique Ingres, a pupil of David. He believed that historical painting was the highest form of painting, but he became most famous for his captivating portraits.

The movement ended around the year 1830 as Romanticism (page 88) began to take the forefront of the art world. Ingres himself had a known rivalry with French Romanticist painter Eugène Delacroix.

I look so sharp. Maybe I should add this to my wardrobe. What do you think?

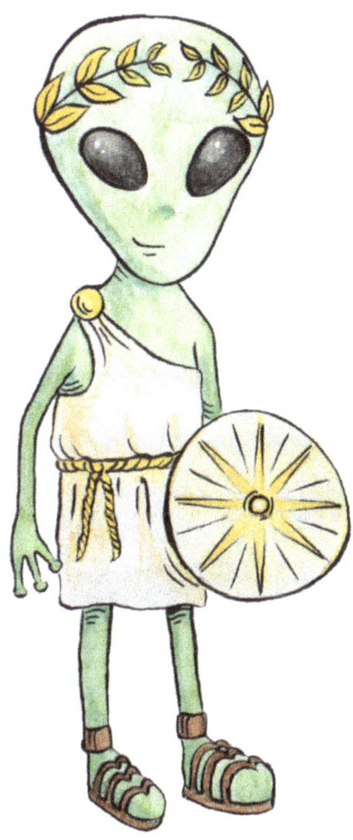

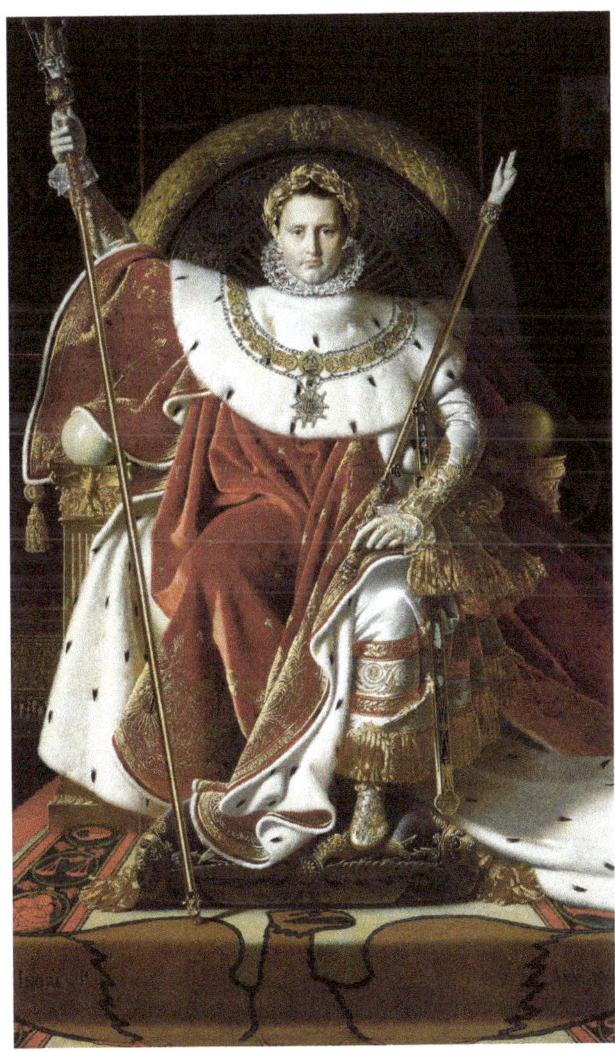

Élisabeth Louise Vigée Le Brun
Julie as Flora, Roman Goddess Of Flower, 1799
Oil on canvas

Romanticism

Can you believe how many beautiful artworks we have seen so far?

Now, we are going to explore another one of my favorite movements from art history, Romanticism... Because aliens can be romantic too, you know!

When you hear the word Romanticism, you might think of people falling in love, but that's not what Romanticism means when we're talking about art.

Romanticism was an art movement that began in the late 1700s and lasted into the mid-1800s. It was a reaction to previous art movements, like Neoclassicism, which was more focused on reason and order. Romanticism in art, instead, emphasized emotions and imagination. Romantic artists often used bold colors and brushstrokes to paint landscapes and nature. They also often depicted scenes from literature, mythology, and history. Romantic paintings were meant to evoke feelings of awe, wonder, and even terror! Romanticism also influenced poetry, books, music, and architecture. It was most prominent in Germany, France, Great Britain, and Switzerland.

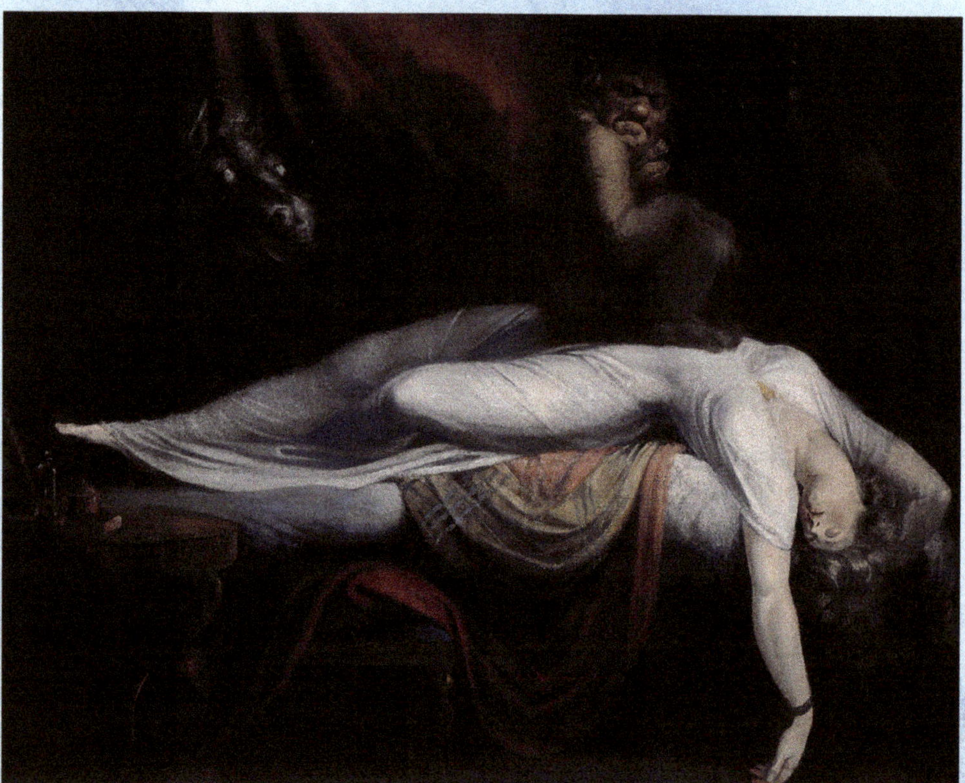

Henry Fuseli
The Nightmare, 1781
Oil on canvas

Henry Fuseli's *The Nightmare* is considered a Romanticism masterpiece. The Romantic author of *Frankenstein* (1818), Mary Shelley, may have been influenced by *The Nightmare* because her parents knew Fuseli, and she was probably familiar with the painting.

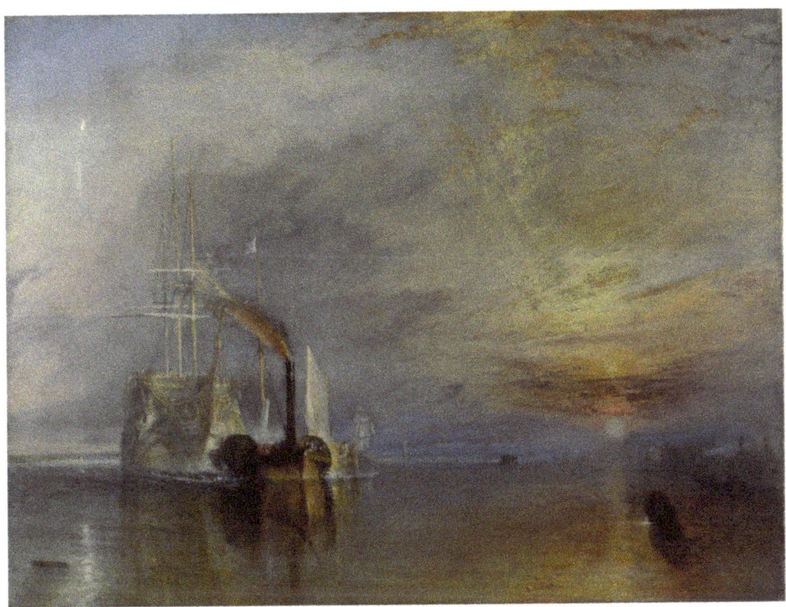

At the same time as Romantic art, something big was happening in the world called the Industrial Revolution. This brought new machines that made things easier, but it also made people feel less important and powerful. This feeling of powerlessness also influenced Romantic artists, and they often painted nature and landscapes to show the beauty and strength of natural things, in contrast to machines that were created during the Industrial Revolution.

English artist Joseph Mallord William Turner created seascapes (paintings of the sea) to show the power of nature.

J.M.W. Turner
The Fighting Temeraire, Tugged to Her Last Berth to Be Broken Up, 1839
Oil on canvas

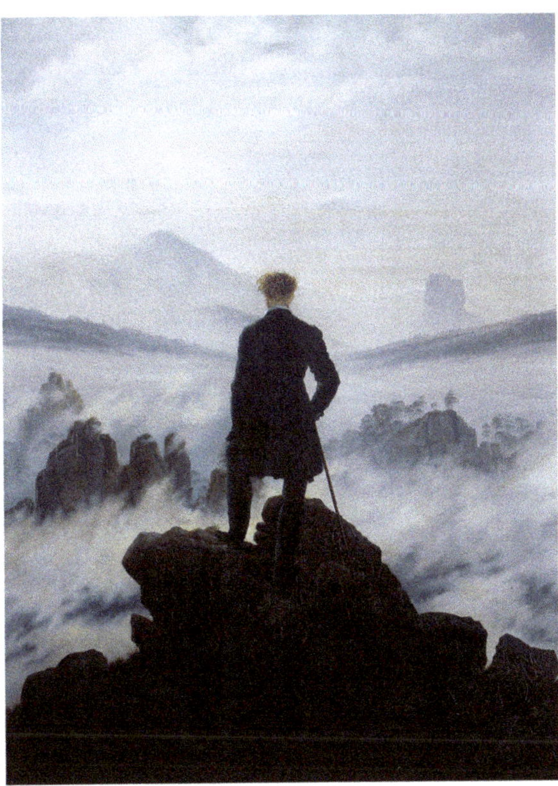

Caspar David Friedrich
The Wanderer above the Sea of Fog, 1818
Oil on canvas

Does this Romantic painting look familiar?
Perhaps you've seen something like it on a book cover?

Activity

Cutout Landscapes

One main theme of Romantic art was landscapes. For this activity, you will create a unique landscape using magazines!!

What you'll need:

- **Used magazines**
- **Scissors**
- **Glue**
- **Paper**

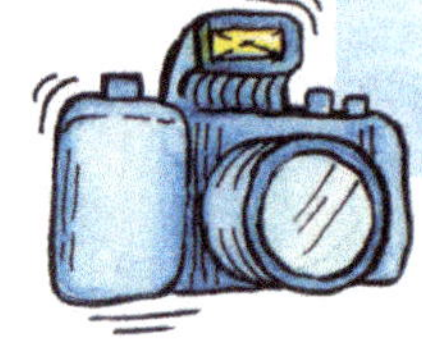

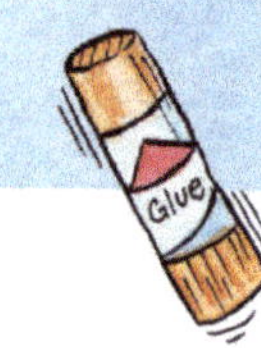

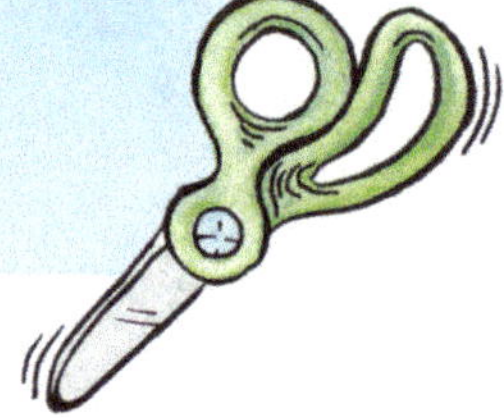

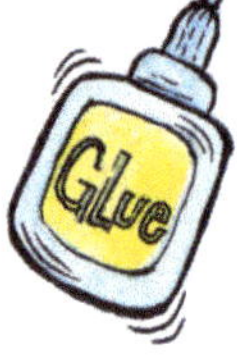

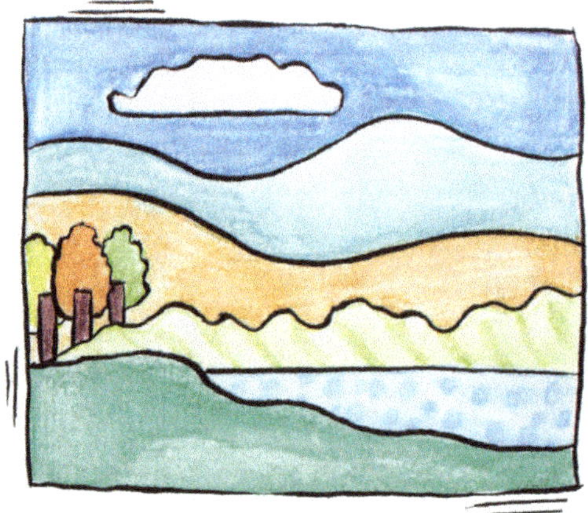

How to create your landscape:

1 First, you must define what kind of landscape you want to portray. Using a reference image can help. You can go outside and take photos or search for landscape images on
.

2 Once you have chosen the reference landscape or image, choose your color pallet. You can use colors similar to your reference or change them according to your imagination!

3 Go through the magazines and start cutting out every image with the colors you wish to use in your landscape. Cut out only the areas with the colors you need. For example: If you want yellow cut-outs and find a picture of a man wearing a yellow shirt, you should only use the shirt.

4 Create a collage by combining all of the cut-outs. Glue the magazine pieces to your paper and see your landscape take shape!

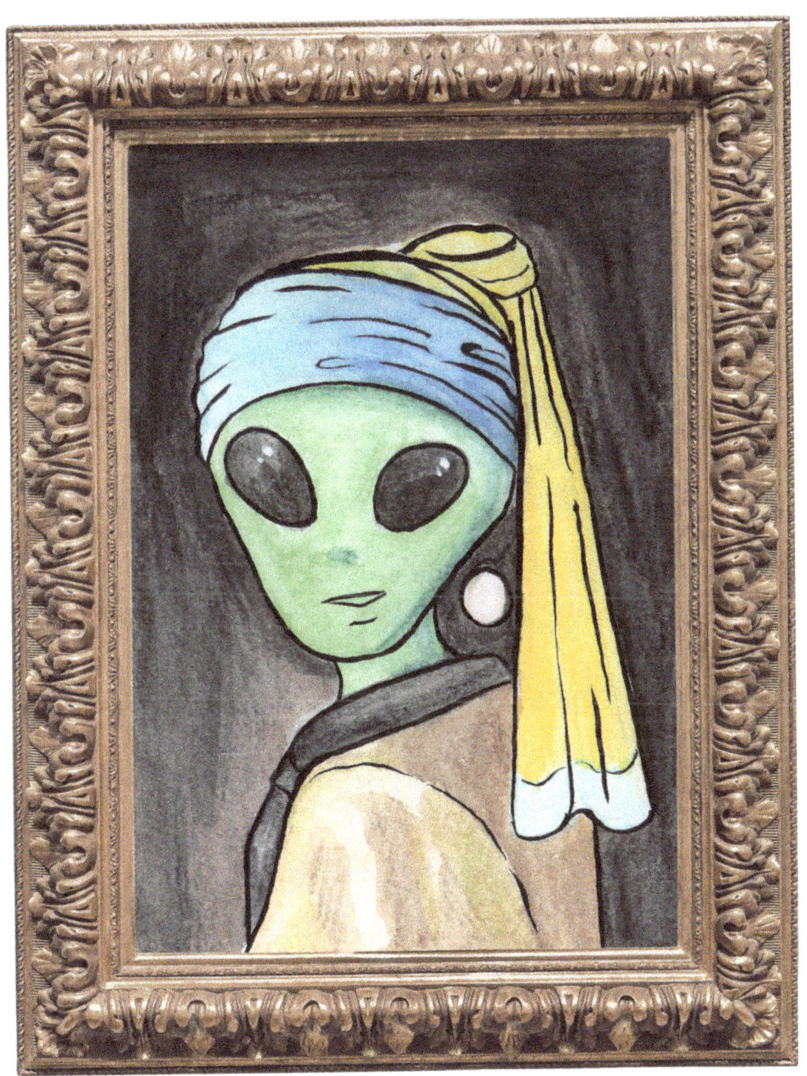

Where on Ea

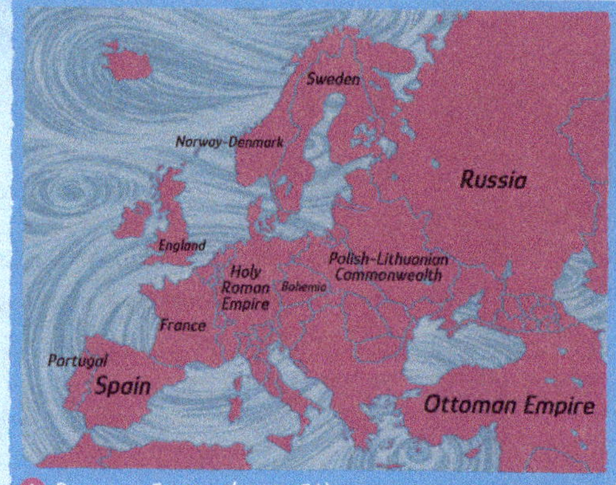

1 Baroque Europe (page 76)

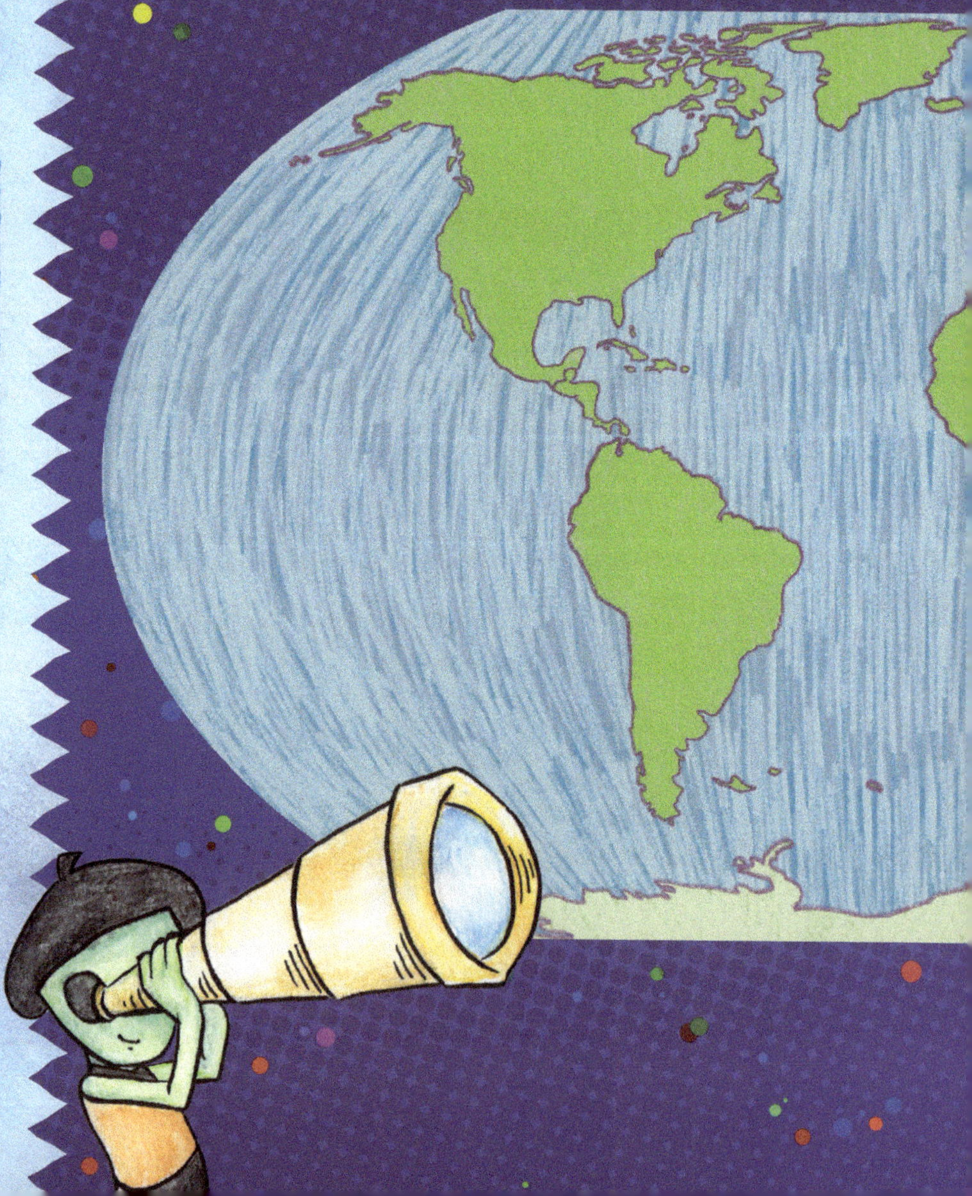

th are We?

Maps: Art from around 1600 - 1800

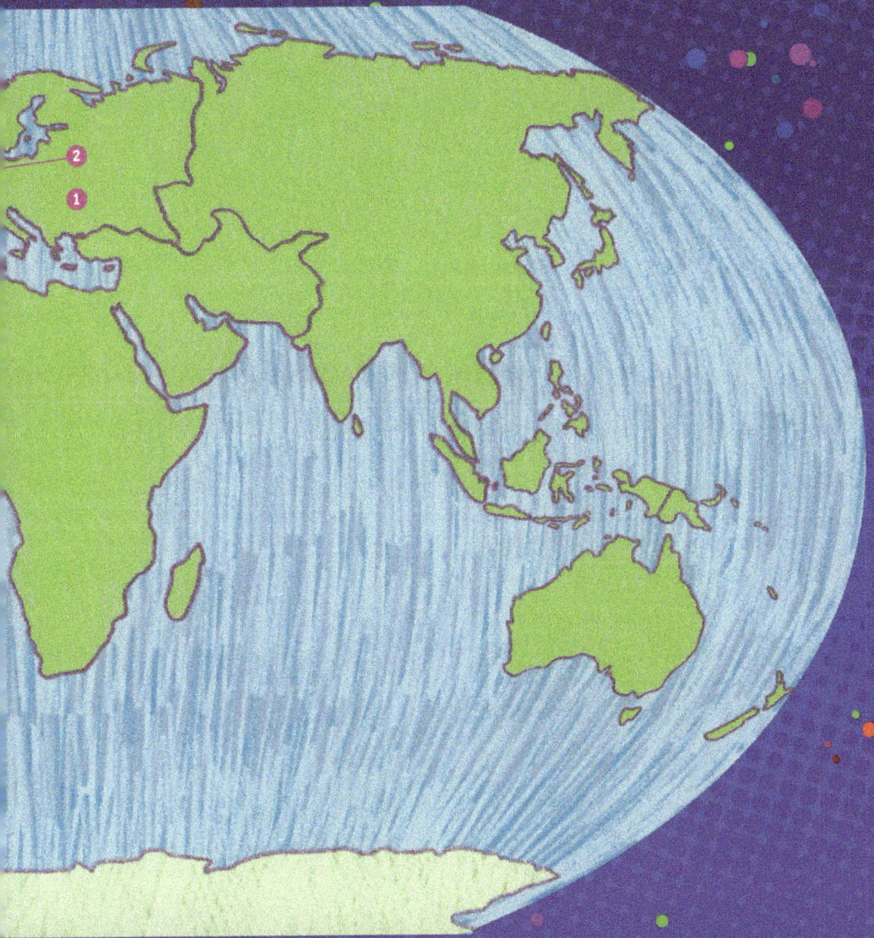

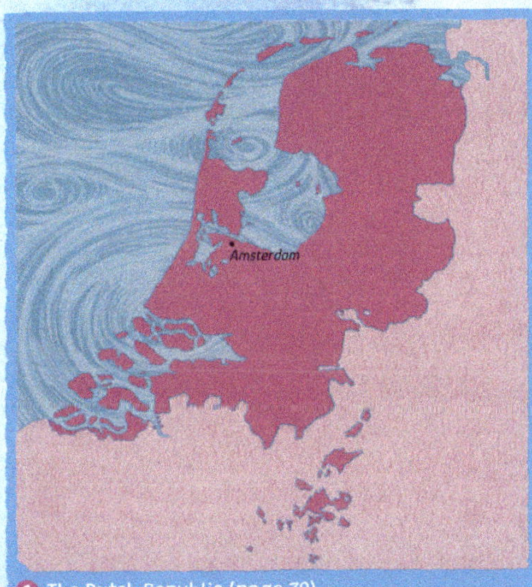

2 The Dutch Republic (page 79)

Art from the 1800s

Academic Art

And here we are, Earthlings; we've reached the 1800s!

I think this is an excellent time to talk a bit about Academic art, a tradition that began in the 1500s and flourished during the 1800s. This movement is directly linked to the artists who studied and were teachers at European academies during this time period.

Remember how we learned about Classical art from ancient Greece and Rome? Academic art was greatly inspired by Classical art and set standards for artists to follow.

Academic art came directly from art academies. In 1816, two French institutions in Paris joined to create the Académie des Beaux-Arts-which translates to the Academy of Fine Arts in English. Art students still study there today!

European art academies replaced Medieval methods of teaching art (page 50) and eventually became the safest way to ensure a successful career as an artist. In order to study at any art academy, students had to pass a series of exams, and the most famous academies had the hardest entry exams. After being accepted to an academy, art students dedicated many years to their craft.

To get better at painting or drawing, art academy students would study works by famous artists from the past. These famous artists are known as the Old Masters.

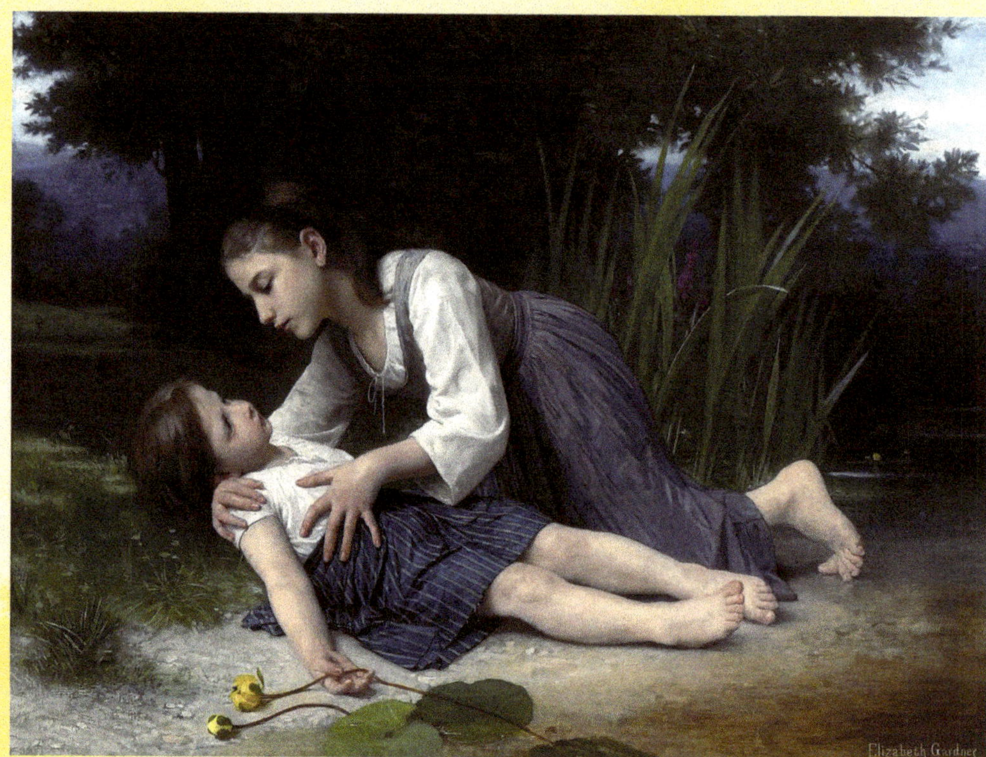

Elizabeth Jane Gardner
The Imprudent Girl, 1884
Oil on canvas

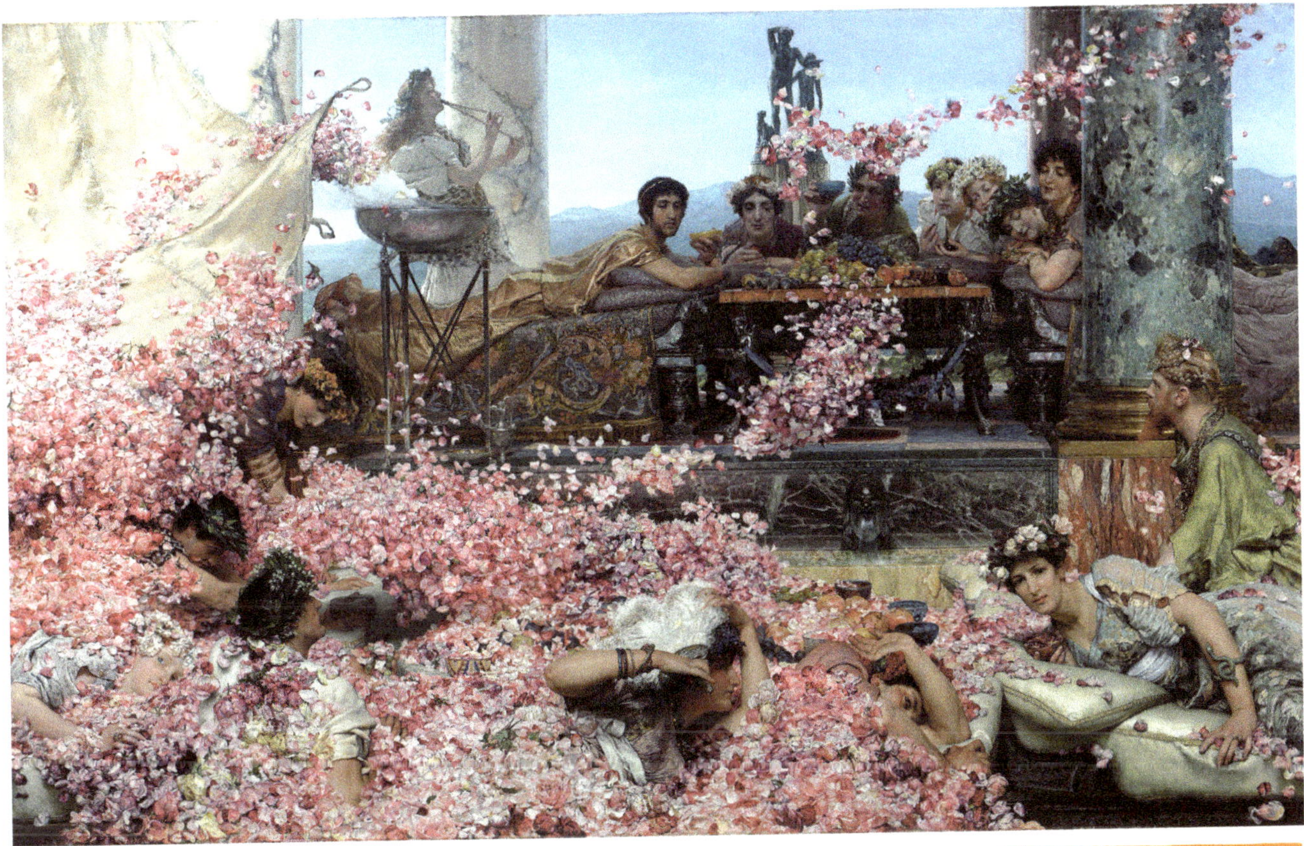

Lawrence Alma-Tadema
The Roses of Heliogabalus, 1888
Oil on canvas

To understand the techniques used by the Old Masters, art students often tried to copy their paintings or drawings using similar colors and styles. Among the most celebrated Old Masters are Leonardo da Vinci, Michelangelo and Caravaggio (pages 64, 65 and 77). While there were many other Old Masters, these three are the most famous.

Art students had to work really hard to be recognized. Their art had to be accepted into prestigious art exhibits, and only the most talented were chosen. The most accomplished students were called academics.

Academic art focused on creating art that made people think rather than just look good. Students explored two distinct styles: Neoclassicism (page 86), which focused on making art with perfect proportions, and Romanticism (page 88), which focused on expressing feelings.

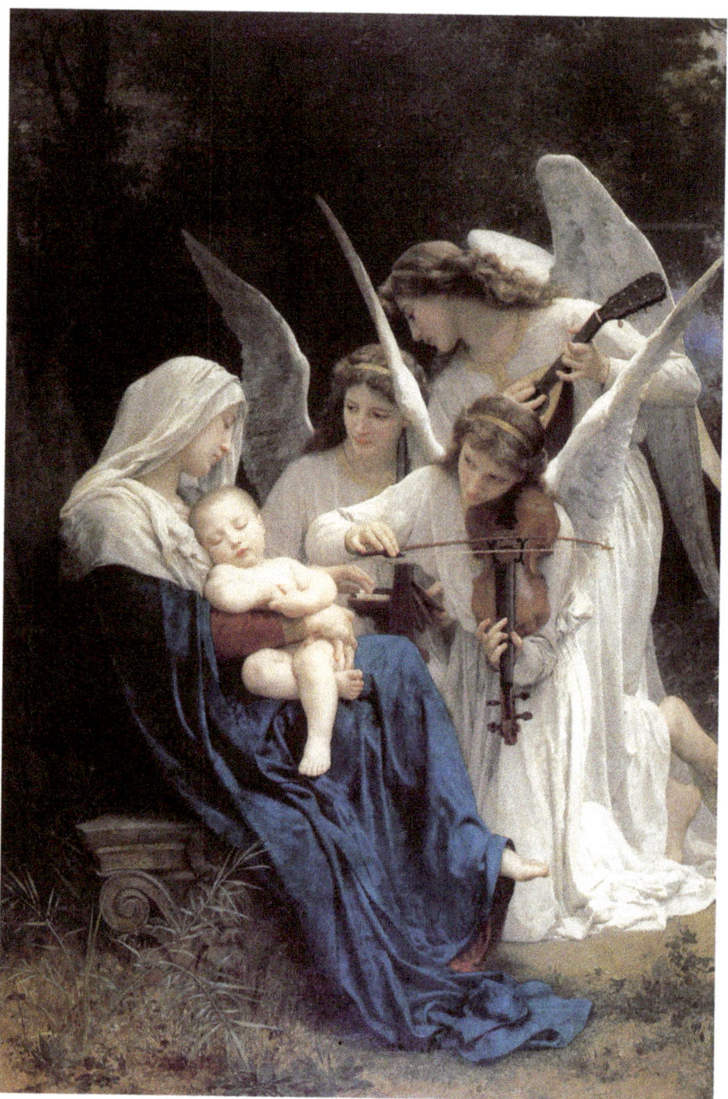

One of the truly remarkable painters of that time was William Adolphe Bouguereau. He was able to portray people in his paintings as though they were made of shiny porcelain. (page 53).

He made many paintings about religion and mythology, as well as about normal people who worked in fields. He also helped women to be able to study art in schools. Bouguereau is often tied to Realism (page 105), which aimed to show things in a lifelike way.

Bouguereau
Song of the Angels, 1881
Oil on canvas

Native North American Art

Now that we have seen what was going on in Europe during the beginning of the 19th century, let's hop over to North America! Native Americans have been making art since 600 BCE. They made many kinds of sculptures, clothes, and pottery. Their art wasn't just meant to look pretty - it was actually useful in their everyday lives.

Native American art often tells stories about their beliefs and how they think the world began. They used their art to share these stories and to celebrate their spirituality.

Throughout history, many Native American groups emerged and thrived, but things became really difficult when European settlers came. Europeans took over their lands and brought many diseases. Interactions between Europeans and Native Americans were also often violent. Europeans did not respect Native American culture and forced Native Americans to stop their way of life.

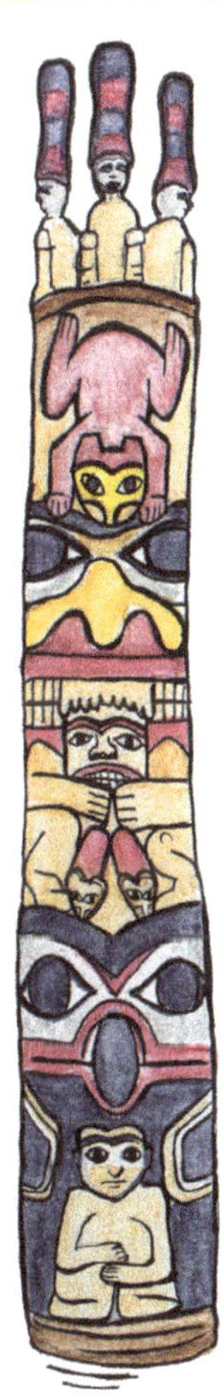

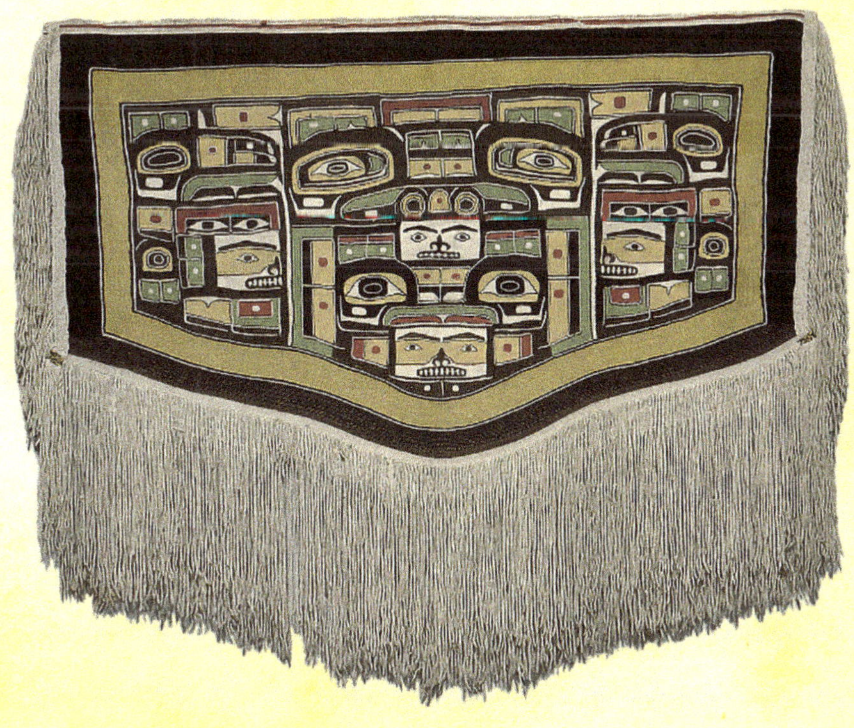

Mary Ebbetts Hunt
Chilkat Robe, circa 1880 – 1890
Goat wool, wool yarn, and cedar bark

This Chilkat robe was created around 1880-1890 by Mary Ebbetts Hunt from the Tlingit culture in Southeast Alaska.

Japanese Art

Let's explore Japanese art during the early 1800s!

Japan has a rich legacy in painting and woodblock printmaking. During this period, a method known as ukiyo-e became really popular. It allowed artists to make prints that looked like watercolors! These prints showed various subjects, like beautiful women, sumo wrestlers, samurais, and actors from traditional Japanese theaters called kabuki.

One of the most famous artists from this time was Hokusai, who was really good at making ukiyo-e prints. Hokusai changed his name 30 times during his career!

When you look at *The Great Wave off Kanagawa*, you might notice some things about the way it's made. The wave is really big, and it takes up a lot of the picture. The boats and the people in them are much smaller, and they look like they're getting tossed around by the wave.

There are different ideas about what *The Great Wave off Kanagawa* means. Some think Hokusai wanted to show that, even though humans think they're in control, nature is still more powerful. What do you think?

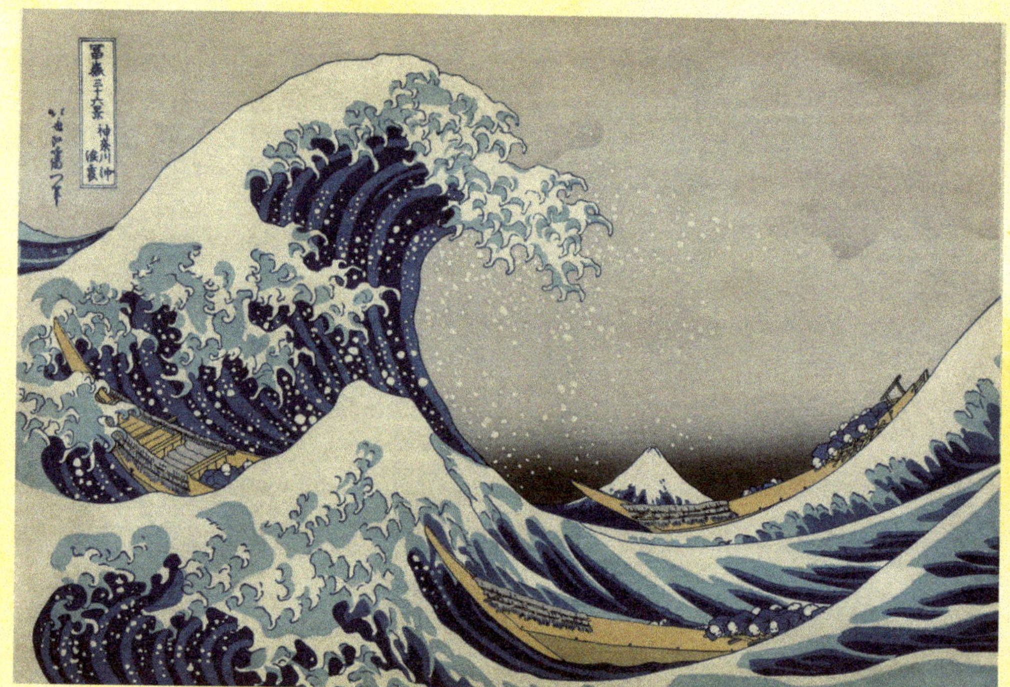

Hokusai
The Great Wave off Kanagawa, 1831
Ukiyo-e (woodblock print)

Perhaps Hokusai's most famous painting is called *The Great Wave off Kanagawa*. It shows a huge wave towering over some boats with people in them. The wave looks really powerful, and it almost seems like it's about to crash down on the boats!

Japanese prints had a big impact on art in Europe in the late 1800s. For example, impressionists and post-Impressionists like Monet and van Gogh (pages 108 and 112) were influenced by them. They liked the strong colors and interesting shapes in Japanese prints and started using some of the same techniques in their own paintings.

Hiroshige Utagawa
Plum Park at Kameido, 1857
Ukiyo-e (woodblock print)

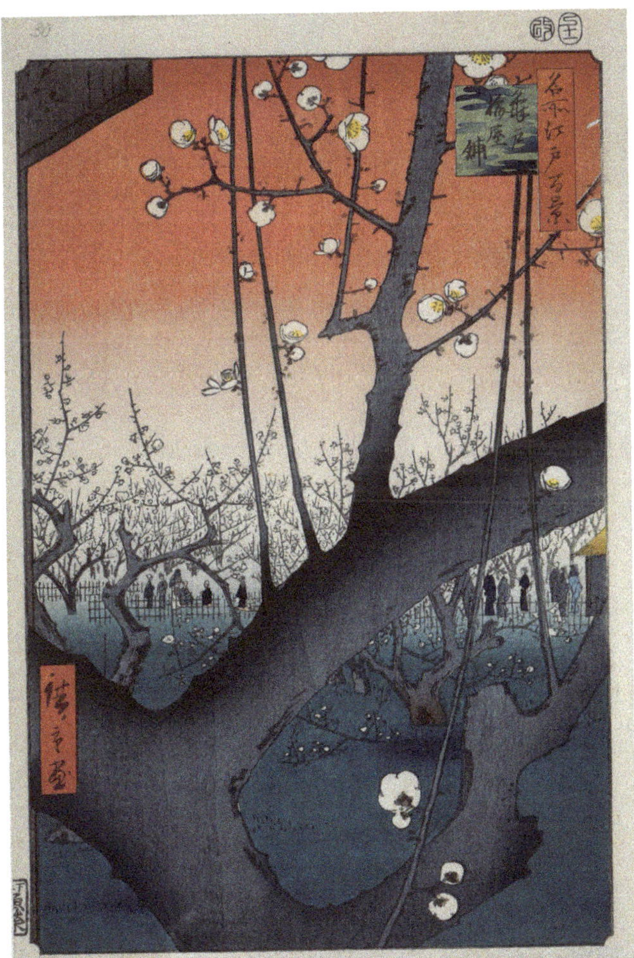

Vincent van Gogh
Flowering plum tree (after Hiroshige), 1887
Oil on canvas

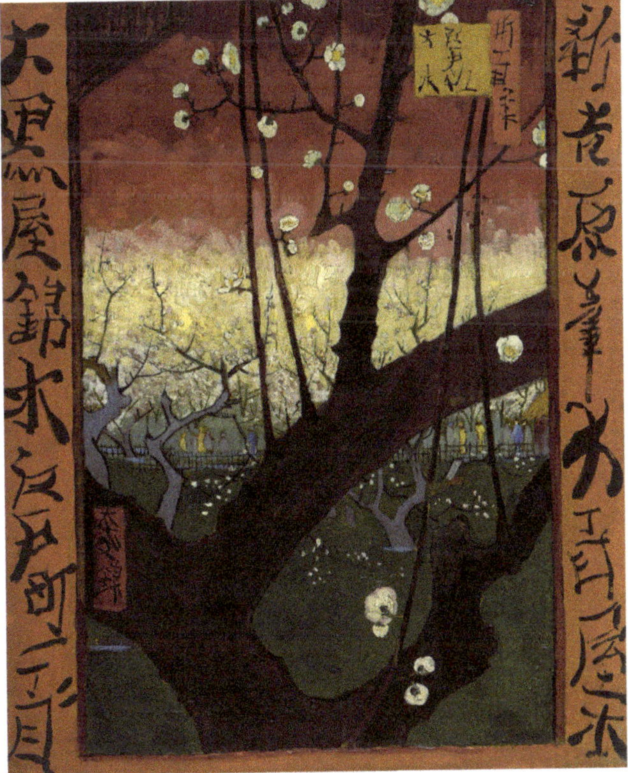

Activity

Homemade Prints

The process of creating woodcut prints is very long and takes many years of practice to achieve. Instead, let's make a print using styrofoam!

What you'll need:

- **Paper**
- **Gouache paint**
- **Scissors**
- **Small foam roller**
- **Styrofoam trays**
- **Paper towels for cleaning**
- **Toothpicks or a sharp pencil**

Get a styrofoam tray.

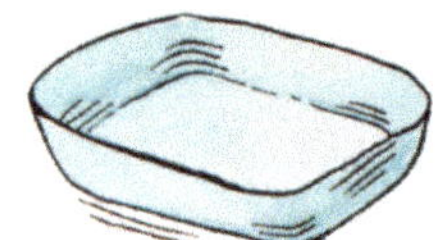

Cut off the edges until you have a flat surface. Transfer your image to the styrofoam using a toothpick or sharp pencil.

Cover the entire surface of the styrofoam with paint using a roller.

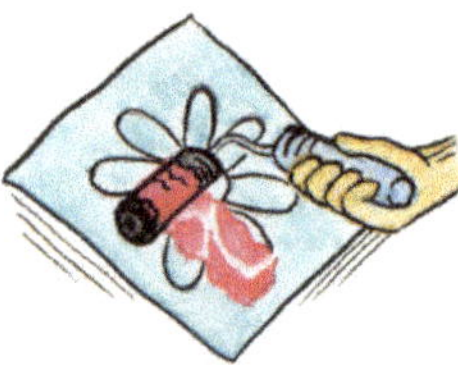

Take a sheet of paper and press it on the styrofoam to transfer your print. Remove it and let it dry.

How to create your print:

1 Take a styrofoam tray and cut off the edges until it looks like a flat sheet. Then, draw a picture on a piece of paper. There's no need to add small details because the styrofoam will not be able to capture them.

2 When you're happy with your drawing, use a sharp pencil or toothpick to transfer it onto the styrofoam by pressing down firmly to make grooves on the surface.

3 Next, on another tray, add a little paint and carefully spread it evenly using a foam roller. Roll the same roller over your styrofoam with the drawing on it so that the paint sticks to the entire surface, and the grooves will still be visible. Then, take a sheet of paper and press it down onto the painted styrofoam. Gently run your hands over it to make it smooth.

4 If the lines on the styrofoam are deep enough, the paint will transfer to everything except for those lines. After finishing, remove the paper and allow it to dry. If there are any mistakes in your print, don't worry! Just try again with more or less paint until you get it right.

Pre-Raphaelite Brotherhood

In 1848, a group of artists in London started a secret society called the Pre-Raphaelite Brotherhood. They were tired of being told how to make art by the Royal Academy, the official art school in England at the time. The Academy had strict rules about what art should look like, and the Pre-Raphaelites wanted to do something different. They wanted to make art with bright colors and lots of details. They didn't like the dark, serious paintings that were popular at the time.

The Pre-Raphaelite Brotherhood wanted to create art that came before the classical style of Raphael (page 66). They were only around for five years, but their impact was big! The Brotherhood loved to paint stories from medieval times and plays by Shakespeare.

John Everette Millais
Ophelia, 1851
oil on canvas

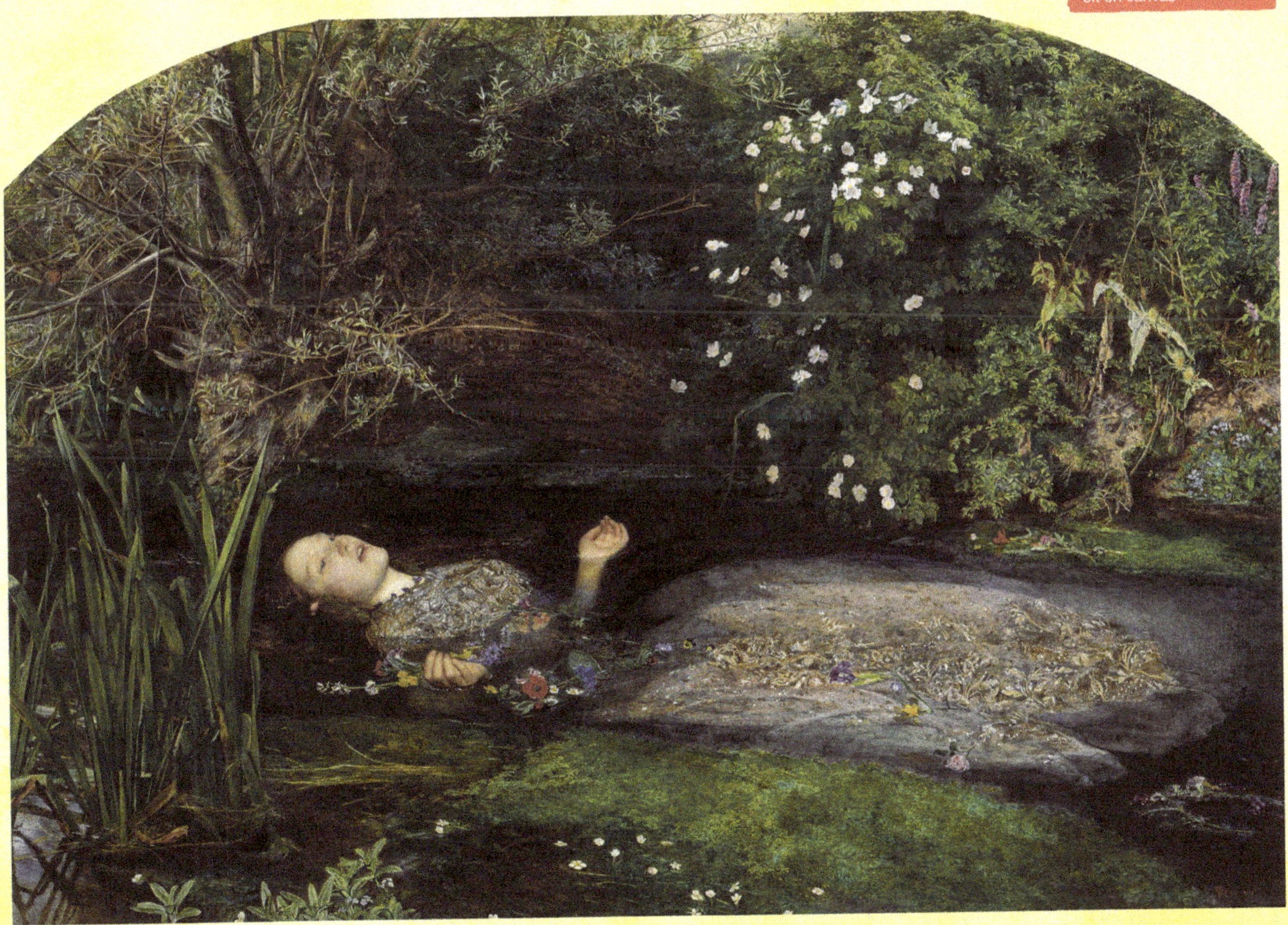

The Pre-Raphaelites painted nature as they saw it, a style that went against Academic norms and later inspired the Impressionists (page 107).

John Everett Millais and Dante Gabriel Rossetti were some of the most famous Pre-Raphaelites. They made many beautiful paintings that people still admire today.

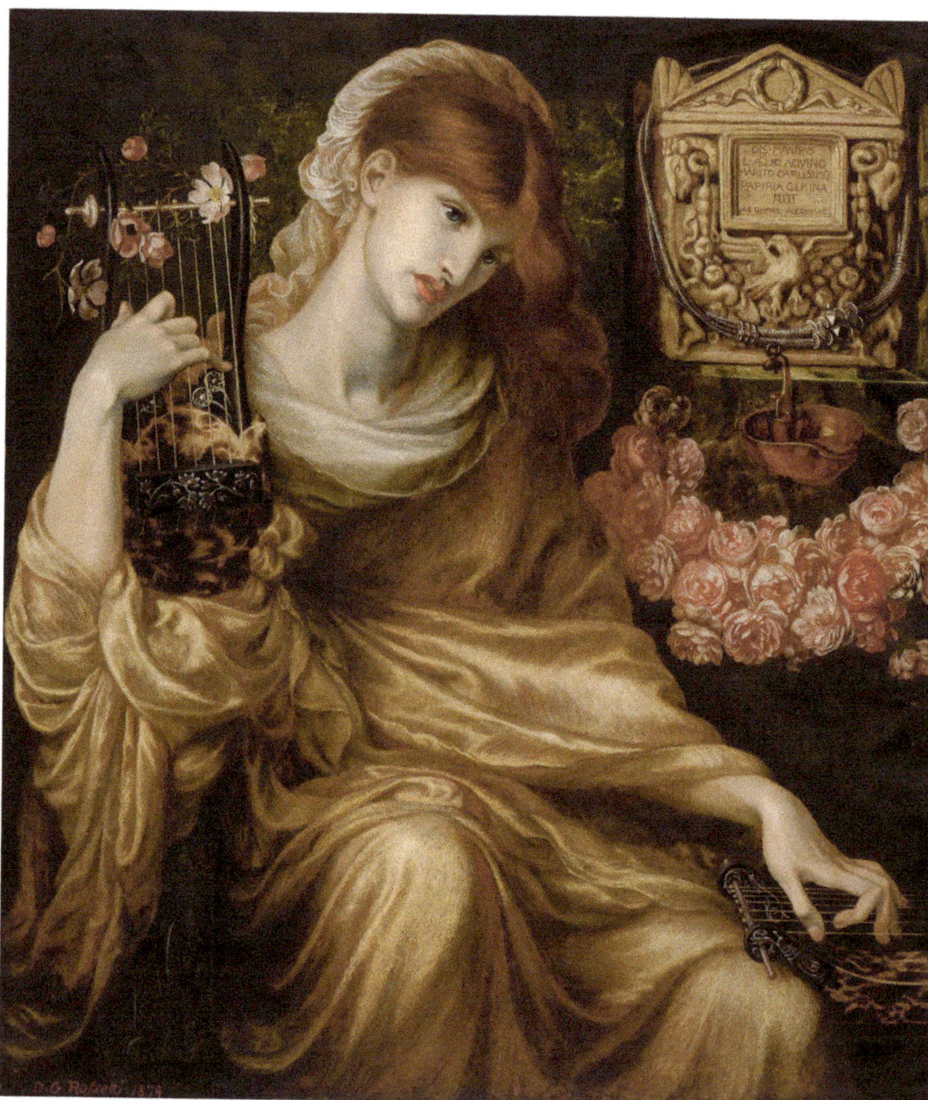

Dante Gabriel Rossetti
Roman Window, 1874
Oil on canvas

Realism

Realism began in Paris in 1830 and sought to portray the world as it really was - without making anything look more perfect or more beautiful than it really was. It was a movement that started because some artists thought Romantic art (page 88) was too emotional and not realistic enough. Instead of painting kings, queens, and mythical creatures, Realist artists painted regular people doing everyday things. They wanted to show that everyone was important, not just the rich and famous!

Realist art often shows people who worked in fields or other jobs as their main subjects. When we look at art, we can learn about what was happening in history at that time too.

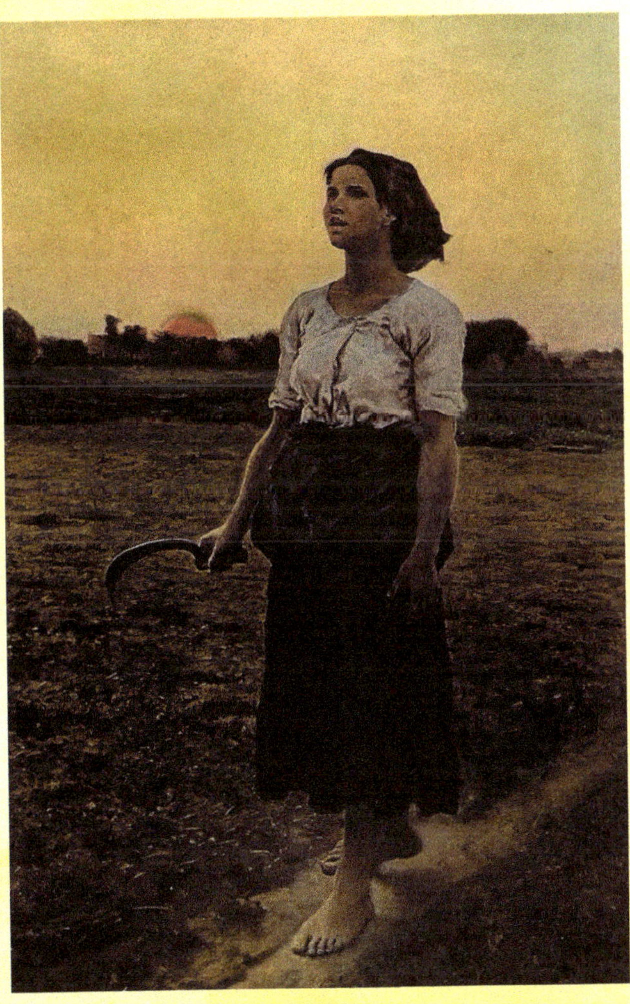

Jules Breton
The Song of the Lark, 1884
Oil on canvas

Gustave Courbet was a famous Realist artist who didn't like the way that art was usually made. He thought that paintings should show real life, even if it wasn't always pretty. In 1848, the Paris Salon exhibit accepted more than 10 of his artworks.

A group of artists who wished to portray the countryside and distance themselves from Romanticism went to a village named Barbizon. They became part of a group created by Jean-François Millet called the Barbizon School.

The Realist movement inspired future artists like Vincent van Gogh (page 112), who created many versions of Millet's works.

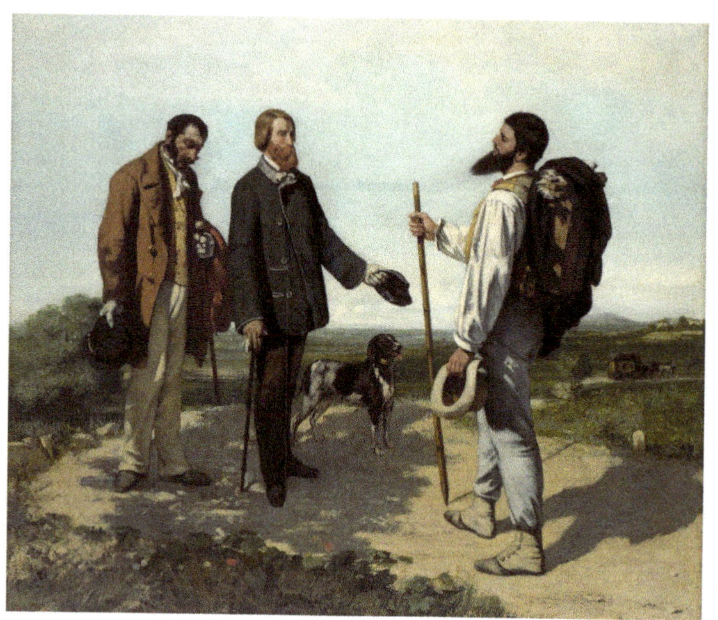

Gustave Courbet
The Meeting, 1854
Oil on canvas

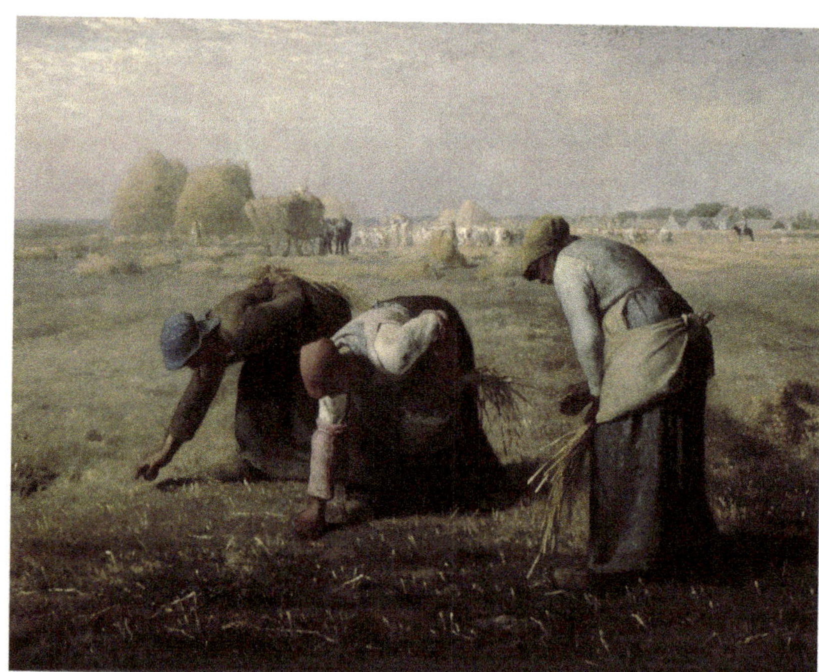

Jean-François Millet
The Gleaners, 1857
Oil on canvas

Impressionism

Let's talk about one of the most famous art movements in Modern art - the Impressionist movement! This is when many humans believe Modern art officially began.

In the 1860s, a group of French artists used to hang out at local cafés. They all studied art but didn't like the strict rules of the Academy.

These artists were tired of not being allowed to show their art at big exhibits, like the Paris Salon, which was the main way to become a successful artist at the time. So in 1863, they decided to have their own exhibit called the Salon of the Refused. This exhibit was filled with artworks that were not accepted into the official Salon of Paris, and it was financed by Napoleon III.

The leading Impressionist artists were Claude Monet, Camille Pissarro, Alfred Sisley, Auguste Renoir, Mary Cassatt, and Edgar Degas.

The Impressionists changed the way that people thought about art. They showed that art could be more about feelings than about making realistic images, and they showed that ordinary peoples' lives were just as important as the lives of kings and queens.

Impressionists explored the effects of light and atmosphere in their paintings. The use of light and color was an essential element of Impressionist paintings, whether created indoors or outdoors.

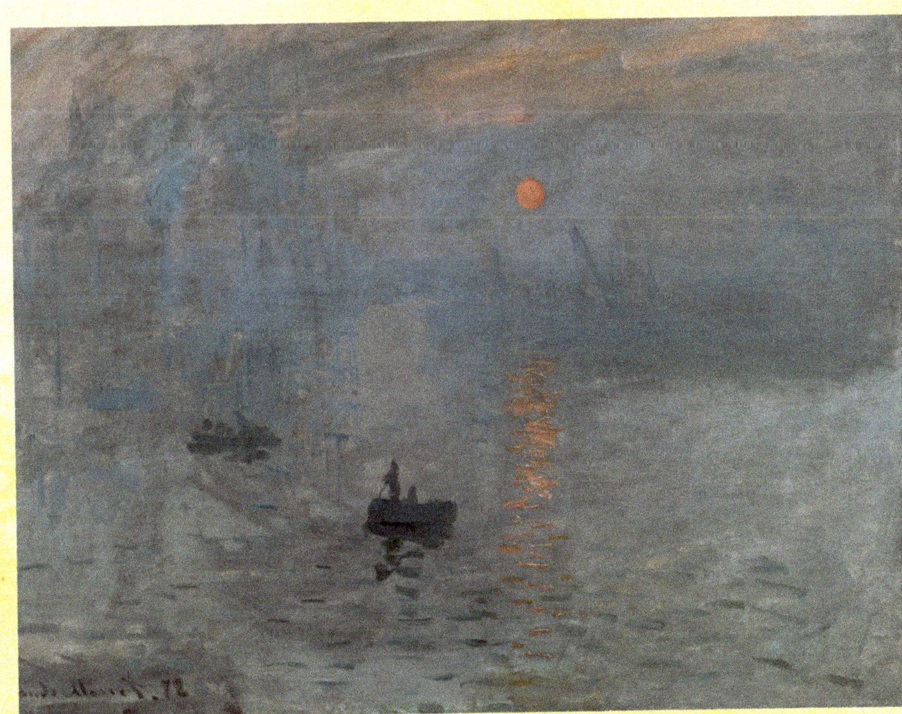

Monet
Impression, Sunrise, 1872
Oil on canvas

This painting was so important to the Impressionist movement that it gave it its name! At first, not everyone liked it though. Some people thought the painting looked sloppy and unfinished.

Born in Paris in 1840, Claude Monet grew up in a town called Le Havre in Normandy. Later on, he built a beautiful garden near Paris, where he loved to paint. When he got older, his eyesight started to get worse. He was diagnosed with cataracts in 1912, which made it hard for him to see clearly. Even so, he kept on painting, using his blurry vision to create beautiful works of art.

As one of the Modern artists who wanted to break free from the rules of Academic art, Monet didn't want to paint only history, religion, or mythological stories. He wanted to paint everyday life in a new way. Instead of painting in a studio, he wanted to paint outside, in nature.

Oh! And don't get Claude Monet (pronounced "Mo-nay") confused with Édouard Manet (pronounced "Man-nay"). Manet was an influential artist that helped start Modern painting. He did not consider himself an Impressionist, although he supported the movement.

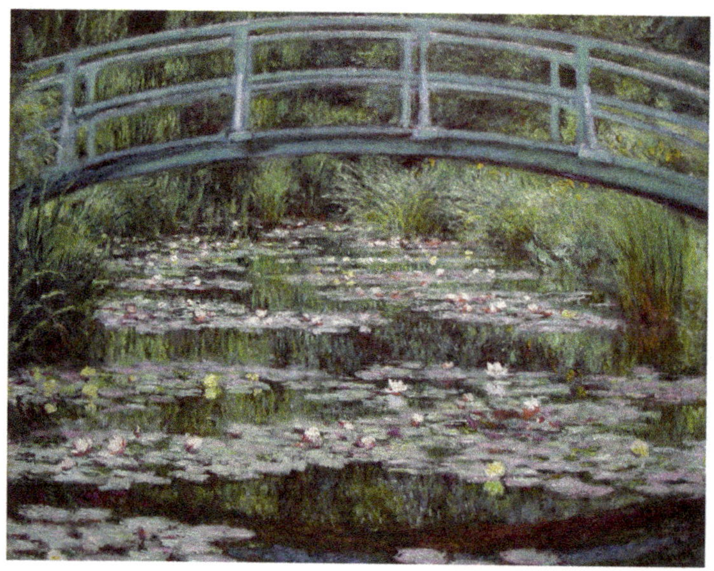

Claude Monet
The Japanese Footbridge, 1899
Oil on canvas

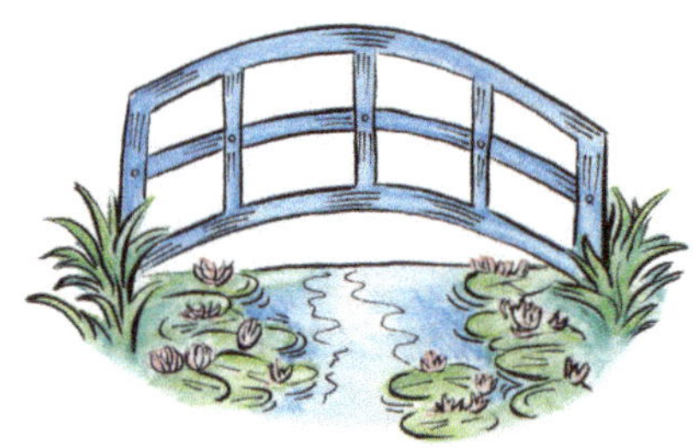

Did you know that photography also influenced the Impressionists? When cameras became more common, some artists began to wonder if it was still important to paint things exactly as they looked, since photos could already do that perfectly.

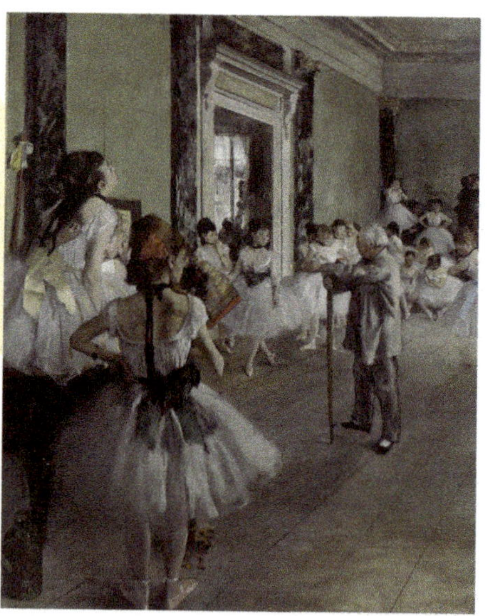

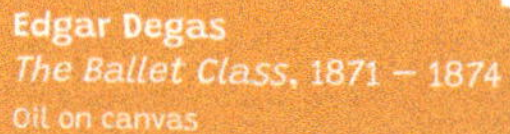

Edgar Degas
The Ballet Class, 1871 – 1874
Oil on canvas

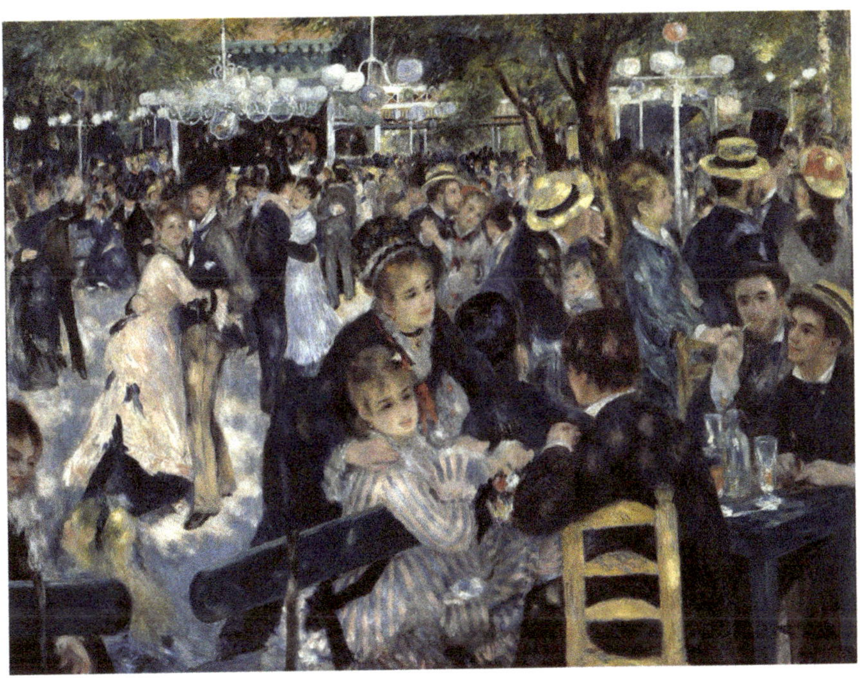

Pierre-Auguste Renoir
Dance at Le Moulin de la Galette, 1876
Oil on canvas

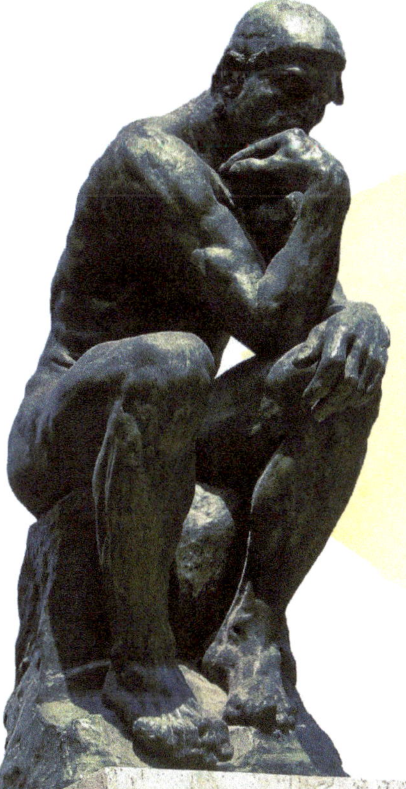

Did you know that Impressionism also had an influence on sculpture? Auguste Rodin was a famous sculptor who experimented with the effects of light on surfaces, just like the Impressionist painters. He used this knowledge to create his own unique sculptures that were very different from traditional sculptures of the time.

Rodin
The Thinker, 1904
Bronze statue

Activity

Creating a Color Wheel

The Impressionists were masters of color, and you can be too! To understand a bit more about color, we need to create our own color wheel!

What you'll need:

- **Gouache paint: magenta, yellow and blue**
- **Paper towels for cleaning**
- **Paintbrush**
- **Tray for mixing**
- **Colored pens**

Using the space on the next page, add the three primary colors: magenta, yellow, and blue. Put each color in a circle on the paper. Now, mix two colors together to make new colors in the empty squares. The new colors you created are called secondary colors.

Write the name of each color with your colored pens.

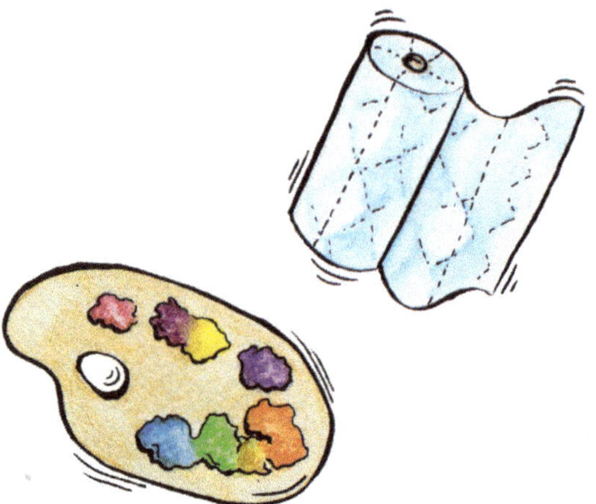

Did you know?

People often mistake one of the three primary colors! Many humans use red instead of the correct primary color, magenta. Both colors are a bit similar, but it makes a lot of difference, trust me. The color magenta looks like a hot pink that, when mixed together with yellow, turns into red!

Primary colors are called primary because they cannot be created by mixing other colors. In other words, the three primary colors are the starting point to create all of the other colors of the wheel.

Some colors make us feel cool, like blue and green - these are called cool colors. Other colors make us feel warm, like yellow and red - these are called warm colors. Think about summer and winter and the colors you see more during each season. Then, find the cool and warm colors on your wheel and write them with your pens.

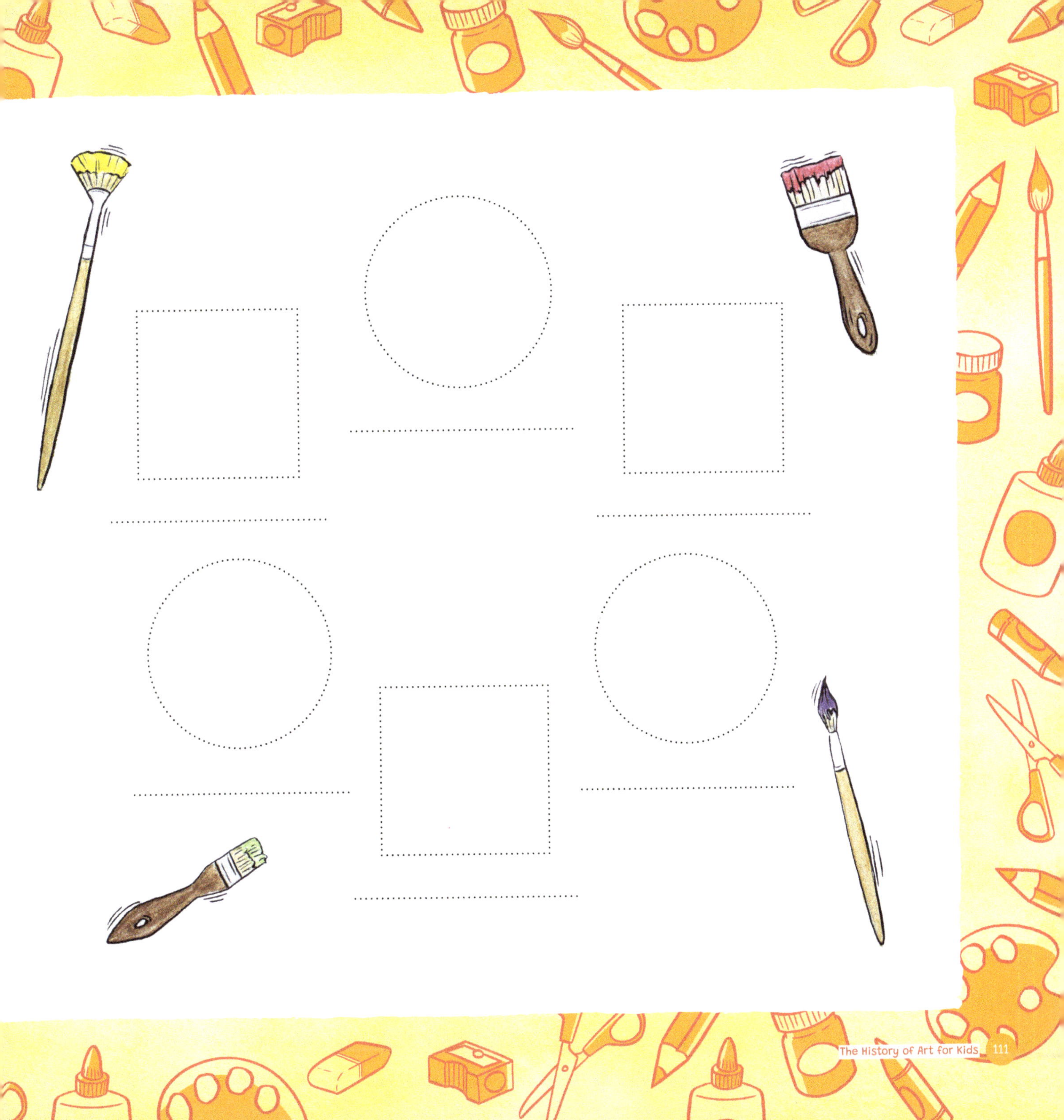

Post-Impressionism

MODERN art is so cool and so free! It makes all three of my hearts pound!

After the Impressionist artists, there were lots of new ideas and styles in art. Some artists continued to explore new possibilities, and this time period is called Post-Impressionism.

Post-Impressionist artists were all different and didn't follow the same style. They used bright colors and thick layers of paint to make their art stand out. Four of the most famous Post-Impressionist artists are:

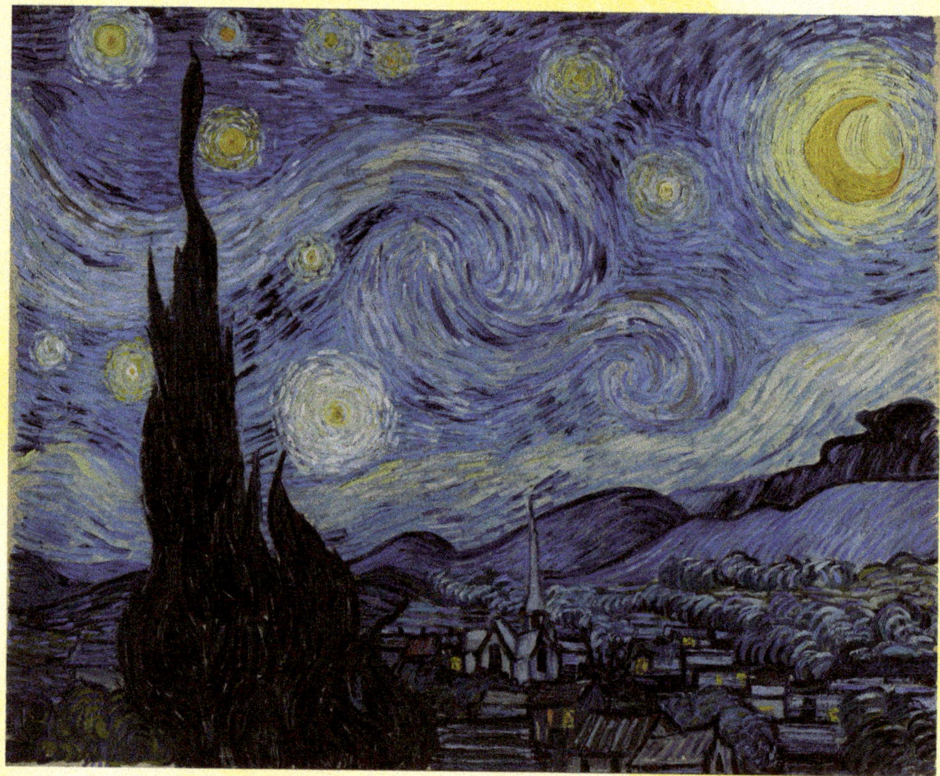

Vincent van Gogh
Starry Night, 1889
Oil on canvas

Vincent van Gogh

I'm sure you've heard of van Gogh before! He made incredible masterpieces that reflected his feelings and emotions. He used lots of bold colors to create beautiful landscapes.

Paul Cezánne

Cezánne participated in some Impressionist exhibits, including the very first one. He worked with blocks of colors to create almost abstract pictures. His style was unique and different from other artists.

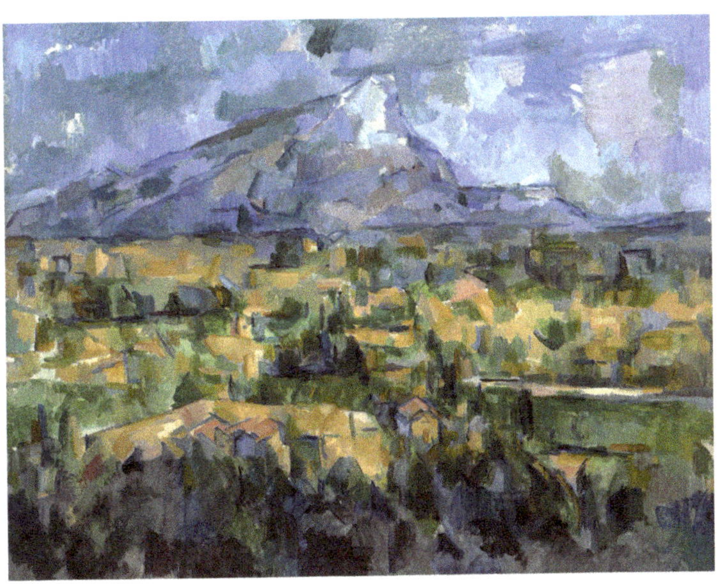

Paul Cezánne
Montagne Sainte-Victoire, 1904
Oil on canvas

Paul Gauguin

Because of his Spanish-Peruvian heritage, Gauguin spent part of his childhood living in Peru, which influenced his later work. He never studied painting but was able to create a style of his own. In 1891, he moved to Tahiti, where he created paintings of the natives and landscapes.

Paul Gauguin
When Will You Marry?, 1892
Oil on canvas

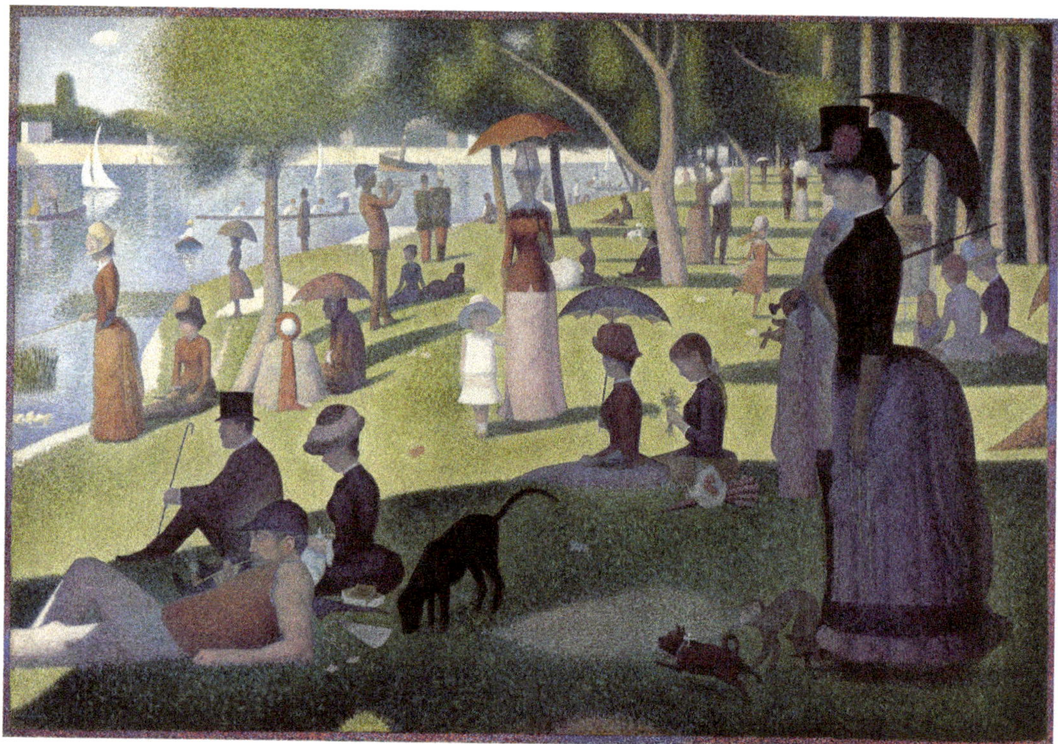

Georges-Pierre Seurat
A Sunday Afternoon on the Island of La Grande Jatte, 1884 – 1886
Oil on canvas

Georges-Pierre Seurat

Seurat studied art since he was 19 years old. Along with his friend and fellow artist, Paul Signac, he created a new technique of painting called Pointillism. This technique used many tiny dots of complementary colors to create a picture.

When we look at modern art, we can see all kinds of colors and styles. Some colors might remind us of summer, like bright yellows and oranges, while others might make us think of winter, like deep blues and purples. We can also find out which colors look good together by seeing the color that is opposite of it on the color wheel, which indicates they are complementary colors.

Examples of complementary color combinations are: red and green; yellow and purple; orange and blue.

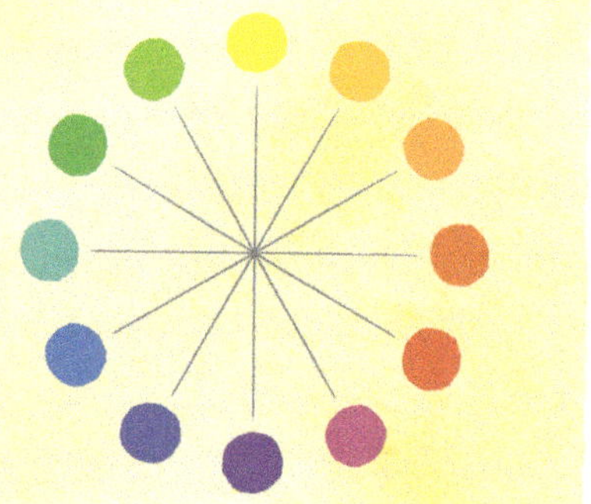

Creating a Pointillist Painting

Let's create our own Pointillist painting!

What you'll need:

- **Gouache paint**
- **Pencil**
- **A cork**
- **A tray for paint**
- **A large piece of paper**

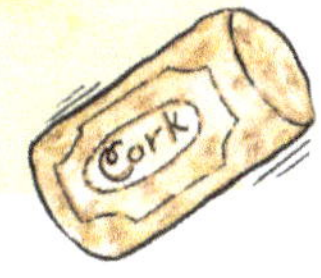

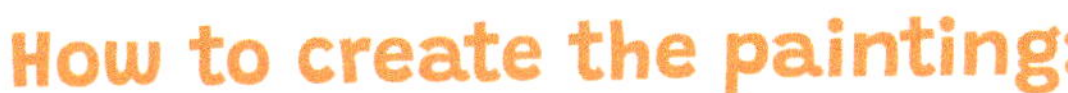

1 Before starting your painting, first think about what kind of image you want to create. The Impressionists and Post-Impressionists loved painting landscapes, so feel free to go outside and use a pencil to sketch your favorite spot!

2 A sketch is just a rough drawing to plan out your painting, so keep your lines light and simple. No need to worry too much about getting everything perfect.

3 When your sketch is done, get your paint ready on a tray - just a dab of each color will do. You can use a cork to create colorful dots throughout your artwork or experiment with using the pencil's tip to make smaller dots. Simply dip the cork into the paint and apply some dots onto the paper. When the paint starts to fade, just dip the cork into the paint again.

4 This activity is even more fun with friends!

5 After you finish your painting, take a moment to look at it up close and then from farther away. Do you see any differences in how it looks?

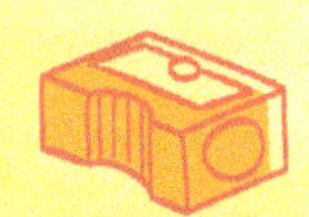

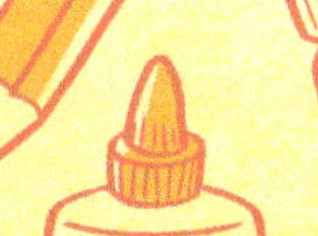

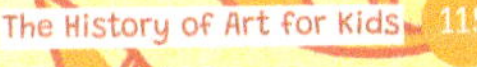

Art Nouveau

In the late 1800s, a fascinating art movement called Art Nouveau emerged. It became popular in paintings, design, and architecture. Art Nouveau, meaning "new art," is noted for its decorative style. It started in Europe and found its way into the hearts of many in the United States.

Art Nouveau drew inspiration from a variety of sources, including Japanese ukiyo-e artworks (page 100) and the stylized paintings created by influential Post-Impressionist artists like Vincent van Gogh and Paul Gauguin (pages 112 and 113).

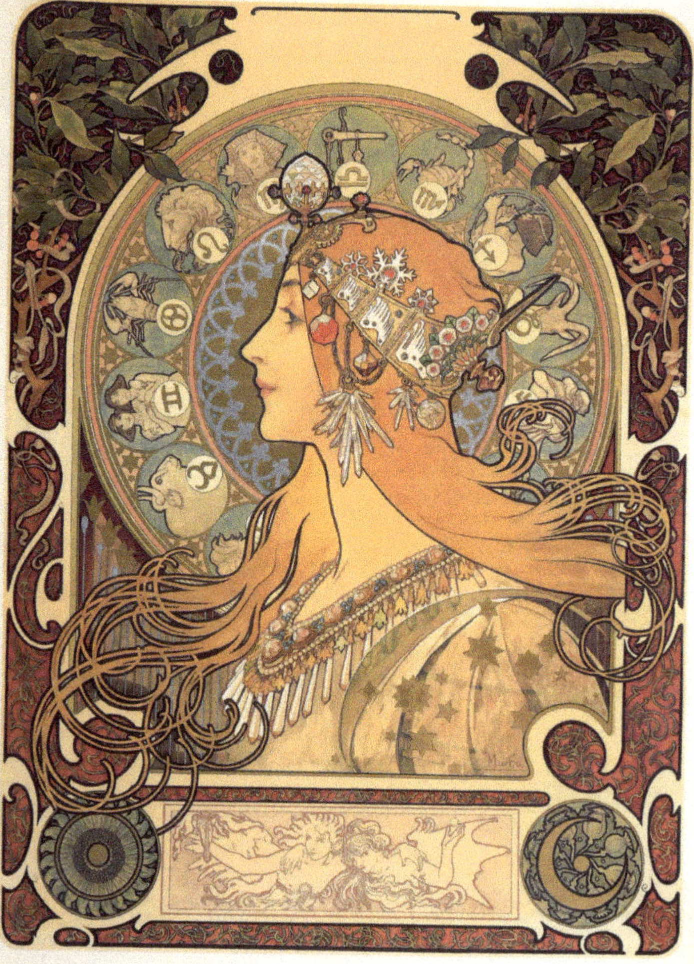

Alphonse Mucha
Zodiac calendar for La Plume, 1897
Lithographic print

Vienna Secession

The Vienna Secession was a movement that started in Austria by a group of artists who wanted to break away from the traditional art style of their time. They believed that art should be more expressive and modern. One of the most famous artists from this movement was Gustav Klimt. He created beautiful paintings with lots of gold and bright colors. The Vienna Secession artists liked to use natural shapes and patterns in their work, just like the Art Nouveau artists.

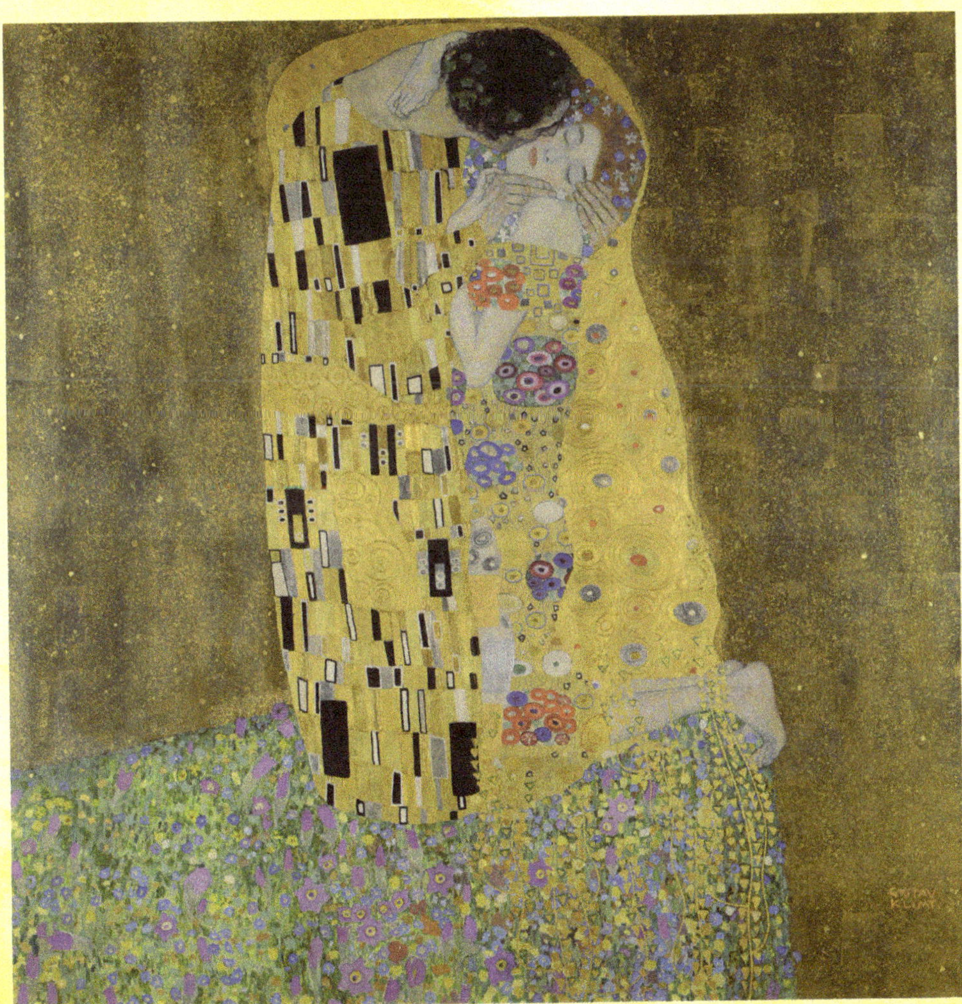

Gustav Klimt
The Kiss, 1907 – 1908
Oil on canvas

Where on Ea

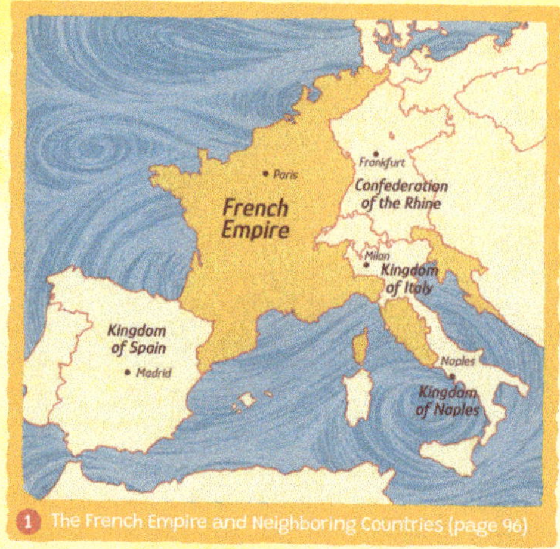

1 The French Empire and Neighboring Countries (page 96)

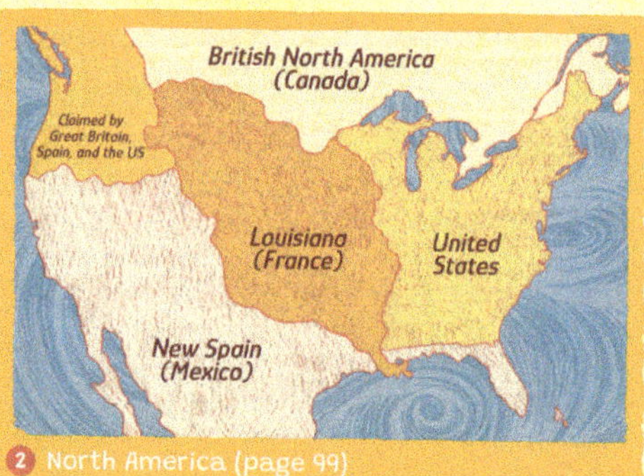

2 North America (page 99)

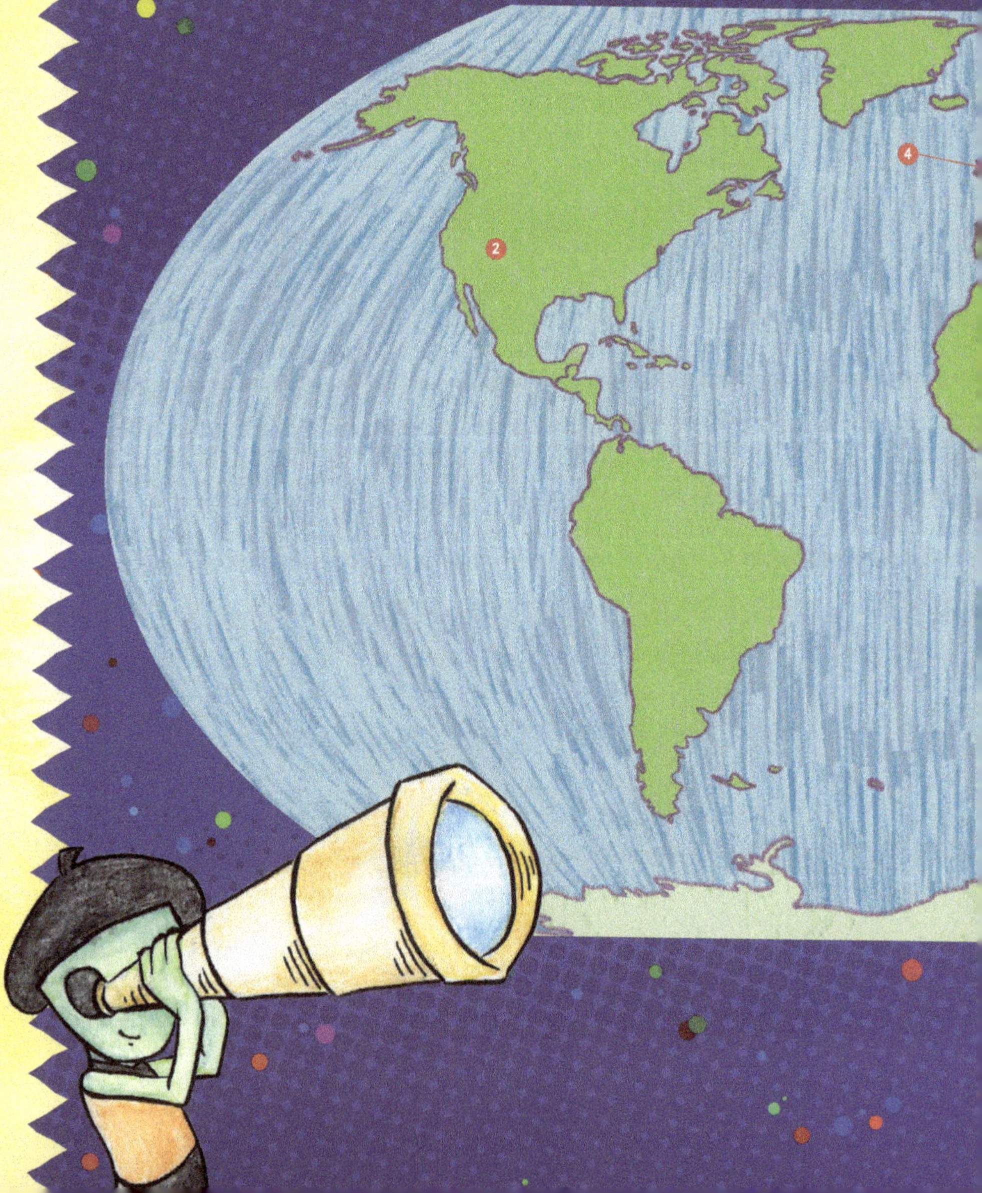

th are We?

Maps: Art from the 1800s

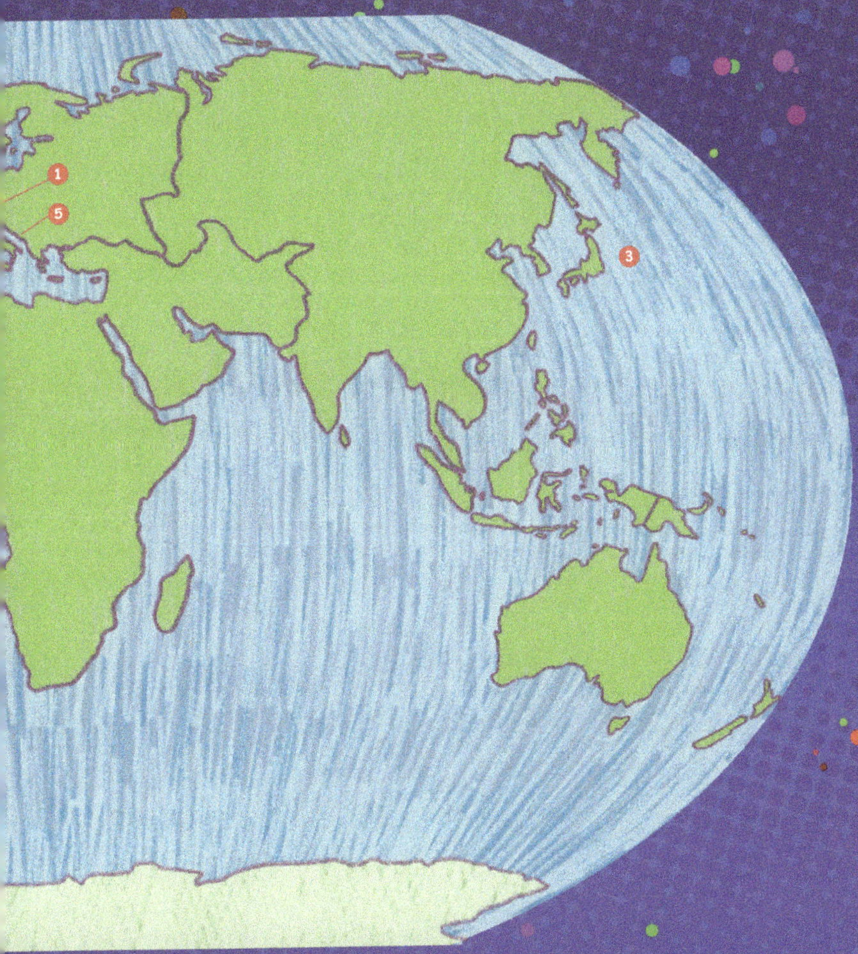

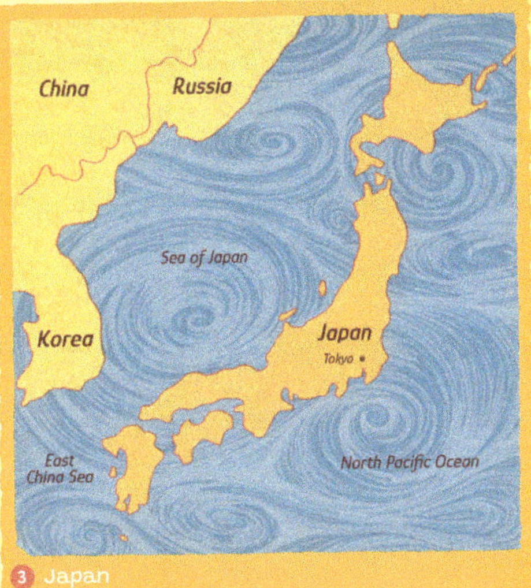

3 Japan

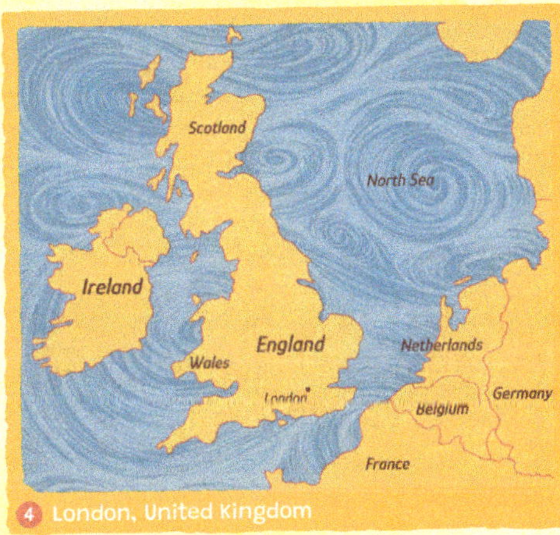

4 London, United Kingdom

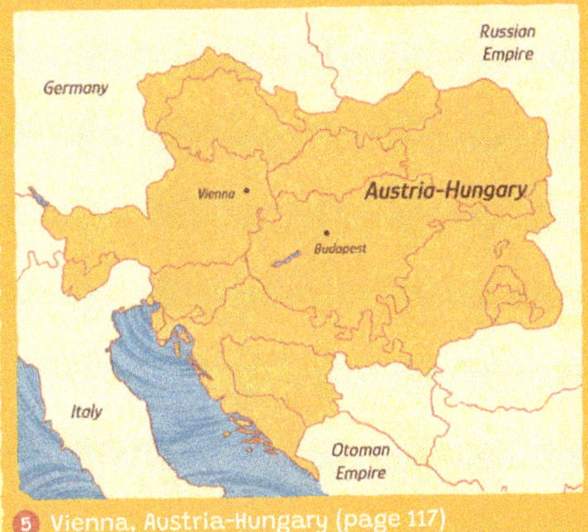

5 Vienna, Austria-Hungary (page 117)

Art from 1900 – 1940

Expressionism

Wow, we went through another century of humankind's amazing art!

Germany is our next stop. Let's learn about the German Expressionist movement. It all started with two groups of artists in Munich and Dresden who loved old German folk art and wanted to bring it back to life. They wanted to feel a connection to their roots and bring new energy to older art styles.

The German Expressionist artists were also influenced by other famous artists. They loved the bright colors used by Paul Gauguin (page 113) and the emotional style of Vincent van Gogh (page 112). They were also inspired by earlier German artists like Albrecht Durer from the Renaissance (page 60). Durer was famous for his woodcut prints, which is like creating a stamp by carving an image onto a block of wood and transferring it onto paper. This technique is similar to the Japanese ukiyo-e but with a different result.

An interesting example of a woodcut print from the Expressionist movement is *The Shepherd* (or "*Der Hirte*" in German), crafted by the German artist Richard Seewald in 1919. It uses watercolors on top of the woodcut.

The Expressionist artists were inspired by many different things, including industrialization, which made them question the purpose of art. Industrialization was a time when machines started doing work that people used to do by hand. Expressionists used bright colors and twisted shapes to simplify art while also breaking away from what was traditionally thought to be beautiful.

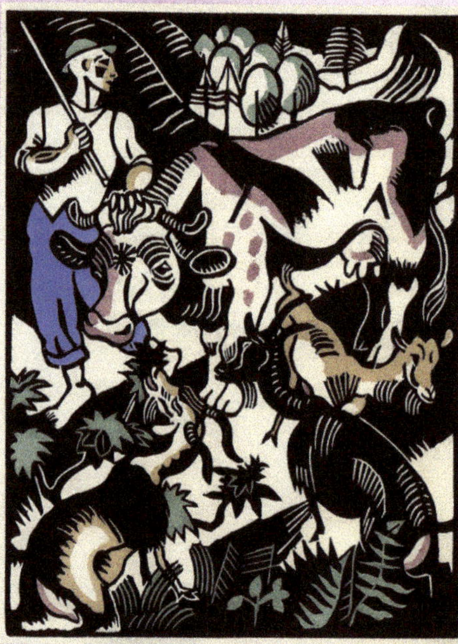

Richard Seewald
The Shepherd, 1919
Woodcut

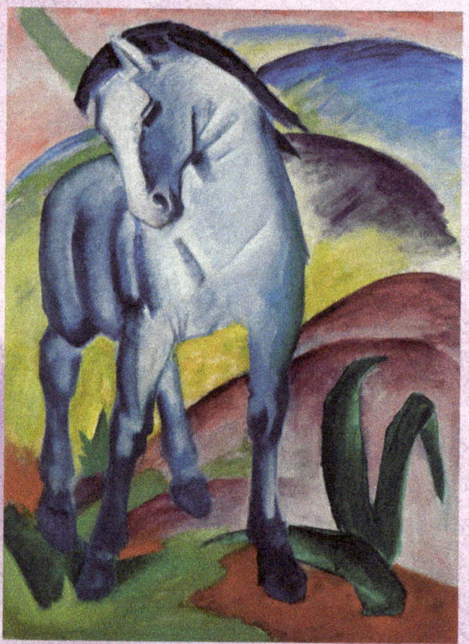

Franz Marc
Blue Horse, 1911
Oil on canvas

Expressionism wasn't just in Germany; it was happening all across Europe! People were expressing their emotions through all kinds of art, like stories, poetry, plays, movies, and music.

The Scream is a very famous Expressionist painting by Norwegian artist Edvard Munch, created in 1893. Today, *The Scream* is a well-known symbol of anxiety in popular culture. What kind of emotions do you think Munch wanted to express when he painted *The Scream*?

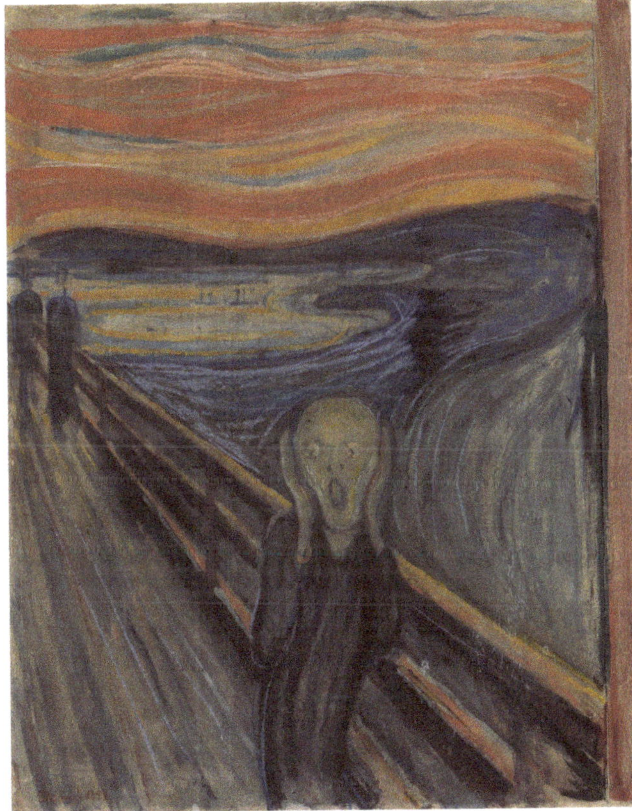

Edvard Munch
The Scream, 1893
Oil paint, tempera, crayons and pastel on cardboard

I always wondered what the person in Munch's *The Scream* was screaming about. So I put myself in the painting to see it with my own eyes! AAHHH!

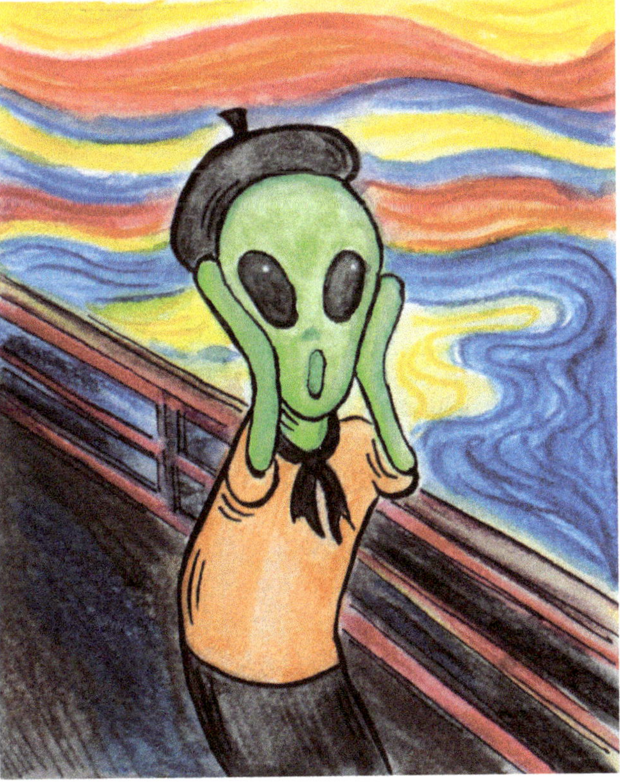

Cubism

Have you heard of Pablo Picasso? He gained fame as a painter, but he was also involved in creating sculptures, designing play sets and even writing poetry.

Some Pablo Picasso works include *Three Musicians* (1921) and *The Weeping Woman* (1937). During the early 1900s, Picasso collaborated with his friend Georges Braques to establish a groundbreaking art movement known as Cubism in Paris.

When Picasso and Braques started making Cubist art, they wanted to do something that hadn't been done before. They wanted to take ordinary things, like people and objects, and make them look more interesting by using lots of shapes and angles. This approach makes the viewer feel they are seeing something from different angles at the same time

Some people did not appreciate Cubism because it was so different from what was considered normal. However, it became more accepted over time and eventually emerged as one of the most significant art movements of the 20th century!

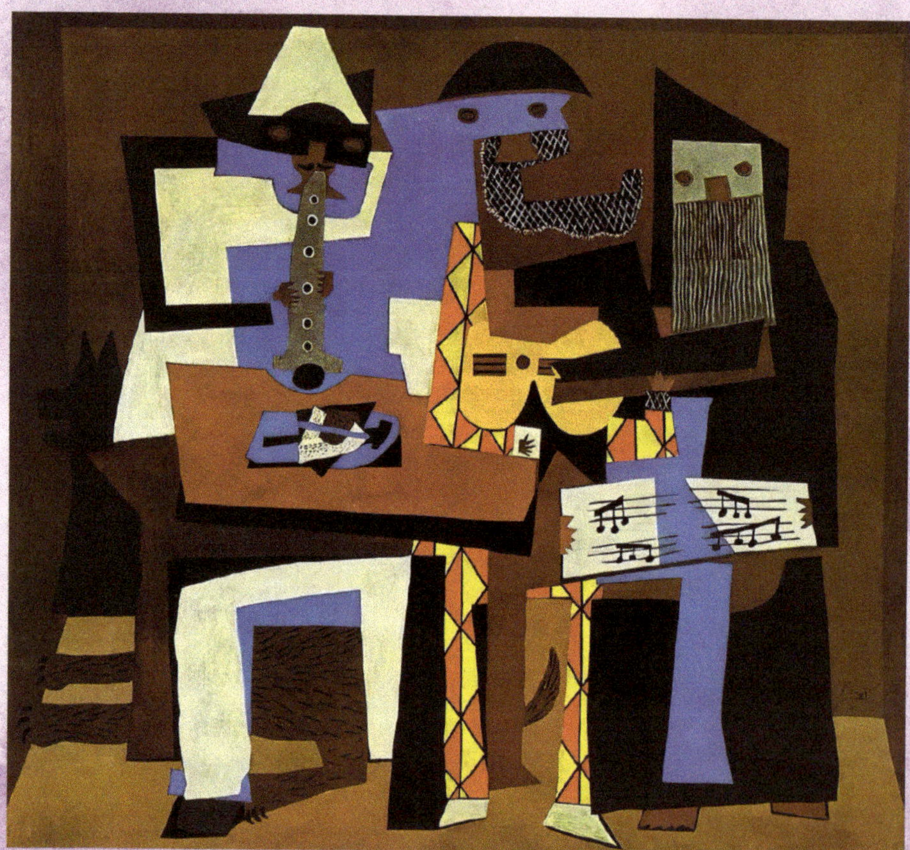

Pablo Picasso
Three Musicians, 1921
Oil on canvas

Picasso and Braques were partly inspired by Paul Cézanne (page 113) because he could make paintings that looked flat while also having a lot of depth and dimension.

African masks also inspired Picasso and Braques. They liked the way the masks were simple and abstract, but still powerful and expressive.

Another thing that Picasso was really good at was making collage art. That means he would cut out pictures and shapes from different things and glue them together to make a new picture.

Picasso was a really hardworking artist. He made a LOT of art over the course of his life - more than 130,000 artworks!

Georges Braques
Violin and Candlestick, 1910
Oil on canvas

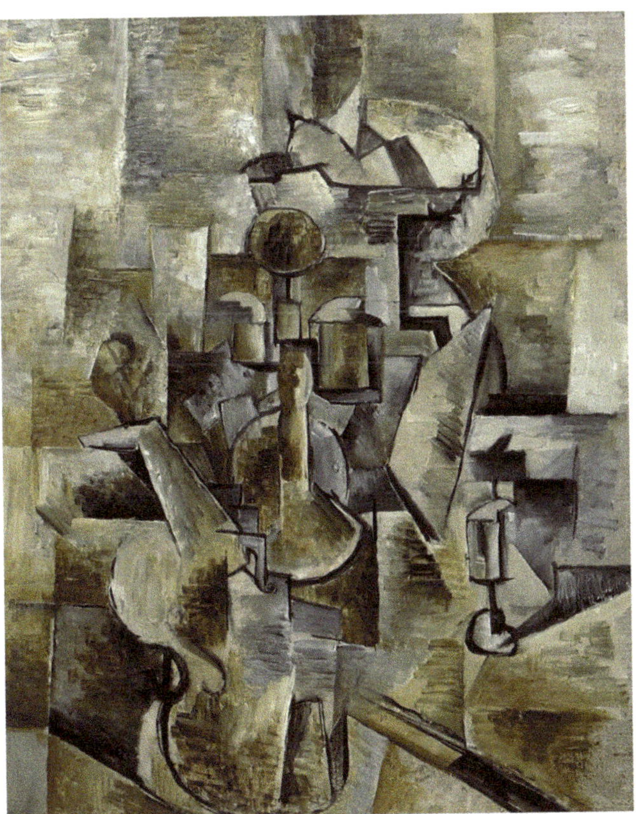

Pablo Picasso
The Bottle of Vieux Mar, 1913
Cut-and-pasted printed wallpapers, newspaper, charcoal, gouache, and pins on laid paper

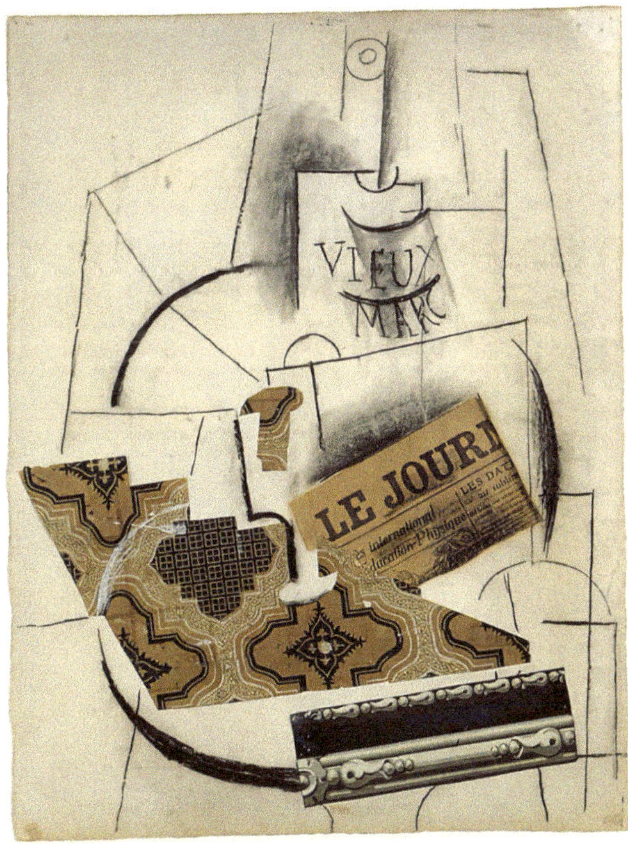

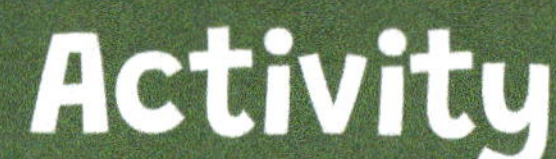

Activity

Cubist Animals Collage

This is a fun activity in which we will create a Cubist collage that can be cut up and put together in different ways. Let's get started!

What you'll need:

- **Paper**
- **Pencil**
- **Eraser**
- **Scissors**
- **Colored pencils**
- **Colored pens**

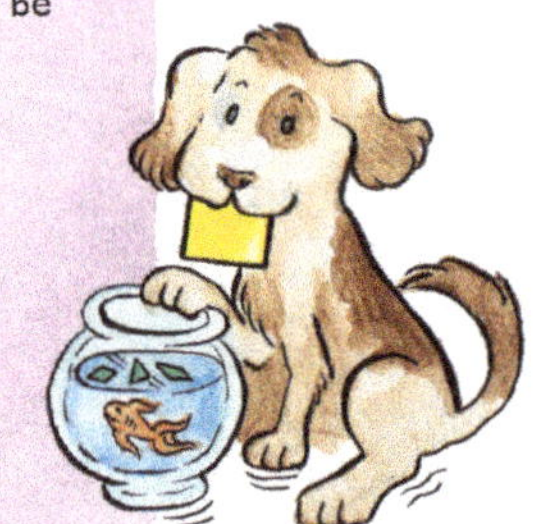

(You can make your sketch here)

How to create your Cubist collage:

1 First, think of an animal and sketch it with a pencil on a piece of paper. Keep it simple; no need for details!

2 Then, on a separate piece of paper, re-draw your animal using only geometric shapes like squares, triangles, and rectangles. Make sure your animal is still recognizable, even if it's made up of simple shapes. For example, a cat's head could be made up of a square and two triangles for the ears.

3 Next, use colored pencils and pens to add color to your animal. Be creative, and feel free to use different colors for each shape!

4 When your animal is complete, use scissors to cut out each shape. Then, try putting the pieces back together in different ways. The more shapes you have, the more possibilities there are for rearranging them!

5 If you're doing this activity with a friend or family member, try swapping some of the pieces with each other and see what new Cubist creatures you can create together!

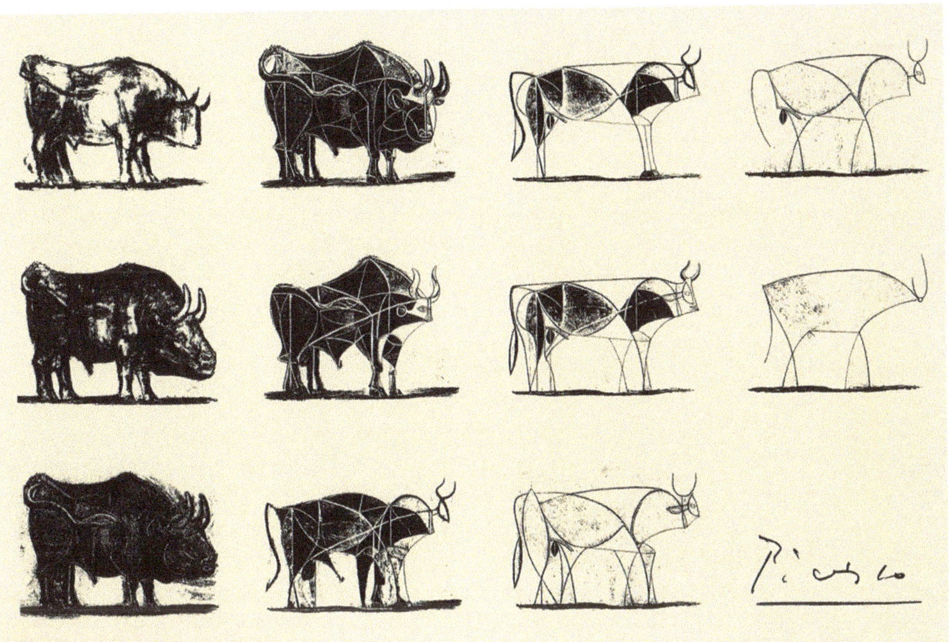

Pablo Picasso
Bull, 1945
Lithographic print

Pablo Picasso made a series of 11 bull drawings where he gradually made each image more abstract.

Have you ever seen a Cubist alien? I think this is how Picasso would paint me if we'd met. I feel like a work of art.

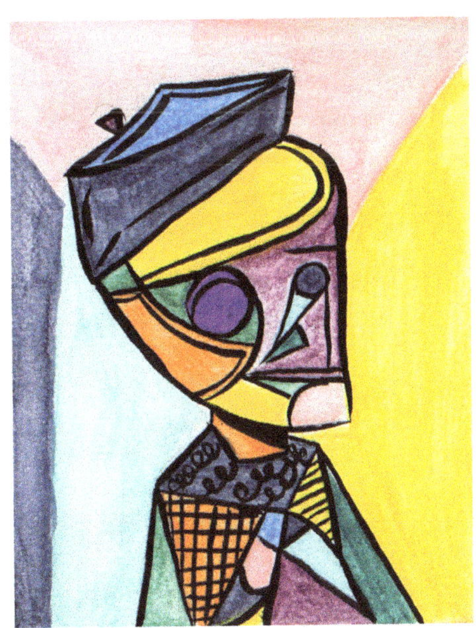

Surrealism

WHILE we are still in Paris, let's check out the Surrealist movement!

The Surrealist movement was really important in the art world, and its ideas have been used in lots of art all over the world. It started when a poet named André Breton wrote a paper called "The Surrealist Revolution" in 1924. He and another poet named Louis Aragon believed that artists should express themselves by tapping into their deepest thoughts and feelings, even if it didn't make sense to others. They thought that art should be wild and imaginative, helping people see the world in new ways. This concept became popular and inspired many to create dreamlike art.

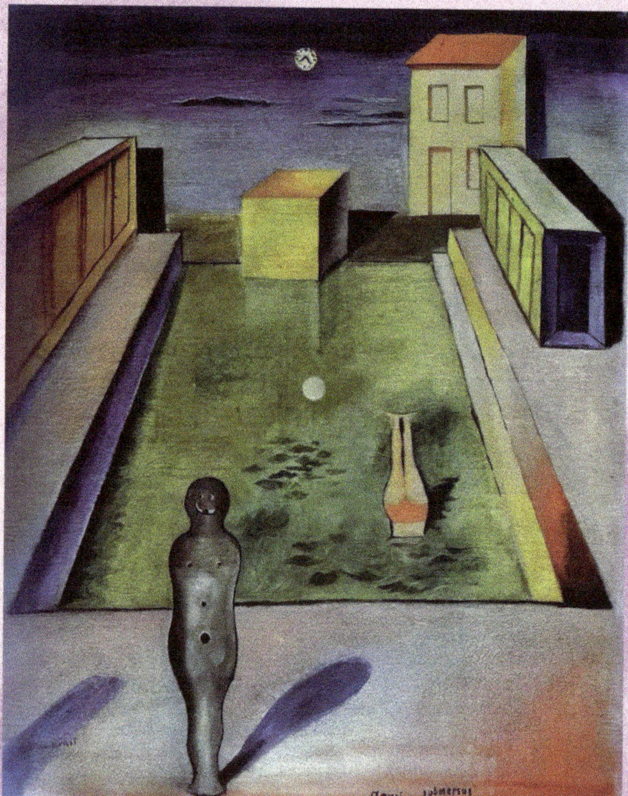

Max Ernst was a German Surrealist artist. His paintings often had hidden meanings, and he liked to include things from his childhood or from his dreams.

Max Ernst
Aquis Submersus, 1919
Oil on canvas

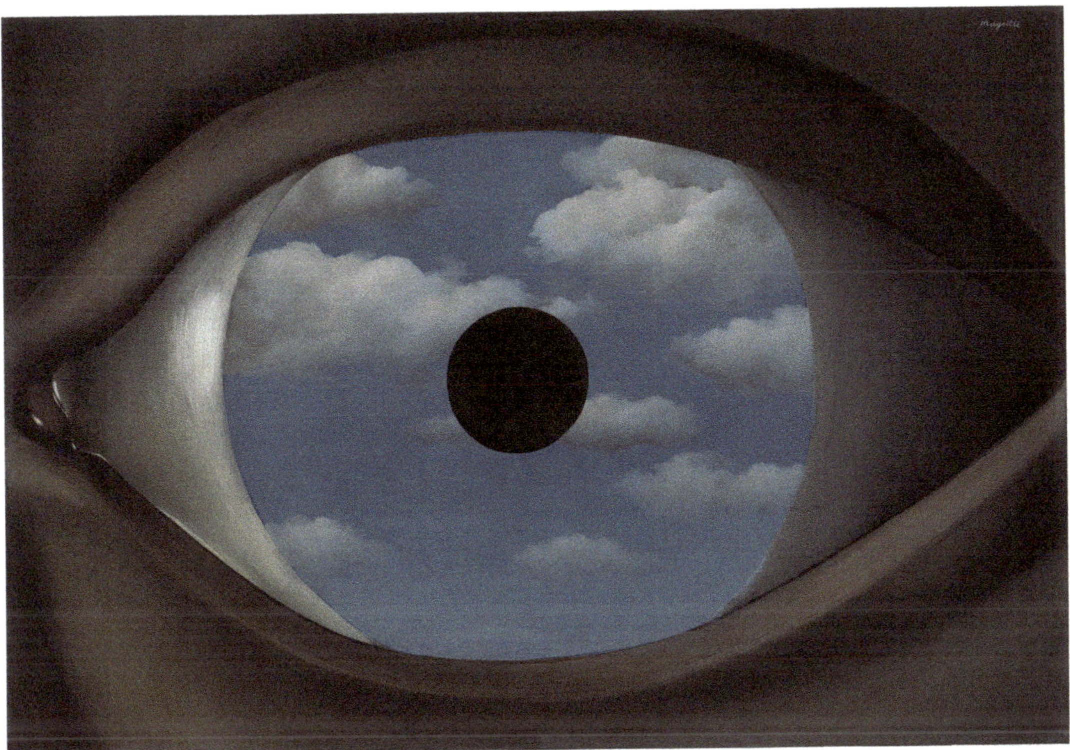

Rene Magritte
The False Mirror, 1928
Oil on canvas

The False Mirror by Magritte is a surrealistic painting completed in 1928. Can you guess why it's titled *The False Mirror*?

The title stems from a couple of concepts that can be found in the painting: the eye is not an actual mirror, even though it seems to reflect the sky and clouds. Also, the eye itself is not real because it is just a representation of an eye in a painting. *The False Mirror* highlights how what we see is not always the same as reality, and how easily our senses can trick us.

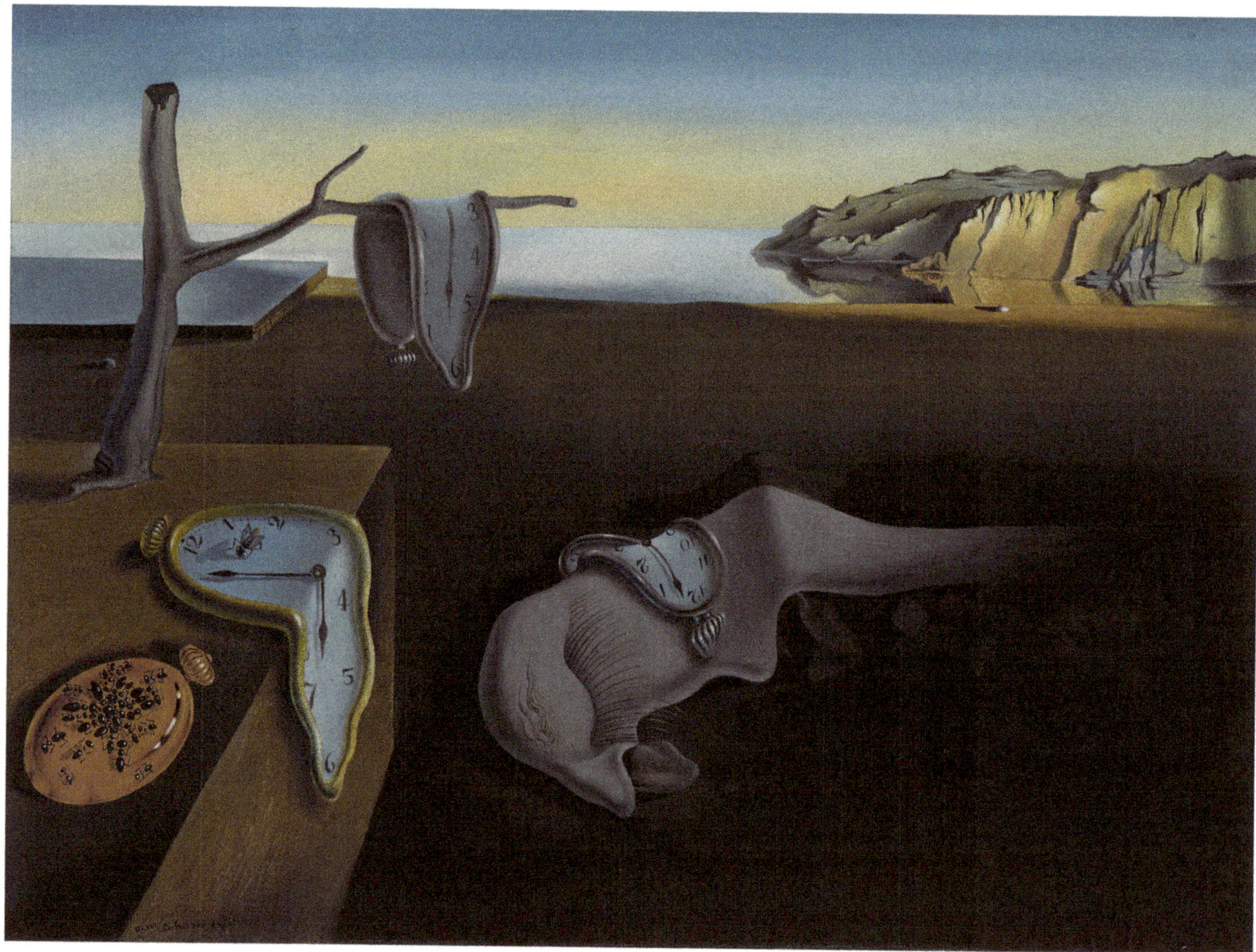

Salvador Dalí
The Persistence of Memory, 1931
Oil on canvas

Salvador Dalí is one of the most famous Surrealist artists. He was born in Spain in 1904 and began painting as a child. Dalí was most known for painting but also worked with photography, sculpture, printmaking, and cinema. He even worked with Walt Disney to create a surreal animated short film!

The Persistence of Memory is considered one of the most influential Surrealist paintings because of how it portrays the aspect of time in a dreamlike atmosphere.

Can you see the self-portrait* in the painting?? Dali painted himself as a strange figure laying on the ground underneath a melted clock. Can you see his closed eye and nose?

* A self-portrait is a painting that an artist created of themselves. See pages 80 and 134 for examples of self-portraits.

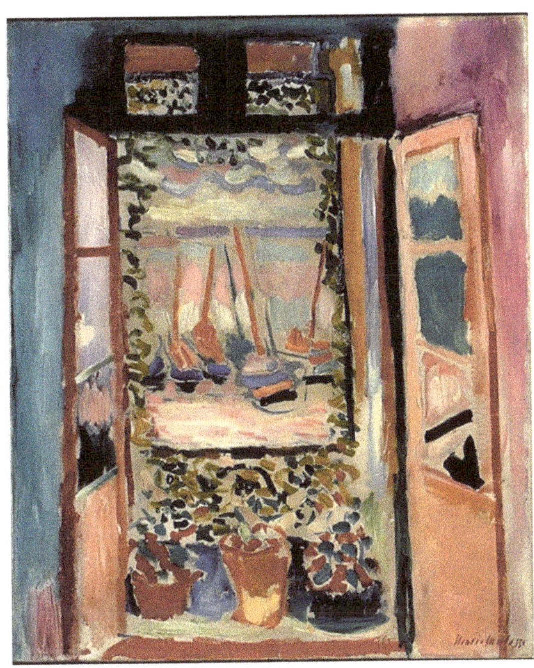

Henri Matisse was a French artist who was part of a movement called Fauvism. Fauvist's wild use of color inspired the rise of Surrealism.

Henri Matisse
The Open Window, 1905
Oil on canvas

Marc Chagall was a famous artist who was born in Russia in 1887 and lived until 1985. He was known for his colorful and imaginative paintings, which often featured dreamlike images of animals, people, and objects floating in the sky.

Many of Chagall's paintings reflected the Jewish traditions and culture he grew up with. He also was inspired by his travels, particularly the time he spent in France, where he became friends with other famous artists like Pablo Picasso.

In 1954, Picasso said: "when Matisse dies, Chagall will be the only painter left who understands what color really is."

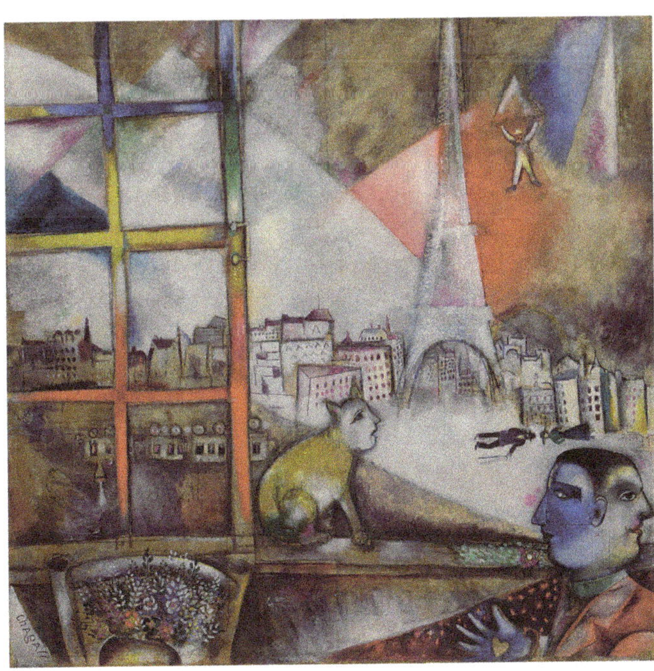

Marc Chagall
Paris Through the Window, 1913
Oil on canvas

Chagall made a masterpiece titled *Paris Through the Window* in 1913. This beautiful painting shows a colorful view of Paris as seen through a window.

Mexico's Revolution in Art

Do you know what was happening in Mexico around the same time Surrealism was popular in Europe?

The Mexican Revolution lasted for a decade and ended in 1920. The Revolution inspired artists to make art about the triumphs and struggles of the Mexican people at a time when they were fighting for freedom. It also inspired artists to explore their own Mexican heritage.

During this time, many Mexican artists began to explore their own unique cultural heritage and traditions in their artwork. They were inspired by the ancient civilizations of Mexico, such as the Aztecs and the Mayans, as well as the vibrant colors and patterns of Mexican folk art.

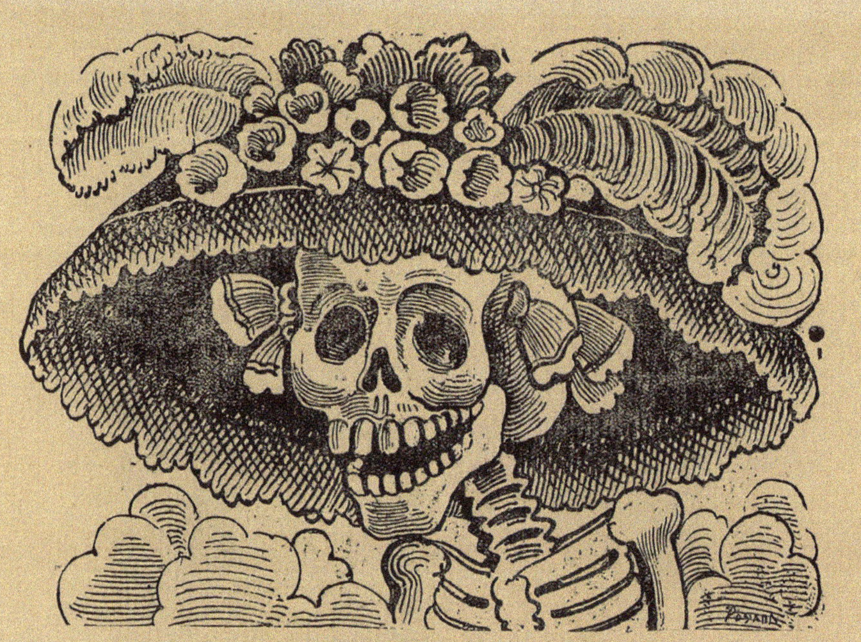

José Guadalupe Posada was famous for his drawings of human skulls, which are called "calaveras". Posada's calaveras were often used to criticize the government of Mexico at the time, which he thought was corrupt. These skull images are also used in a holiday called the Day of the Dead, which is celebrated in Mexico to remember people who have passed away.

Murals, or big paintings made on walls, were popular in Mexico. They have been a part of Mexican art for a long time, but they became even more popular after the Mexican Revolution. The most famous muralist in Mexico was Diego Rivera. He painted murals that showed what life was like for working-class and native people.

José Guadalupe Posada
La Calavera Catrina, 1910
Etching

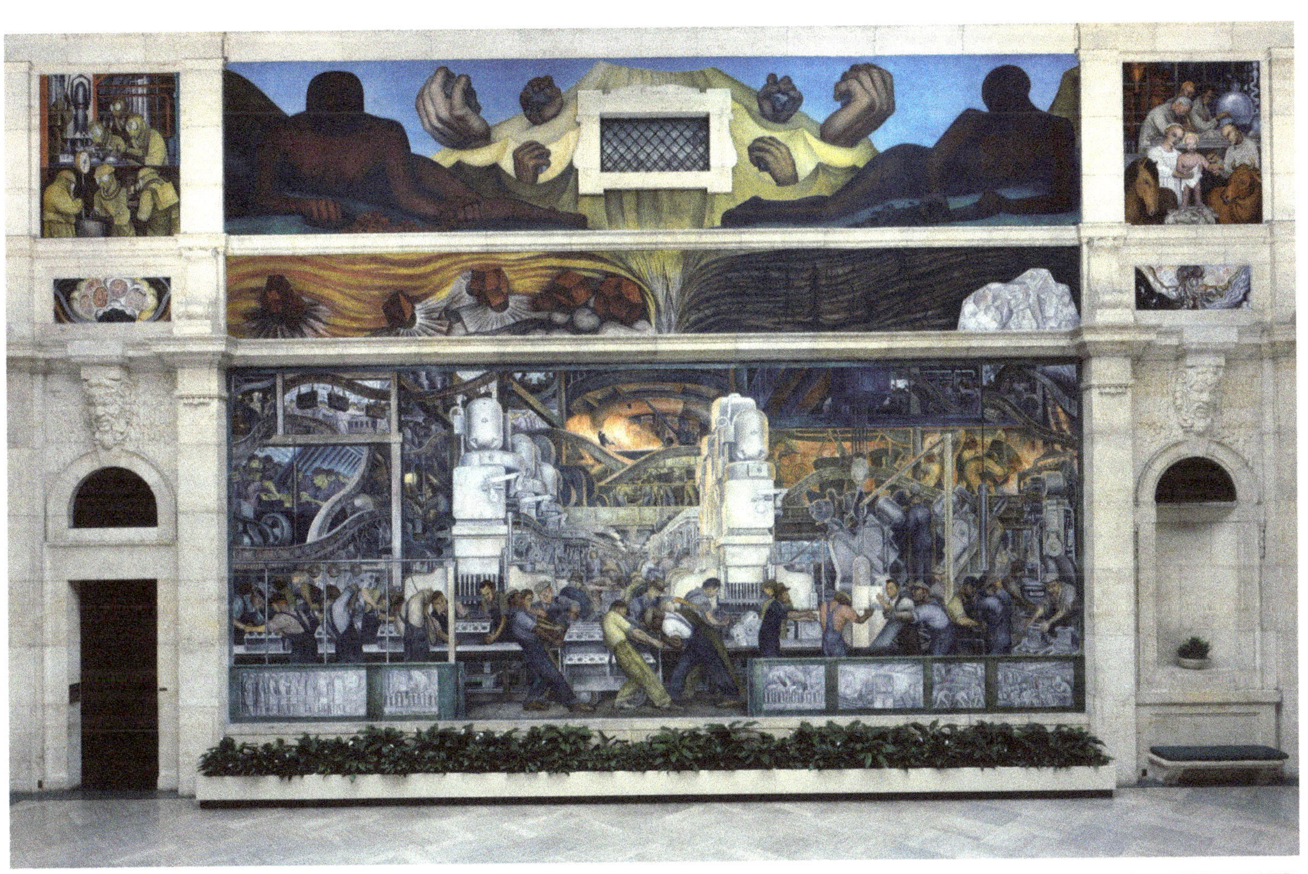

Diego Rivera
Detroit Industry Murals: North wall, 1933
Fresco

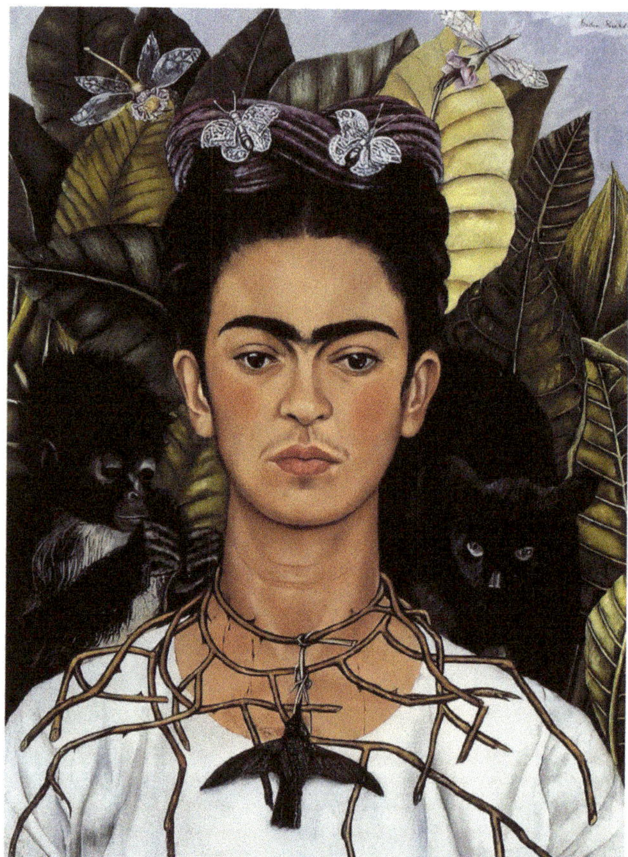

Diego Rivera was married to Frida Kahlo, another famous artist inspired by The Mexican Revolution. Kahlo often created self-portraits expressing pain, love, and loss. Some have called her art surrealist, although Frida preferred to be known for just painting feelings and experiences that were important to her, such as women's rights.

Frida Kahlo
Self-portrait with Necklace and Hummingbird, 1940
Oil on canvas

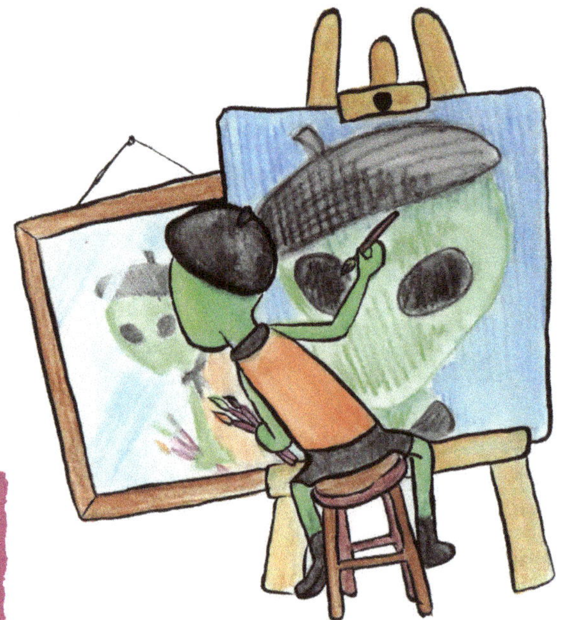

In 1960, the American artist Norman Rockwell created a funny self-portrait called *Triple Self-portrait*, in which he represented himself painting himself in front of a mirror – a self-portrait within a self-portrait. I felt so inspired that I wanted to do it too! How do I look?

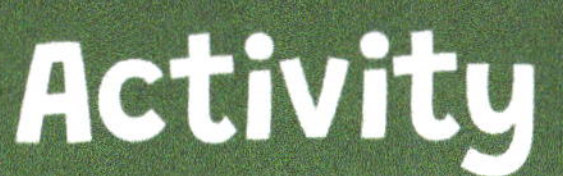

Activity

Creating a Self-portrait

Frida Kahlo was known for her many self-portraits. Let's create one of our own!

For this cool activity, you will need the following:

- **Pencil**
- **Eraser**
- **Paper**
- **Colored pencils**
- **Mirror**

How you'll create your self-portrait:

1 To create a self-portrait, you need to start by looking at yourself in the mirror. Take a good look at your face. How do you feel today, and how do you see yourself?

2 Then, pick up a pencil and use it to measure the different parts of your face. For example, is the length of your nose around the same size as your forehead? Are your eyes around the same size as the gap between your eyes?

3 Once you have observed your face, it is time to start sketching! Begin by outlining the shape of your head and chin and then add features like your eyes, nose, and mouth. Remember to include details like hair, ears, neck and shoulders. You can also include things like beloved pets, instruments, or sports equipment.

4 When you complete your drawing, you can enhance it with colored pencils. Consider using colors that illustrate your emotions – perhaps red for passion, blue for calmness, or green for growth. The most important thing is to enjoy yourself and be creative!

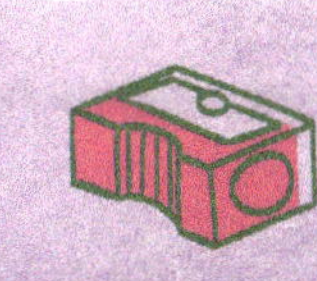

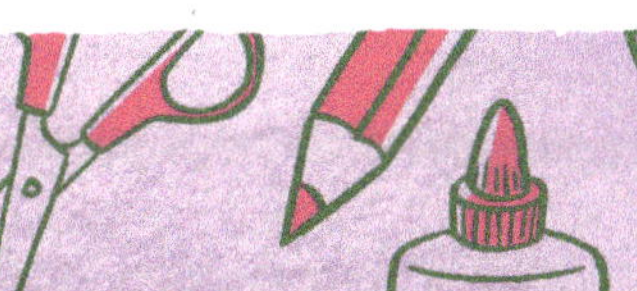

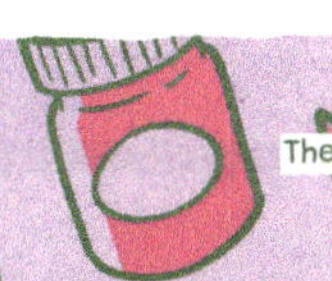

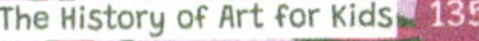

Brazil and the Modern Art Week

Since we're already in Latin America, let's check out Brazil! In 1922, São Paulo hosted an art festival known as Modern Art Week. This event brought together artists, writers, musicians and architects who showcased their work and shared innovative ideas.

Prior to Modern Art Week, most Brazilian artists were loyal to European art styles. The artists who achieved the most success were those who had studied in European art schools and then brought back what they learned to Brazil.

The festival was a huge success and changed Brazilian art forever. It was the most important event that introduced modern art to the general public and to major art critics in Brazil.

Brazilian Modern art was all about breaking away from traditional styles and showcasing Brazilian culture. Artists like Anita Malfatti and Emiliano Di Cavalcanti used bright colors and themes in their paintings to represent their country.

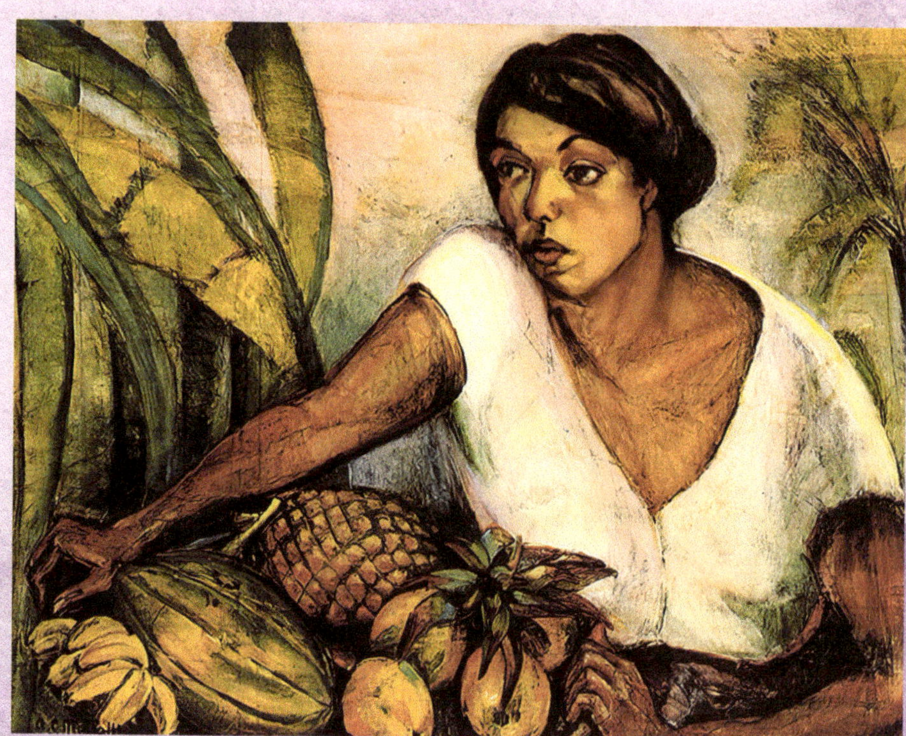

Anita Malfatti
Tropical, 1917
Oil on canvas

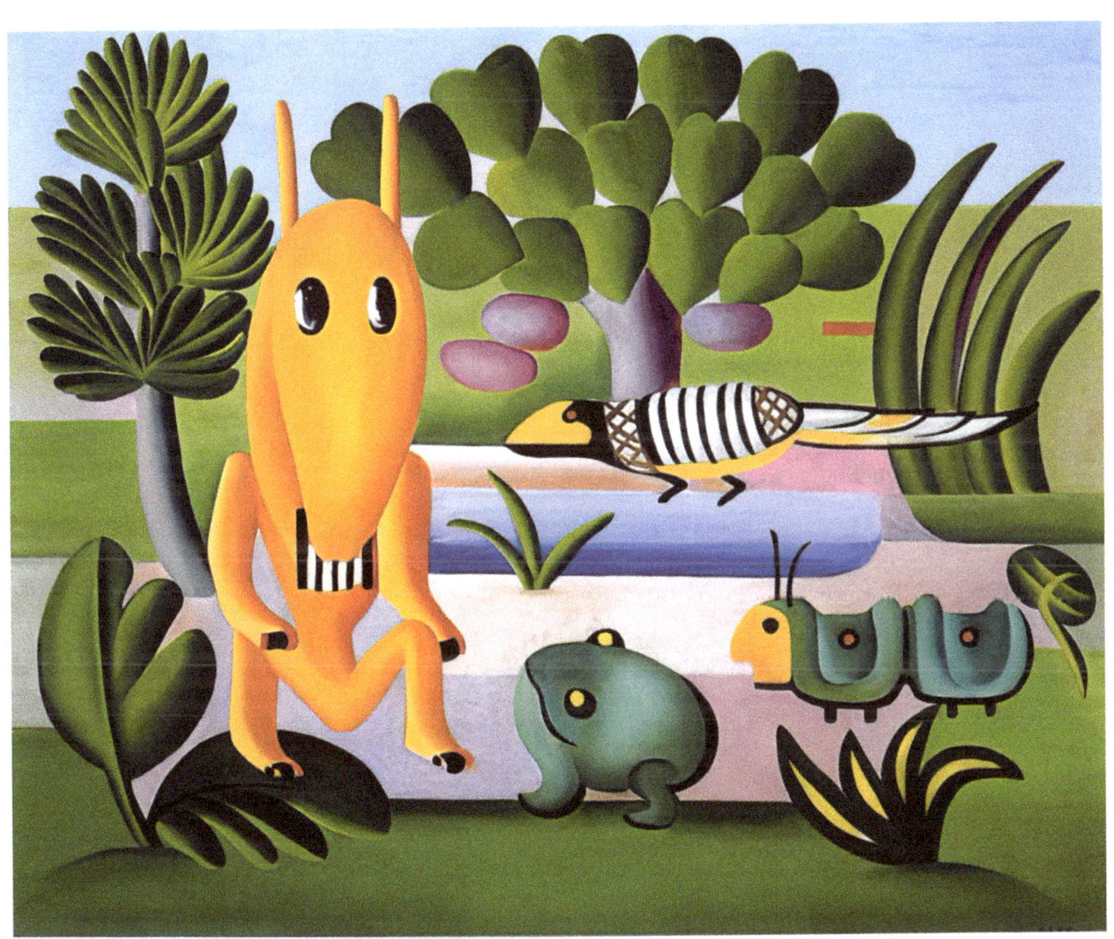

Tarcila do Amaral
A Cuca, 1924
Oil on canvas

Another important Modern artist was Tarcila do Amaral, whose art also reflected the vibrant and unique culture of Brazil.

Contemporary Art

PHEW! What an adventure we have gone through, my human friend. We've gone on a journey from the first prehistoric paintings ever made to now! Have you noticed that artists in the past were more strict about following certain rules when making art? But now, things are different! Artists today feel more free to be unique and do their own thing. There is less pressure to follow any particular movement. So, if you look at a painting today, you might not know what style it is just by looking at it. Isn't that cool?

Abstract Expressionism

Have you heard of Abstract Expressionism? It's a fancy name for a style of art that began in the 1940s in New York City. It's different from other kinds of art because it doesn't try to show things that look real, like pictures of people or landscapes. Instead, artists who use this style create paintings that are all about how they feel and how they move their paintbrushes or drip paint onto a canvas. Many artists in the Abstract Expressionism movement used large canvases and bright colors to express their emotions and depict motion in their artwork.

Renowned artists like Jackson Pollock and Willem de Kooning were notable Abstract Expressionists. They became famous for their unconventional techniques, which challenged traditional art styles. Abstract Expressionism changed the way people perceived art and opened doors for new forms of abstract expression.

Barnett Newman
Vir Heroicus Sublimis, 1950 – 1951
Oil on canvas

Newman also played a big role in Abstract Expressionism. He specialized in making color field paintings that focused on colors themselves rather than things like people or landscapes. What kind of emotions do you feel when you look at this painting?

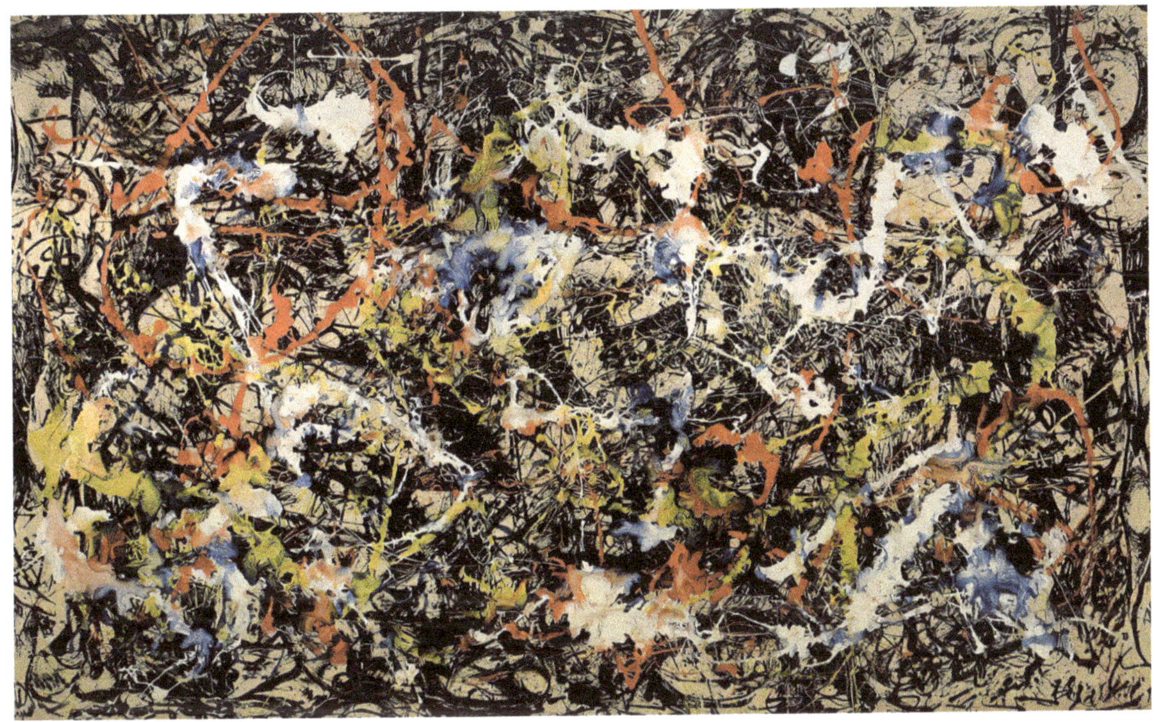

Jackson Pollock
Convergence, 1952
Oil on canvas

Jackson Pollock was one of the famous artists of this time. Pollock demonstrated that the creative process of making art could be just as interesting as the finished painting, dripping and splattering paint onto a canvas placed on the floor. He didn't use a brush, and he moved around the canvas in a very physical way. This technique was very different from traditional painting methods, and it was seen as very innovative.

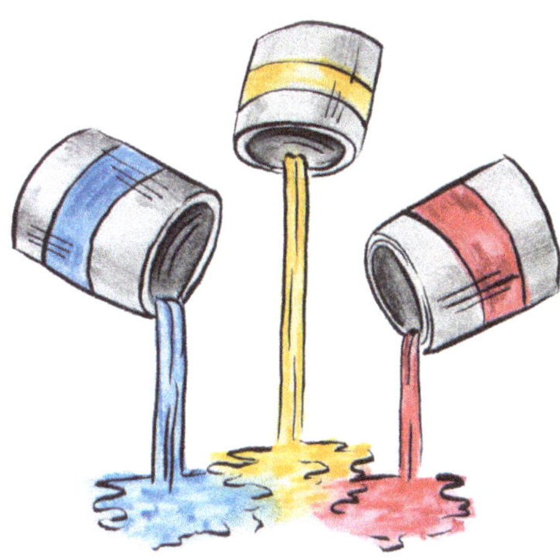

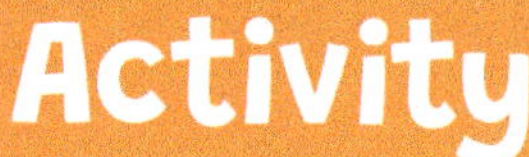

Making an Abstract Painting

I know a really fun way to create an abstract work of art. Let's do it!

What you need:

- String
- Scissors
- Pencil
- Paper
- Colored pencils
- Colored pens of your choice

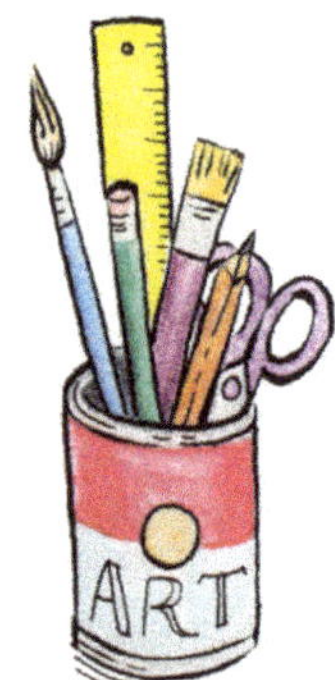

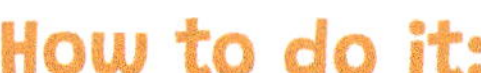

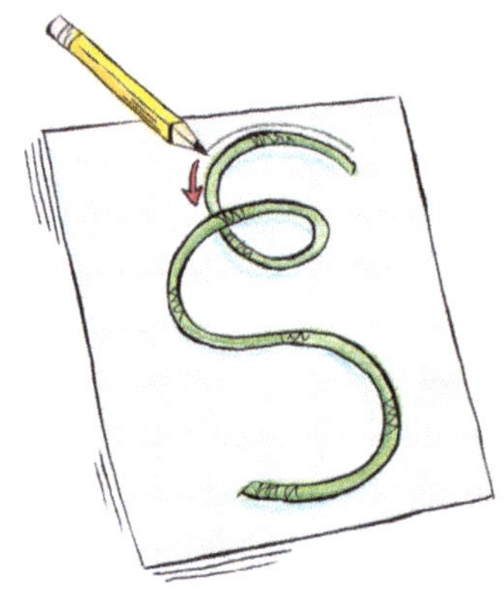

1 First, grab a piece of paper and put it on a table. Cut a piece of string that's at least the size of your hand and place it on the paper. Now, without moving the string, trace one side of it using a pencil. Repeat this step with different strings until you have drawn multiple lines on the paper. You can even use strings with different lengths for different types of lines.

2 Now that you have created these lines, let your imagination take over. Connect or continue the lines however you'd like. Remember, this is your artwork, so feel free to be creative!

3 Once you are satisfied with your lines, it's time to add some color. Use colored pencils to fill in the shapes formed by your lines. If you want to make the lines more prominent, you can also trace over them with a pen.

4 To make your artwork even more interesting, consider shading some areas darker than others or experimenting with different textures using your pencils. Enjoy yourself and see what wonderful creations you can bring to life!

Neo-Expressionism

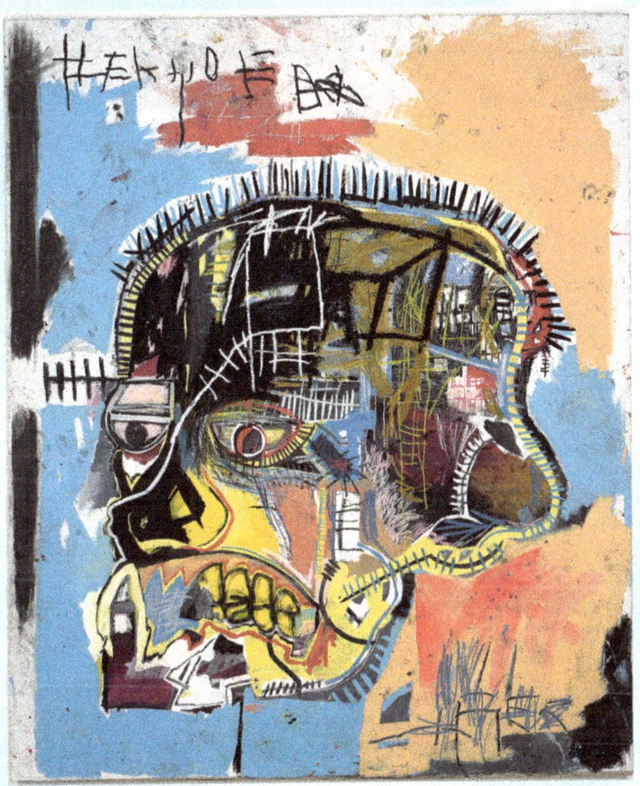

© Estate of Jean-Michel Basquiat. Licensed by Artestar, New York.

Jean-Michel Basquiat
Untitled (Skull), 1981

One of Basquiat's most extraordinary paintings is known as *Untitled (Skull)* from 1982. It is one of the most expensive paintings of all time. In 2017, it was sold for $110.5 million! Basquiat was only 21 years old when he painted it.

Neo-expressionism emerged as an art movement during the late 1970s and remained influential until the mid-1980s. It was a response to the more minimal and conceptual art that had been popular in previous decades.

The aim of Neo-Expressionist artists was to create emotional and expressive art that conveyed deep feelings and emotions. They used bold colors and thick layers of paint to purposely create a sense of messiness.

Neo-Expressionsists also used powerful symbols and used their artwork as a platform to comment on politics or society. Their art addressed issues like war, poverty and inequality.

One renowned artist associated with Neo-Expressionism is Jean- Michel Basquiat. Born in New York City, Basquiat began his artistic journey when he was only 4 or 5 years old. His artistic style differed from that of other artists at the time by using vivid colors and powerful symbols in his paintings. He even used things like doors and cardboard boxes as canvases!

Basquiat's art often portrayed people, animals and things that he saw in the world around him. He also was inspired by popular music and movies as well as political and social issues.

Pop Art

Pop Art emerged as a contemporary art style during the 1950s, a time of significant changes in society. People were enjoying new technologies like televisions and refrigerators as well as buying new things like cars and clothes.

The artists of the Pop Art movement wanted to create art inspired by these everyday things, including comic books, advertisements, and product packaging. They wanted to show that ordinary things could be just as interesting and beautiful as more traditional subjects like landscapes or portraits. Even today, the influence of Pop Art can be seen in many aspects of our lives such as advertising, fashion trends, and films.

Andy Warhol was a Pop artist renowned for his portrayals of objects and famous people. His most iconic work was the Campbell's soup can. Warhol had a special workspace known as the Factory where he made art with a team of workers.

He wanted his art to convey a sense of mass production, as if the artworks were manufactured in a factory. He used a printing technique called silkscreen to make many identical copies of his artworks. Afterwards, he included some unique details by painting each one. This gave every picture a touch of its own uniqueness.

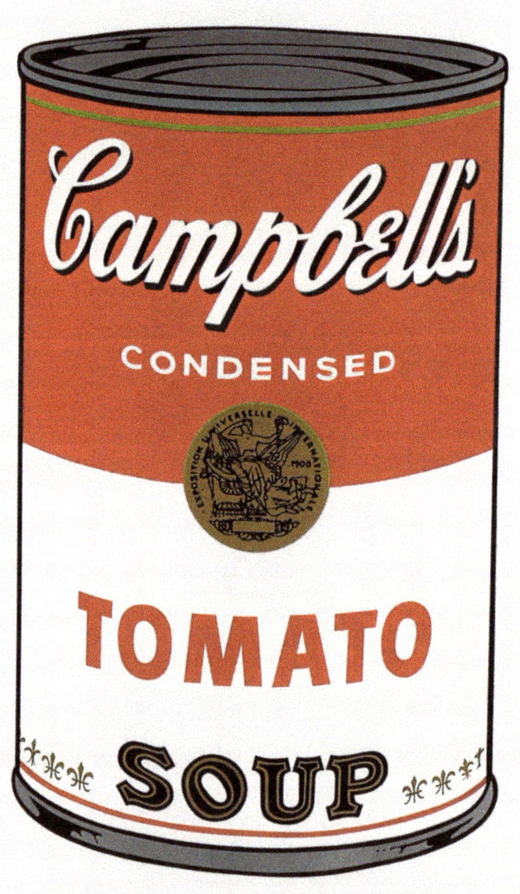

Andy Warhol
Campbell's Soup Cans, 1962
silkscreen painting

Warhol questions the value of art and products by recreating the image of popular soup cans as a work of art. This also brings up the Pop artists' idea that art should imitate life.

Another standout artist was Roy Lichtenstein, who created large paintings of comic book images.

Pop art was also brought to the field of sculpture, with artists like Claes Oldenburg, who created everyday objects on a large scale. He worked with a style called soft sculpture, which is a type of art in which soft materials like fabric, yarn, or foam are used to create sculptures instead of hard materials like wood or metal. They often have a cuddly and friendly feel to them.

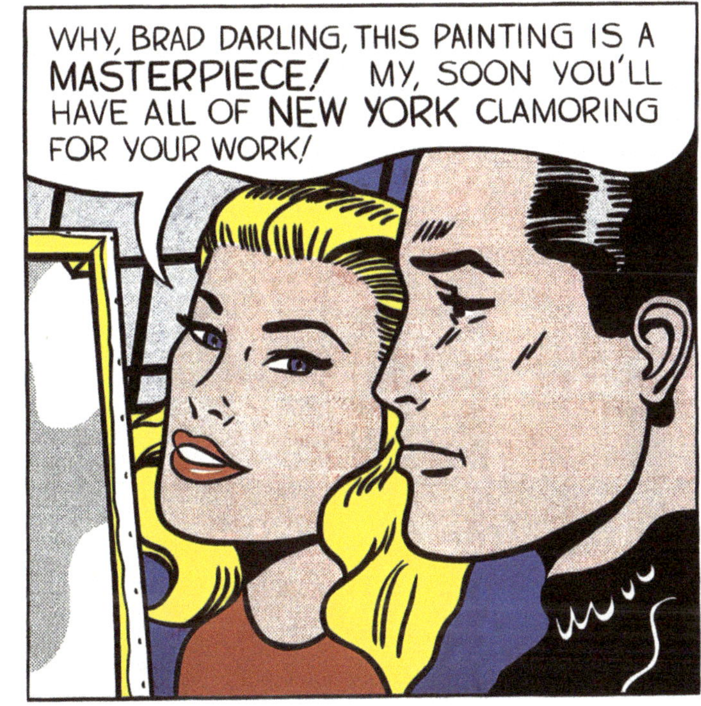

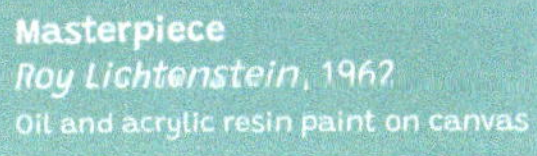
Masterpiece
Roy Lichtenstein, 1962
Oil and acrylic resin paint on canvas

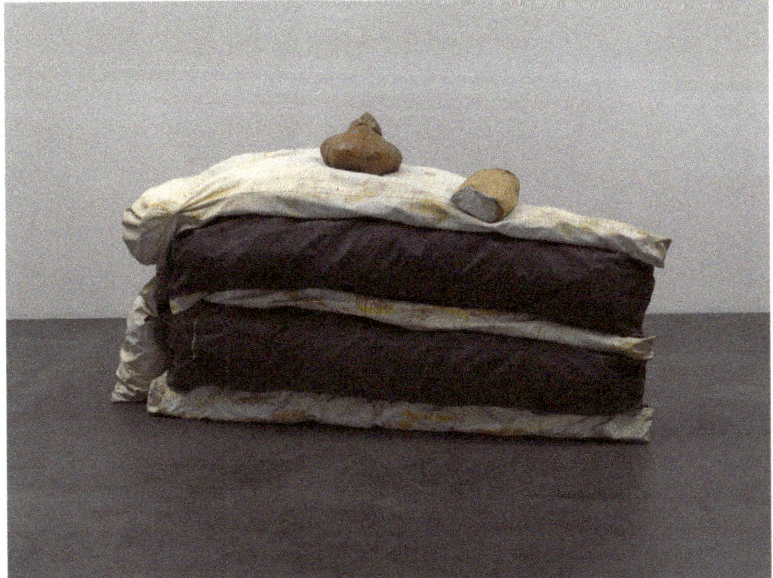

Claes Oldenburg
Floor Cake, 1962
Synthetic polymer paint and latex filled with foam rubber and cardboard boxes

Floor Cake is a tasty example of Oldenburg's soft sculptures.

Contemporary Art Genres

Before we explore modern art from other parts of the world, how about we learn about some new genres of art that emerged in the 20th century?

We all know what painting, drawing, sculpture, photography, and architecture are. But have you ever heard of land art? What about performance art?

Installations

Have you ever walked into a museum or art gallery and seen something really big and impressive that takes up a whole room or even more? That's called an installation! In the 1960s, artists started making these kinds of artworks that are made just for one specific place. Sometimes they use all kinds of things, like objects or sculptures, to create their art. Other times, they just change the space itself in a creative way. Installations are a really cool way for artists to use their imagination and make something unique for people to see!

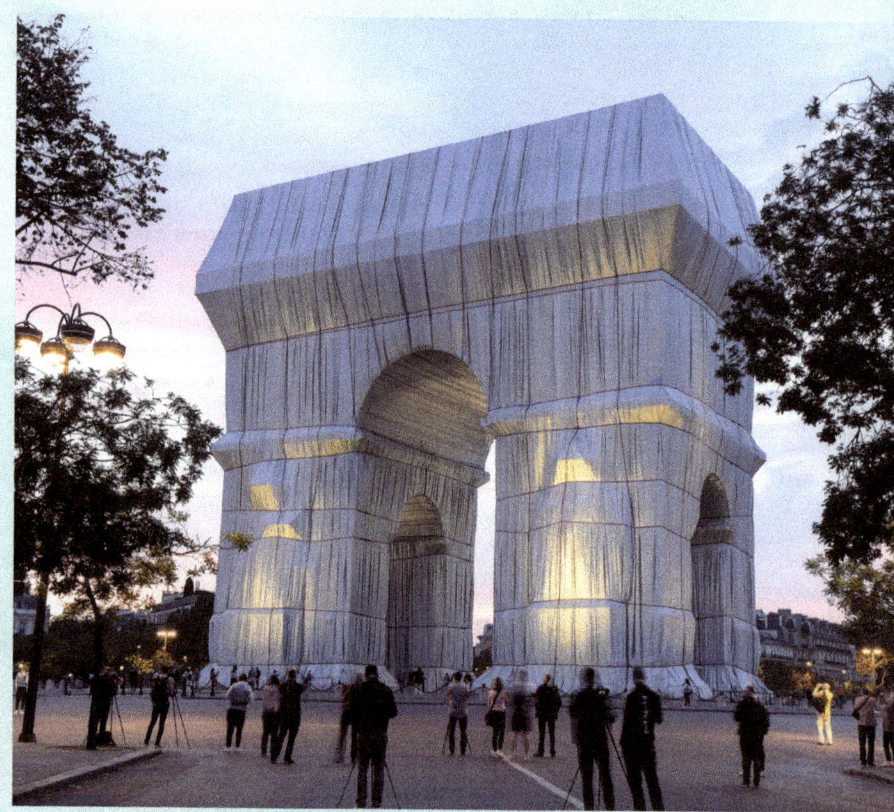

Christo and Jeanne-Claude
L'Arc de Triomphe, Wrapped, 1961
Red rope and recyclable polypropylene fabric

This artist duo created many "wrapped" works of art. This particular installation shows a famous structure in Paris, the Arc de Triomphe, wrapped in silver material.

Performance art

Once upon a time, some artists started doing something wildly different with their art. They didn't just paint or draw or sculpt things; they actually used their own bodies to make art! This kind of art became known as Performance art in 1960, and is still called that today. Some artists did this way back in history, like the Surrealists (page 128), Dadaists, and Italian Futurists.

Being living Sculptures is

our life-blood

our destiny

our romance

our disaster and

our light and life.

As day breaks over us

we rise into our vacuum.

The cold morning light

filters dustily through

the window.

We step into the responsibility suits

of our Art.

- Gilbert & George

Text taken from Gilbert & George: The Singing Sculpture, by Carter Ratcliff and Robert Rosenblum – 1993

Gilbert and George
The Singing Sculptures, 1969

Gilbert & George first presented The Singing Sculpture in 1969, then repeated it over the next three years in the U.K., Europe, and Australia, and for the opening of New York's Sonnabend Gallery in 1971. Mounting a table, their faces and hands painted in metallic colours and wearing neat, if ill-fitting suits, they executed automaton-like movements as a cassette recorder repeatedly played 'Underneath the Arches', Flanagan and Allen's Depression-era song about two down-at-heel drifters who 'dream our dreams away'.

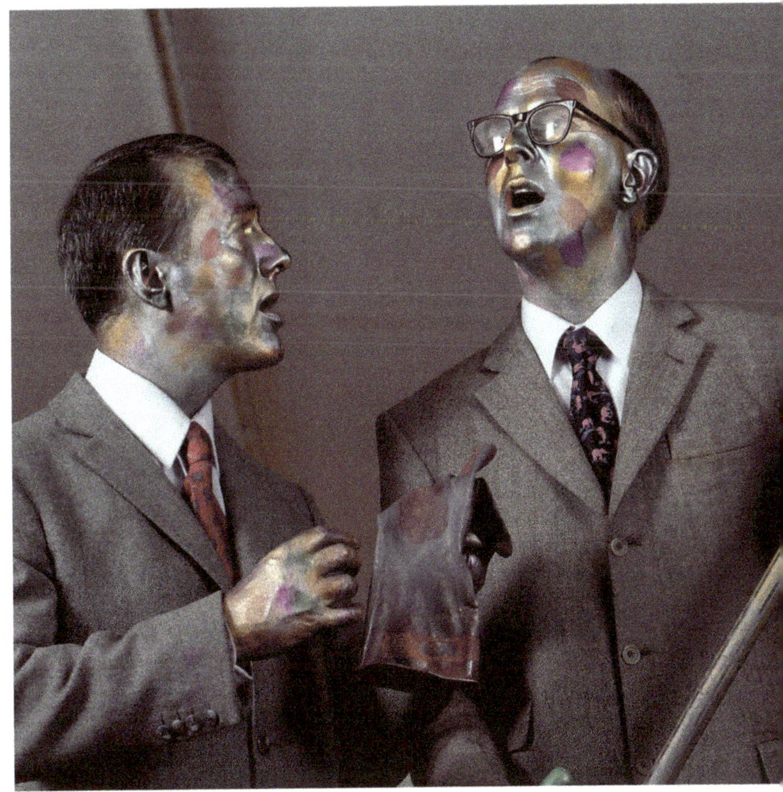

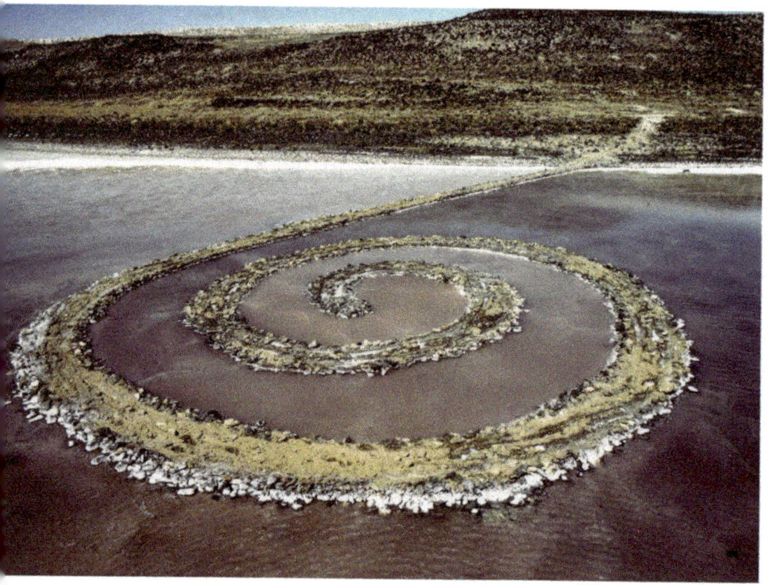

Land art

Land art is a type of art that uses nature as its canvas. Instead of making art on paper or canvas, artists use materials like rocks, leaves, and branches to create their artwork. They might make patterns on the ground or create sculptures that blend in with the natural surroundings.

Land art started in the 1960s and was a way for artists to show how beautiful and amazing nature can be. Some land artists use their artwork to call attention to environmental issues like pollution and deforestation. Land art is a really cool way to make art that's not just beautiful but also helps us appreciate and take care of the world around us!

Robert Smithson
Spiral Jetty, (Rozel Point, Great Salt Lake–Utah) 1970

Hyperrealism

Have you ever seen a painting or sculpture that looks so real, it's like you could touch it, and it would feel like the real thing? That's called hyperrealism! Hyperrealist artists are really good at making their art look super realistic - even more realistic than a photograph.

They use things like photos to help them make their art look so lifelike. They might even use special techniques to make the artwork look like it's 3D or moving.

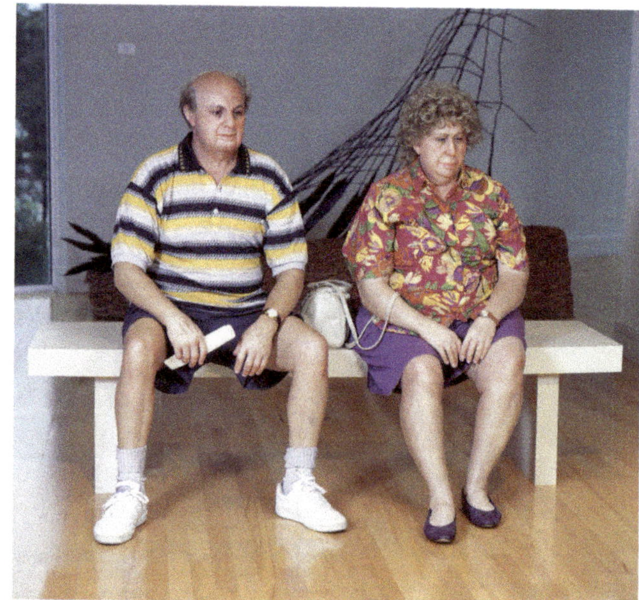

Duane Hanson
Old Couple on a Bench, 1994
Fiberglass

In 2010, Marina Abramovic created the performance artwork *The Artist is Present*, where she sat at a table with an empty chair in front of her. For almost three months, visitors of the Museum of Modern Art in New York were able to take turns sitting across from Abramovic. She did this for eight hours every single day and saw over 1,000 people! I have been sitting here for five minutes and am already thinking about taking a lunch break.

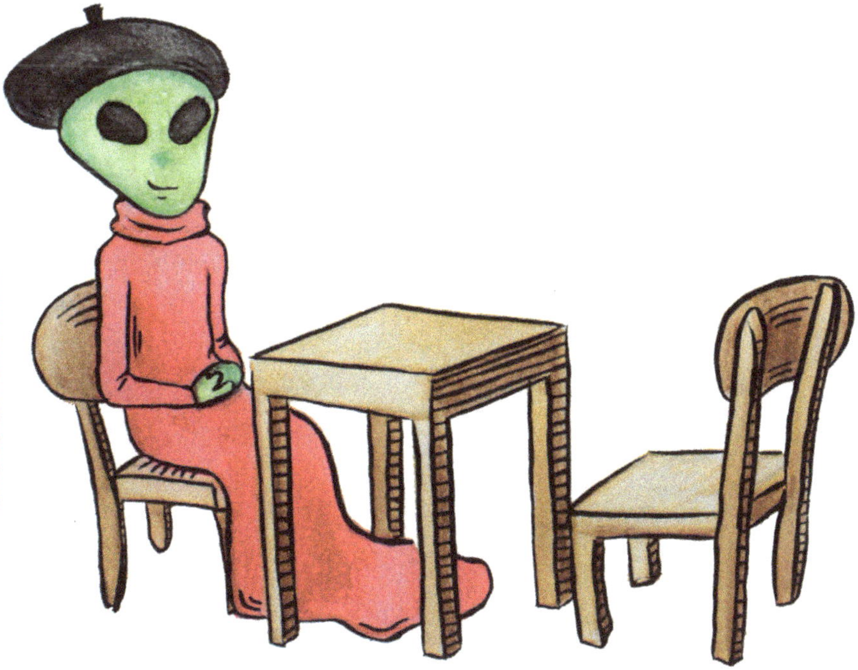

Artists from Africa

Let's take a look at what artists in Africa are creating today! In the 20th century, Africa went through some big changes, like the end of slavery and the formation of many new countries.

All of these important events had an impact on African art. Artists started using new techniques like photography, painting, sculpture, and printing to express themselves.

One artist, Hazoumé, even used old gasoline bottles to make masks that showed how African people were struggling with trash problems. It was a way to call attention to an important issue and make art at the same time!

Photography also became really popular with African artists. They used it to show their own reality and lifestyle in a new way. Contemporary African art is an interesting way to see how art can reflect the world around us and help us understand it better.

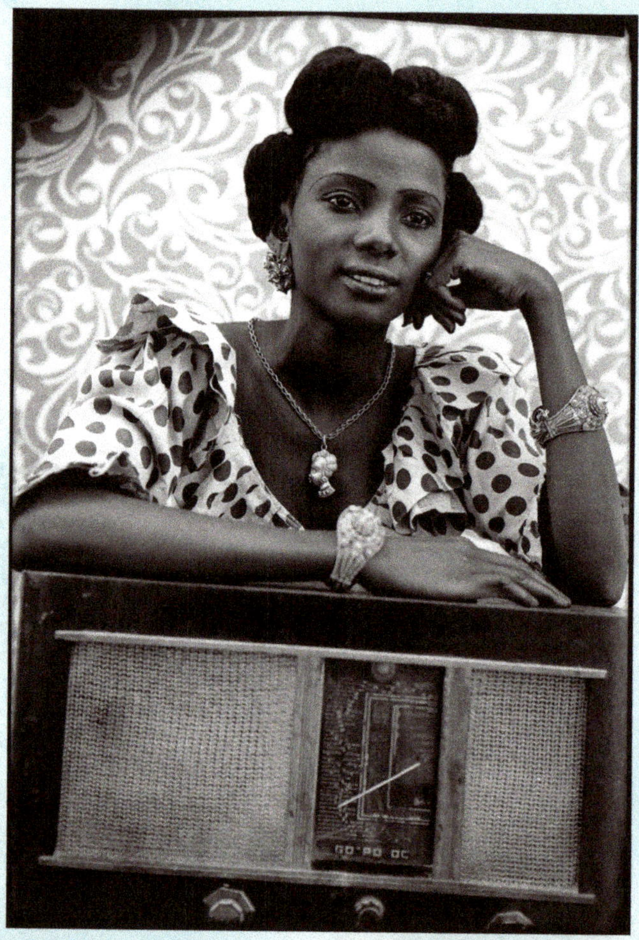

Seydou Keïta
Female portrait, 1949 – 1963
Photography

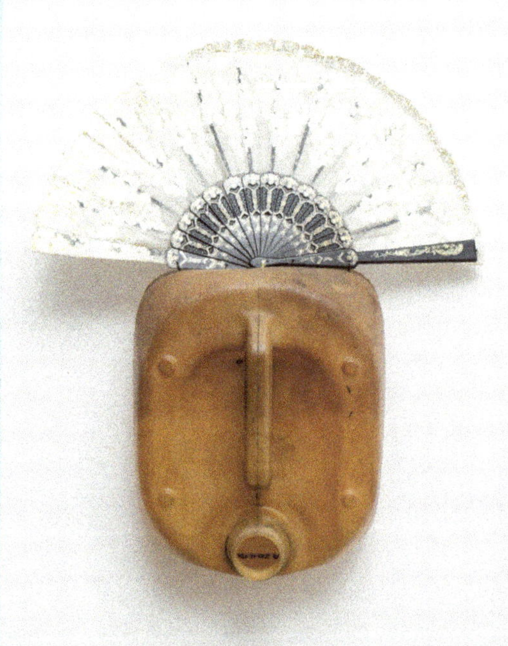

Romuald Hazoumé
(Untitled) Mask, 1962

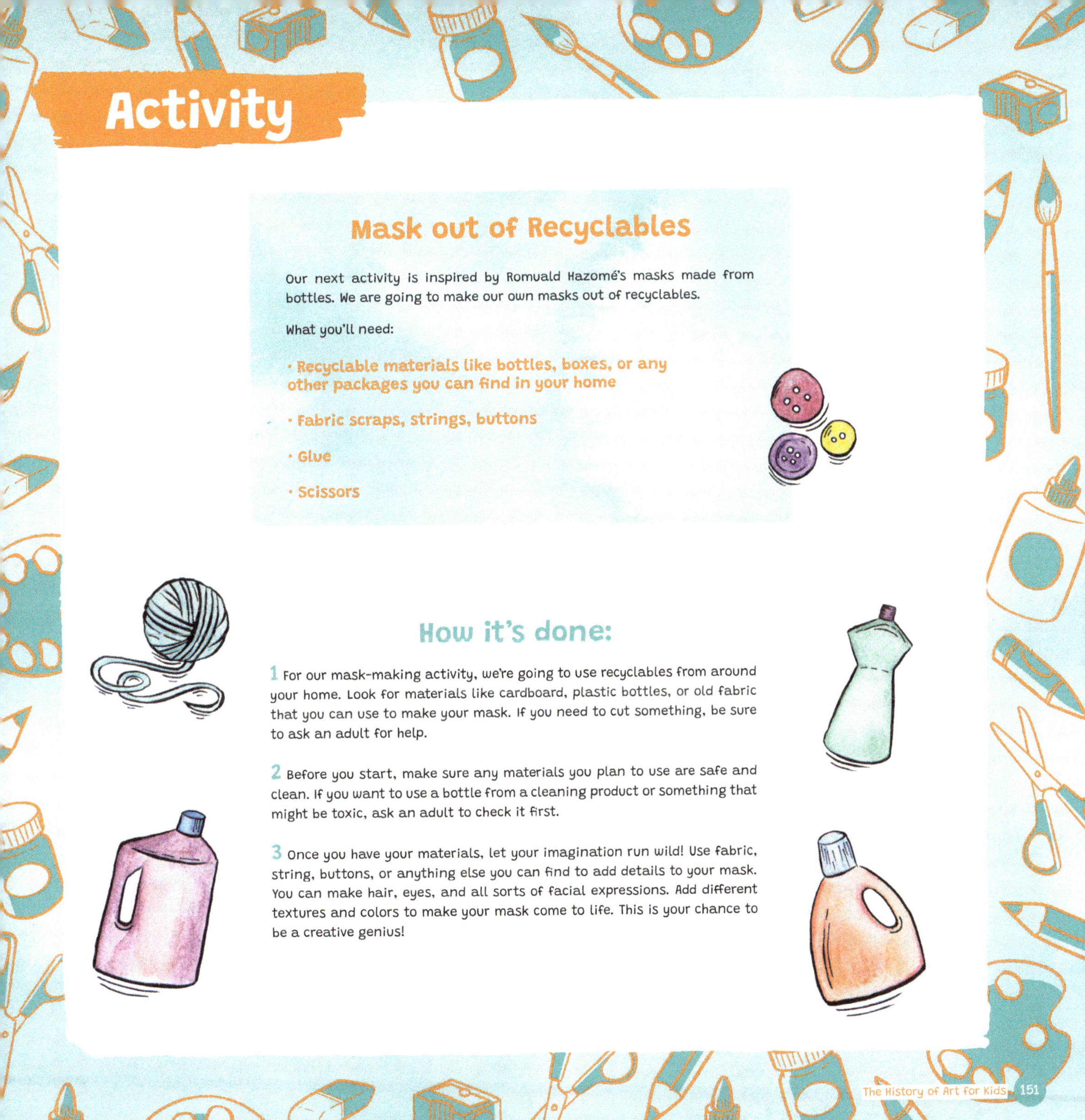

Activity

Mask out of Recyclables

Our next activity is inspired by Romuald Hazoumé's masks made from bottles. We are going to make our own masks out of recyclables.

What you'll need:

- **Recyclable materials like bottles, boxes, or any other packages you can find in your home**
- **Fabric scraps, strings, buttons**
- **Glue**
- **Scissors**

How it's done:

1 For our mask-making activity, we're going to use recyclables from around your home. Look for materials like cardboard, plastic bottles, or old fabric that you can use to make your mask. If you need to cut something, be sure to ask an adult for help.

2 Before you start, make sure any materials you plan to use are safe and clean. If you want to use a bottle from a cleaning product or something that might be toxic, ask an adult to check it first.

3 Once you have your materials, let your imagination run wild! Use fabric, string, buttons, or anything else you can find to add details to your mask. You can make hair, eyes, and all sorts of facial expressions. Add different textures and colors to make your mask come to life. This is your chance to be a creative genius!

Artists from Asia

LET'S take a quick trip to Asia to see the exciting world of contemporary Asian art!

In the late 1970s, Chinese artists began to experiment more with different materials and be influenced by Western art and culture. After the Chinese government violently responded to protests in 1989, artists began to think about their culture and how it was represented in art, sparking a new form of pop art with political themes.

In the 1980s, Japanese artists were inspired by both traditional Japanese culture and modern Western art. They created works that merged the two together in unique ways. Some artists incorporated technology into their art, such as video installations or computer-generated imagery. Others explored themes related to consumerism and popular culture.

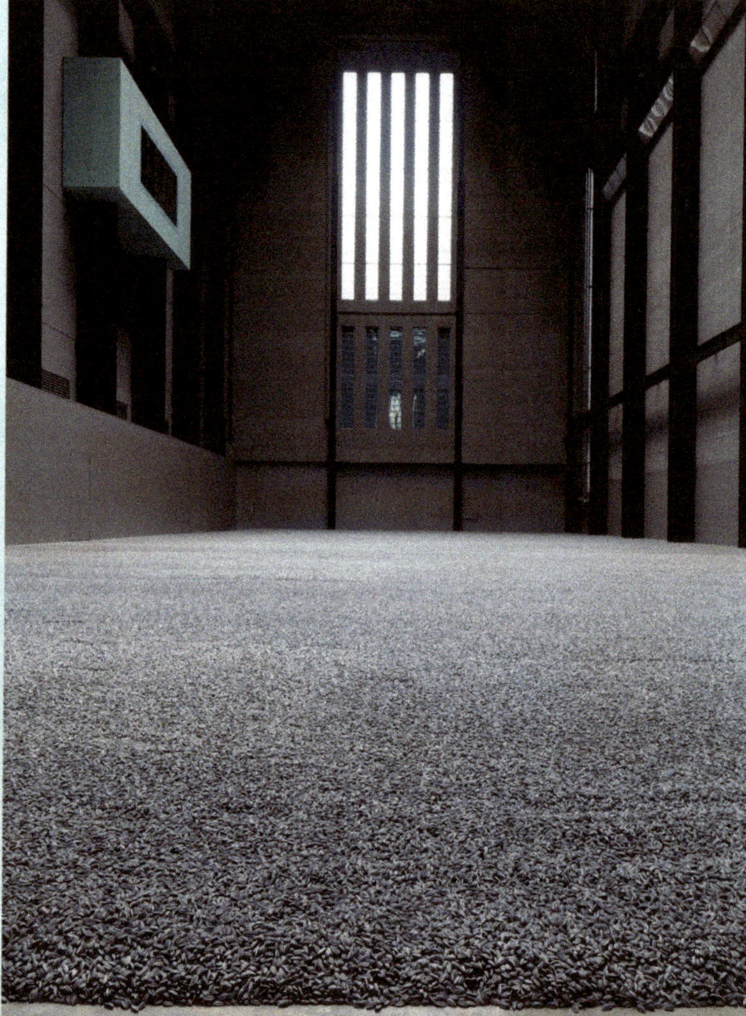

Ai Weiwei
Sunflower seeds, 1961

One of the most significant Chinese contemporary artists is Ai Weiwei, whose work often comments on the Chinese government. He created an installation called *Sunflower Seeds*, which was made of 100,000 handmade porcelain sunflower seeds scattered on the floor of a large room.

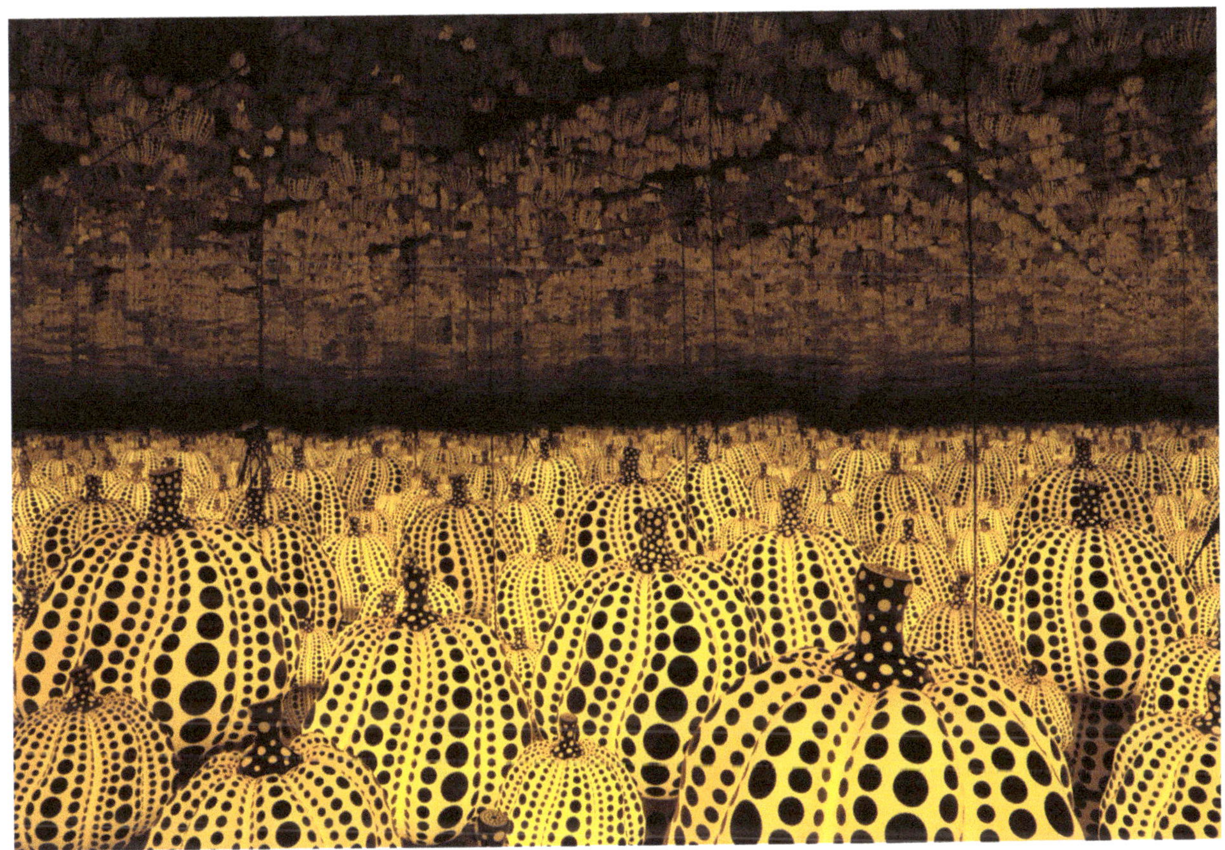

Yayoi Kusama
All the Eternal Love I Have for the Pumpkins, 2016
©YAYOI KUSAMA

Yayoi Kusama is a Japanese artist who is famous for her bright and bold artwork. She creates art using various materials like painting, sculpture, and installations. She started her artistic career in the 1950s, and since then, she has created many famous artworks that people all over the world love.

One of her most famous creations is the *Infinity Mirrored Rooms*, which are rooms filled with mirrors that create the illusion of endless space. When you enter these rooms, it feels like you are in a magical world where anything is possible. Kusama's art is inspired by her personal experiences and feelings, and she often uses dots and bold colors to express herself.

Artists from Latin America

In the 20th century, artists from Latin America wanted to create art that was true to their culture and different from what they learned in European art schools. They looked back to the symbols and images of their Indigenous cultures for inspiration.

Many countries in Latin America, like Bolivia, Argentina, Paraguay, Uruguay, Chile, and Brazil, were ruled by cruel leaders called dictators who took away people's freedom of speech. Some artists left their homes and went into exile to escape dictatorships.

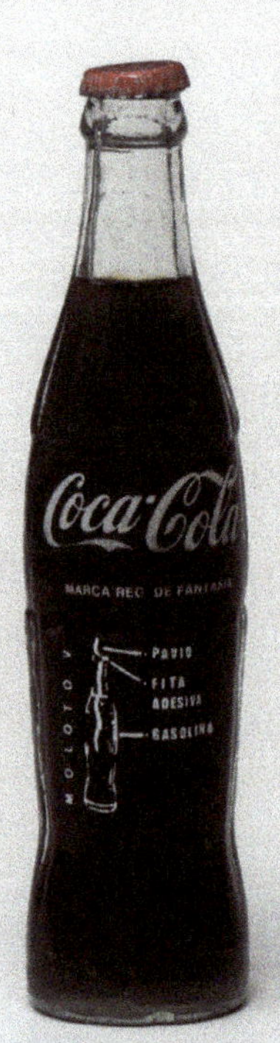

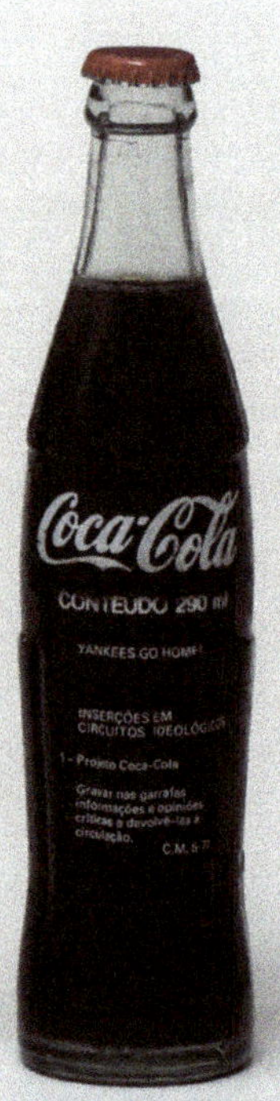

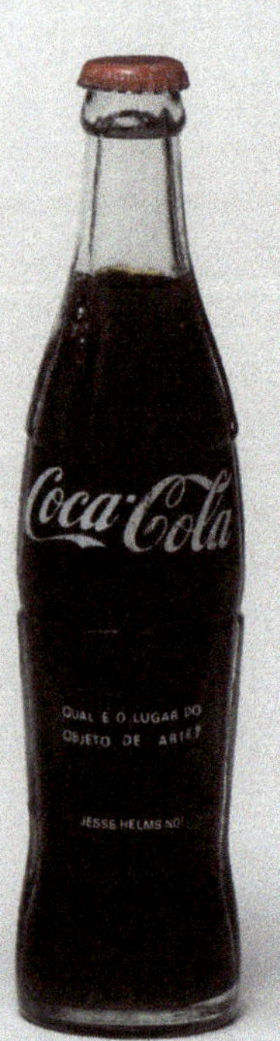

Cildo Meireles
Insertions in ideological circuits: Coca-Cola Project, 1970

Cildo Meireles, a Brazilian artist, printed hidden messages on empty Coca-Cola bottles. The writing was in white, so people could only see it when they filled the bottle again. This was a way for him to secretly protest the dictatorship that ruled Brazil at the time.

Urban Art

We are almost ending our artistic journey, human friend!

Let's explore a cool type of art that comes from cities - it's called urban art! The oldest form of urban art is graffiti, which is when people paint or draw on walls or trains using spray paint. By the 1980s, graffiti was very large and expressive in New York City and other urban areas.

Urban art broke down barriers because it allowed people to have access to art even if they didn't go to museums or galleries. People who live and work in busy cities could now see cool drawings and paintings on buildings, subways, and alleyways.

At first, graffiti artists were thought to be troublemakers and criminals. However, as more street artists emerged and brought their work to museums, graffiti became considered a respectable art form.

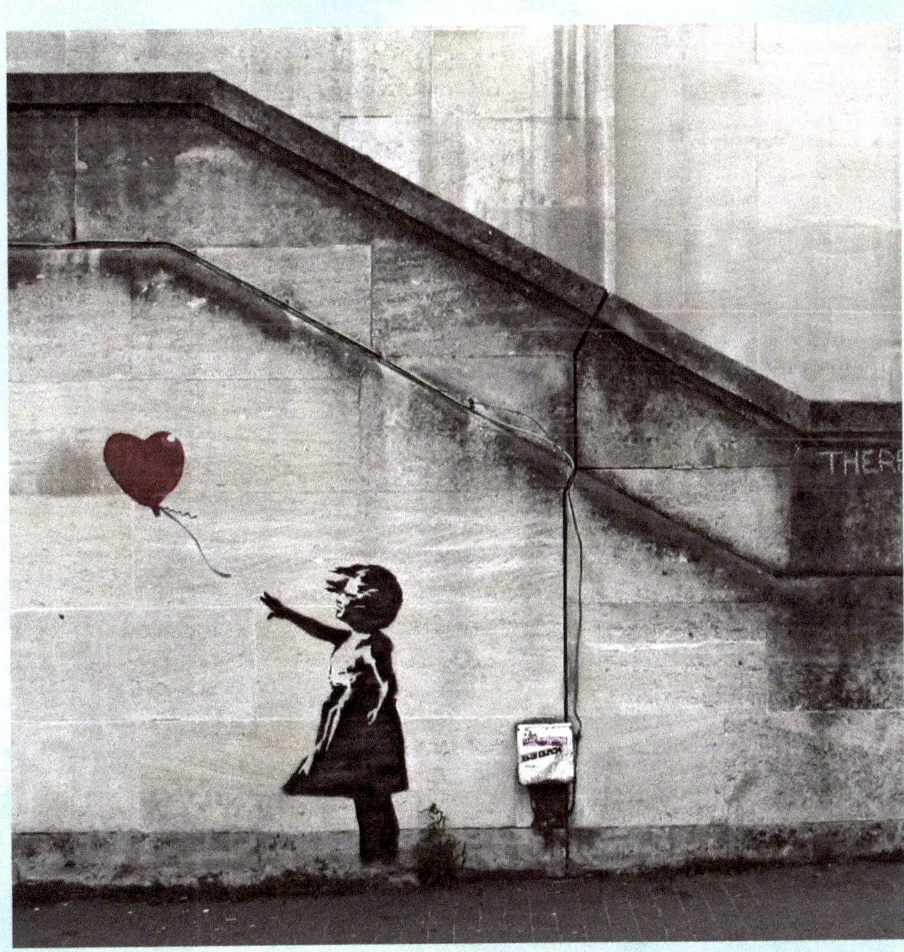

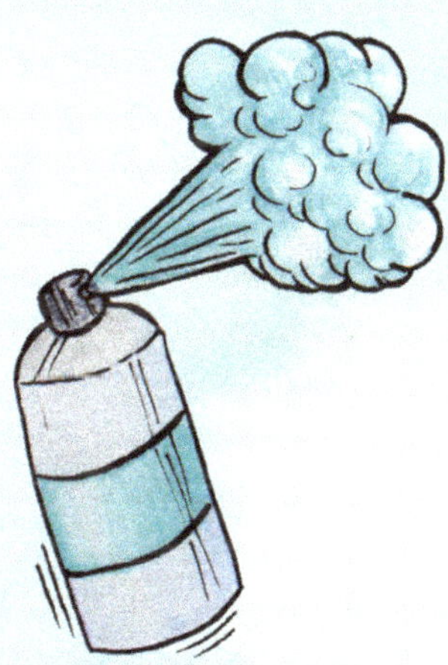

Banksy
Balloon Girl
Courtesy of Pest Control Office, Banksy, 2004
Graffiti

Urban art is still popular today, and one of the most famous urban artists is Banksy. He creates art with a message, but no one knows who he really is!

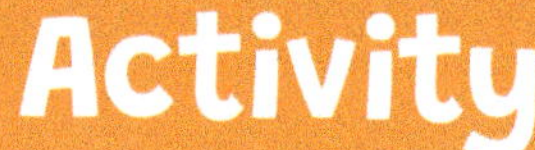

Toy Art

In the 1990s, a new form of art began in Tokyo, Japan, called Toy Art. The artist Michael Lau created limited edition sculptures that were toys.

Let's create our own Toy Art. It will be fun!

- A small block of wood (big enough to fit in your hand)
- Gouache paint
- Paintbrushes
- Pencil
- Colored pencils

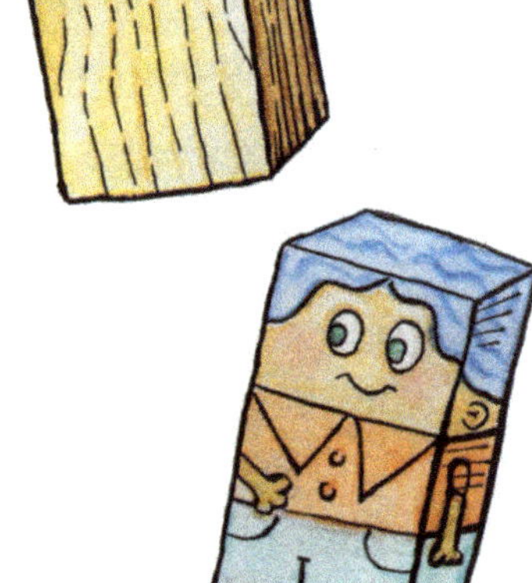

How to create your Toy Art:

1 First, think of a character. Are they human or something else? Where do they live and what do they eat? What's their name? Write down some notes to help you remember.

....

....

....

....

....

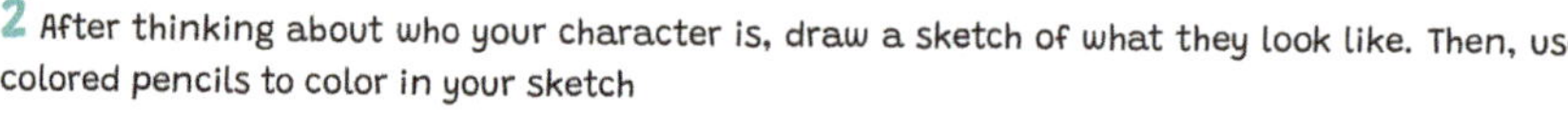

2 After thinking about who your character is, draw a sketch of what they look like. Then, use colored pencils to color in your sketch

3 Finally, it's time to paint your character on a block of wood. Trace your drawing onto the wood with a pencil, then paint it using your favorite colors. Add details to make your character unique and special!

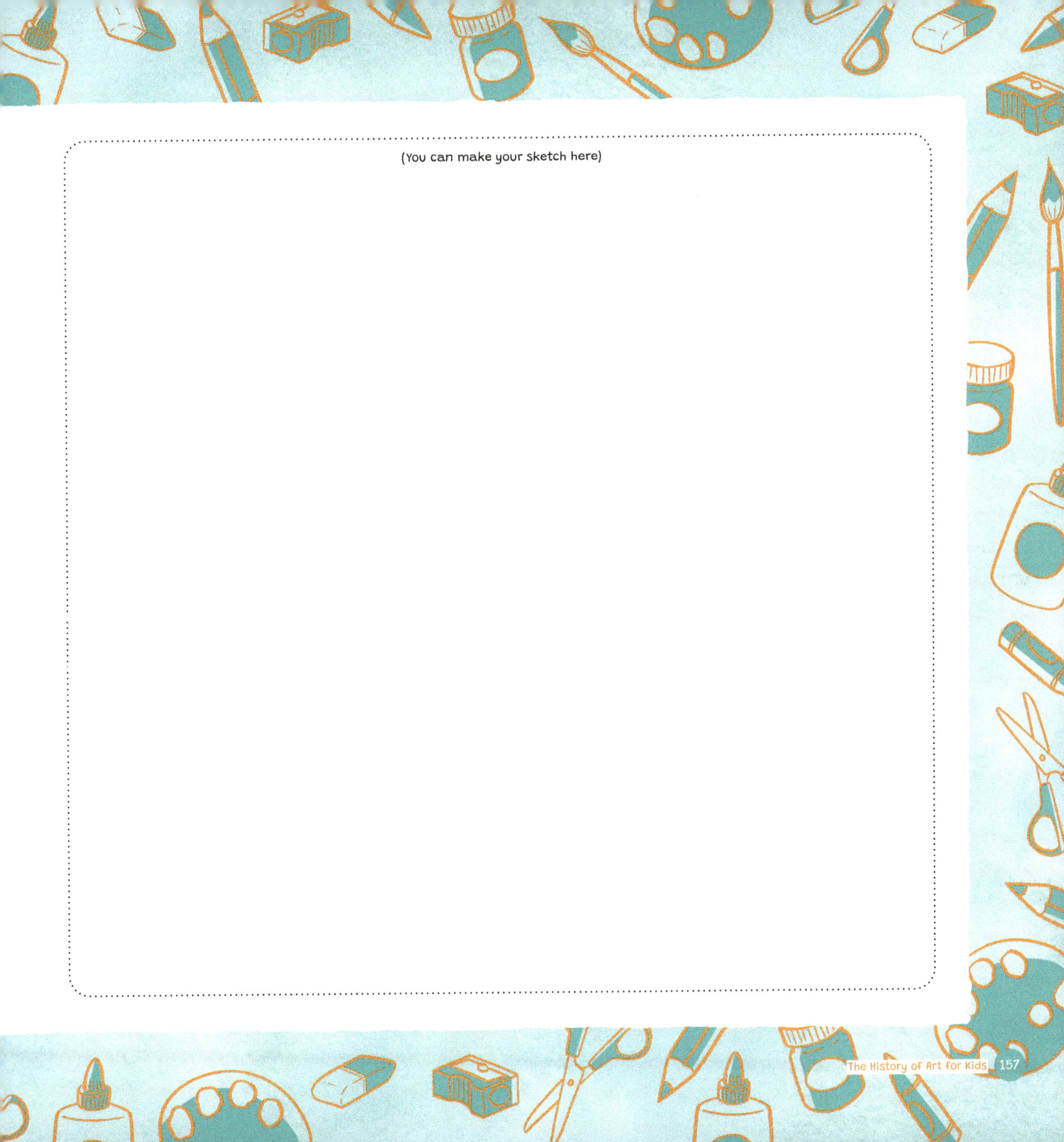

(You can make your sketch here)

Why do we make art?

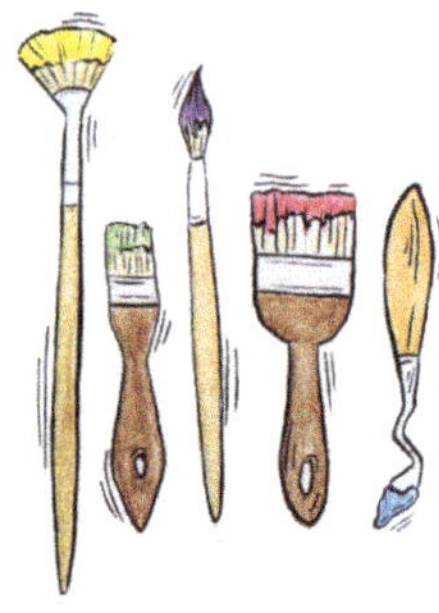

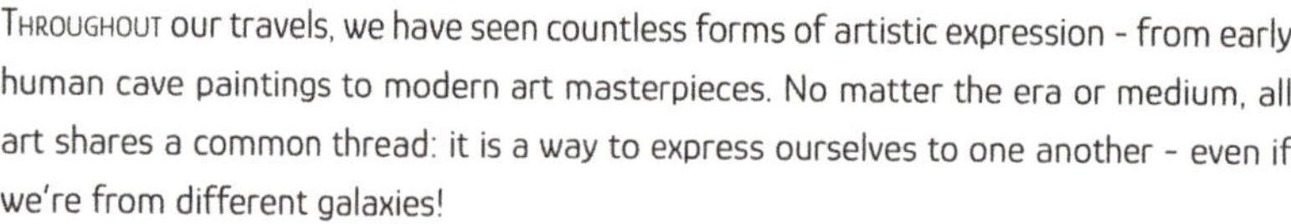

Throughout our travels, we have seen countless forms of artistic expression - from early human cave paintings to modern art masterpieces. No matter the era or medium, all art shares a common thread: it is a way to express ourselves to one another - even if we're from different galaxies!

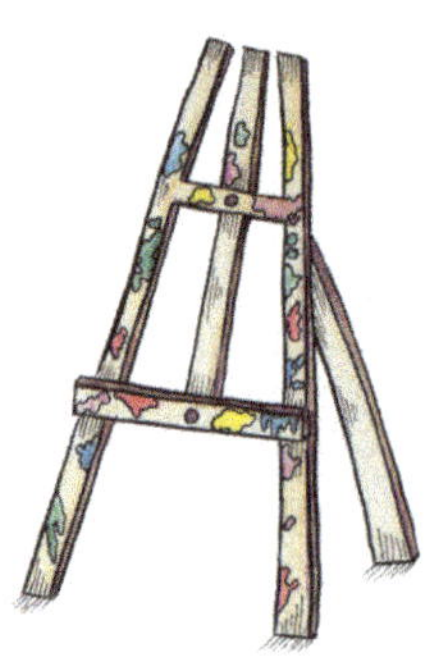

Art conveys emotions and ideas in ways that words cannot. It is how we tell stories, capture moments in time, and communicate across barriers of language, culture, and even solar systems.

As I reflect on my travels throughout Earth, I am reminded of the wise words of Vincent van Gogh, who once said, "I am seeking, I am striving, I am in it with all my heart." This, my human friends, is the spirit of art - a never-ending quest to express ourselves, to connect with others, and to find meaning in the worlds around us.

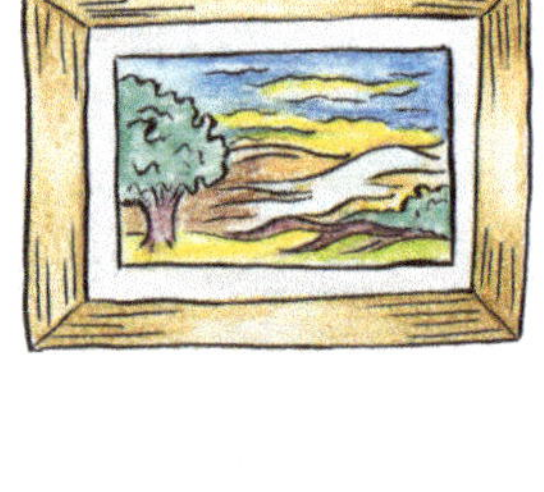

Filled with awe from all I've discovered, I turn my gaze back to the stars, ready to explore the endless universe once more. Wherever my journey takes me, I'll carry Earth's art—and its lessons—close to my heart.

To all of you who joined me on this adventure: keep exploring, creating, and celebrating the art around you. Who knows? Maybe one day you'll even create something that inspires beings from other worlds to visit, like me.

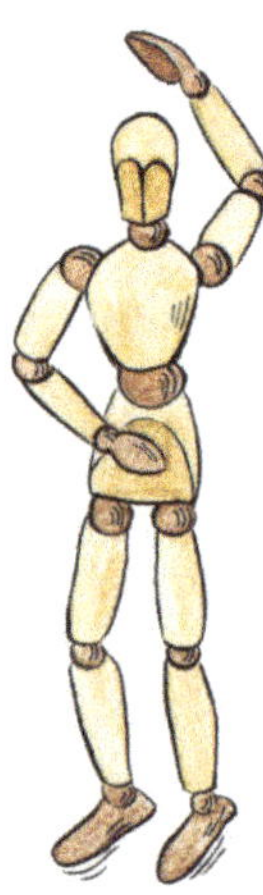

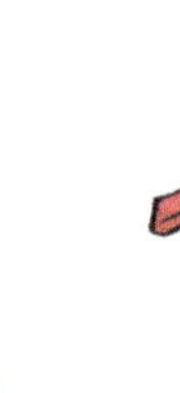

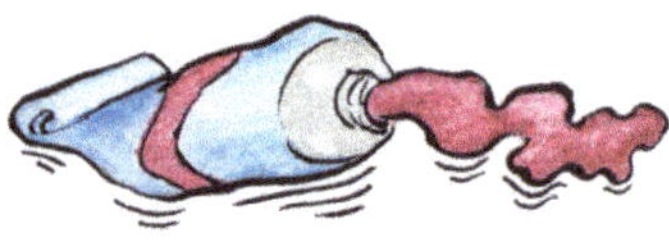

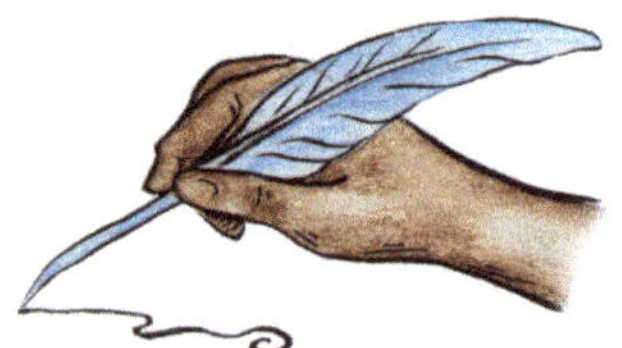

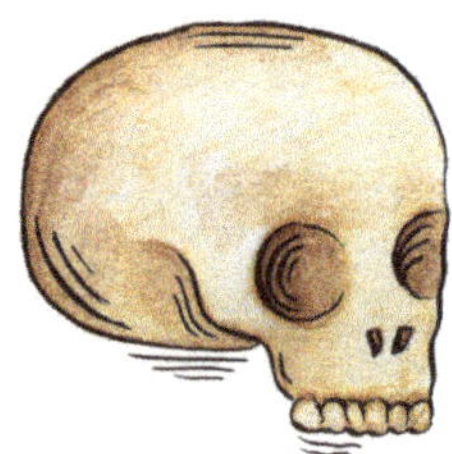

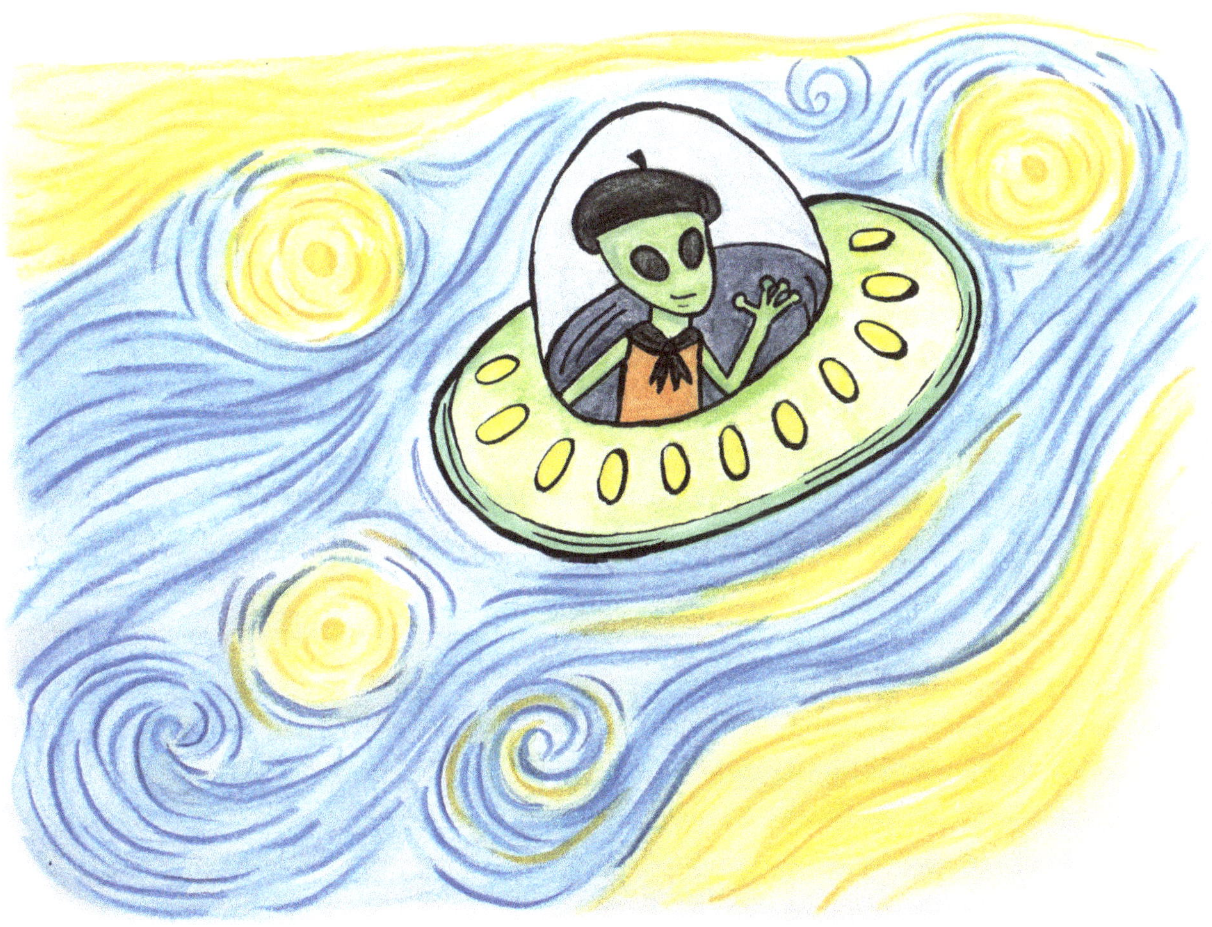

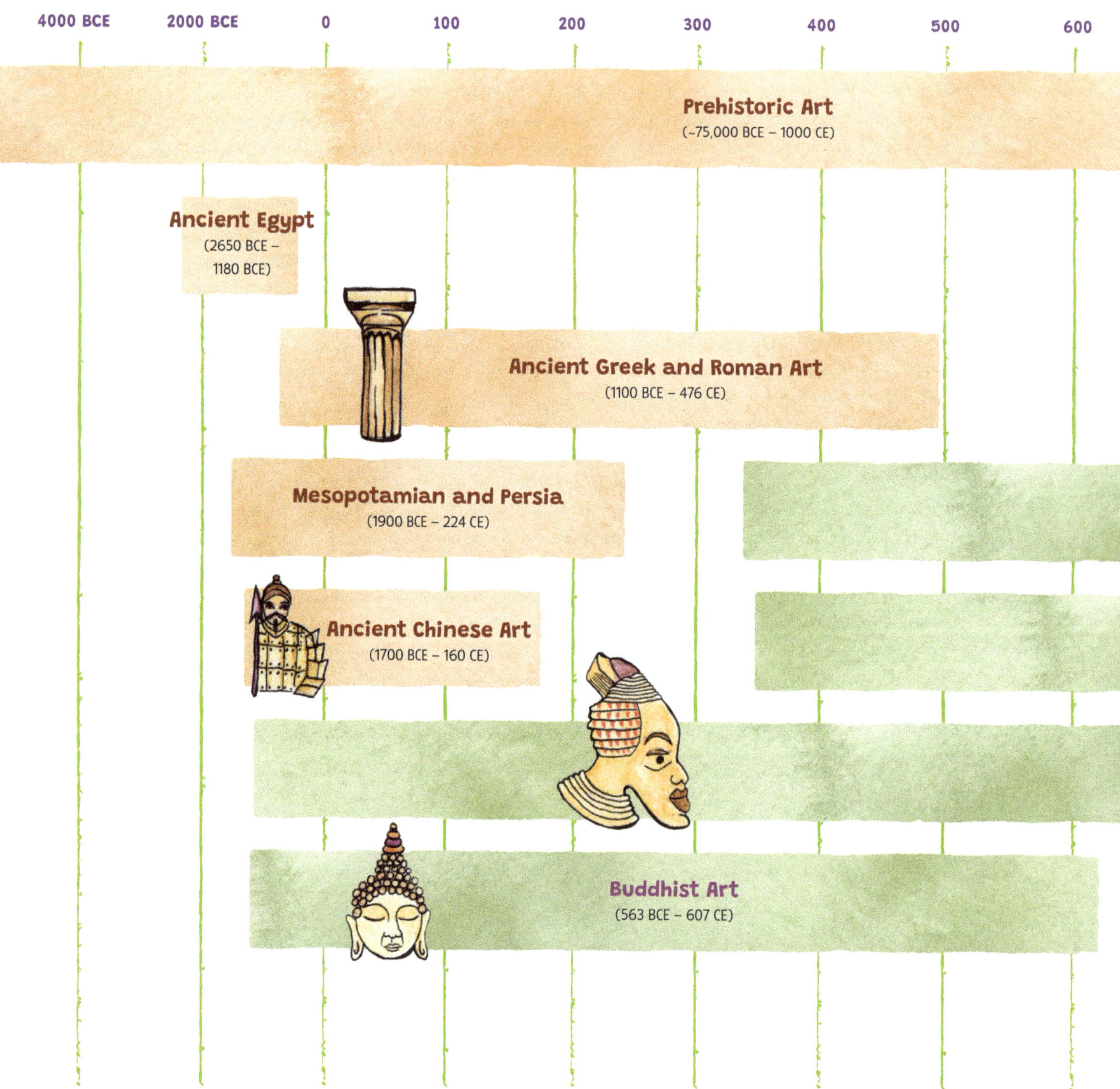
4000 BCE
2000 BCE
0
100
200
300
400
500
600
Prehistoric Art
(~75,000 BCE – 1000 CE)
Ancient Egypt
(2650 BCE – 1180 BCE)
Ancient Greek and Roman Art
(1100 BCE – 476 CE)
Mesopotamian and Persia
(1900 BCE – 224 CE)
Ancient Chinese Art
(1700 BCE – 160 CE)
Buddhist Art
(563 BCE – 607 CE)

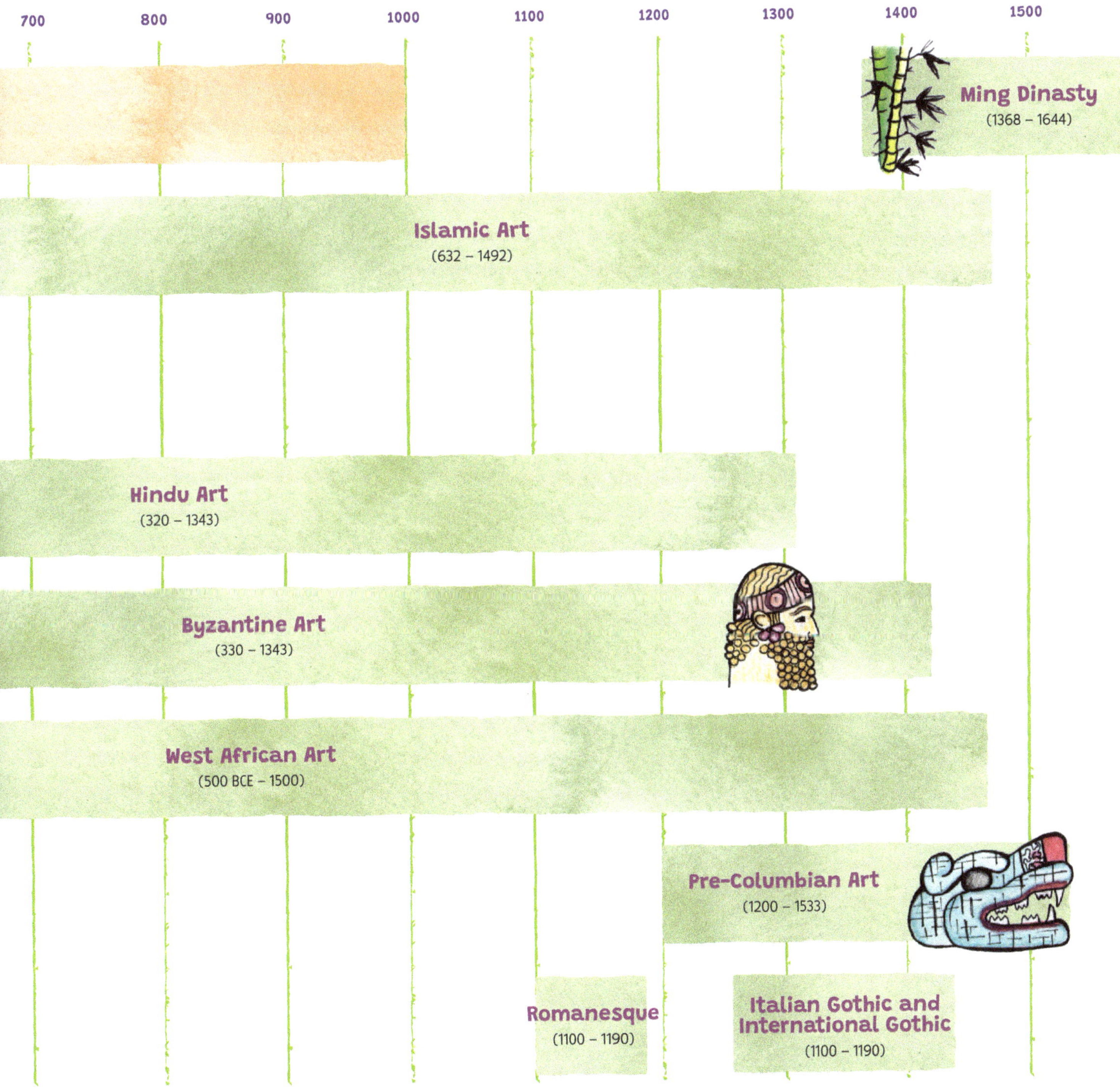

700
800
900
1000
1100
1200
1300
1400
1500
Ming Dinasty
(1368 – 1644)
Islamic Art
(632 – 1492)
Hindu Art
(320 – 1343)
Byzantine Art
(330 – 1343)
West African Art
(500 BCE – 1500)
Pre-Columbian Art
(1200 – 1533)
Romanesque
(1100 – 1190)
Italian Gothic and
International Gothic
(1100 – 1190)

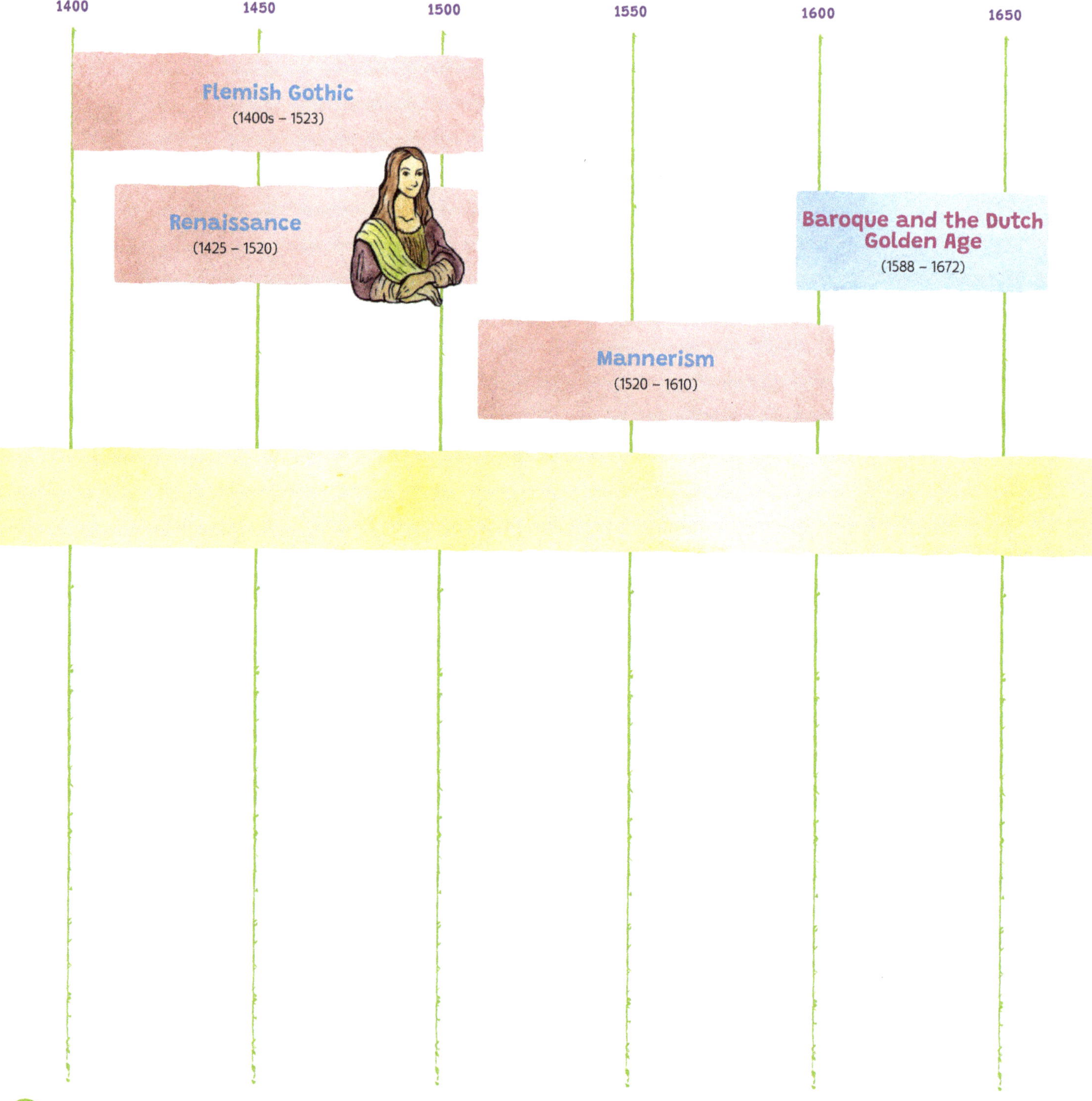
1400
1450
1500
1550
1600
1650
Flemish Gothic
(1400s – 1523)
Renaissance
(1425 – 1520)
Baroque and the Dutch Golden Age
(1588 – 1672)
Mannerism
(1520 – 1610)

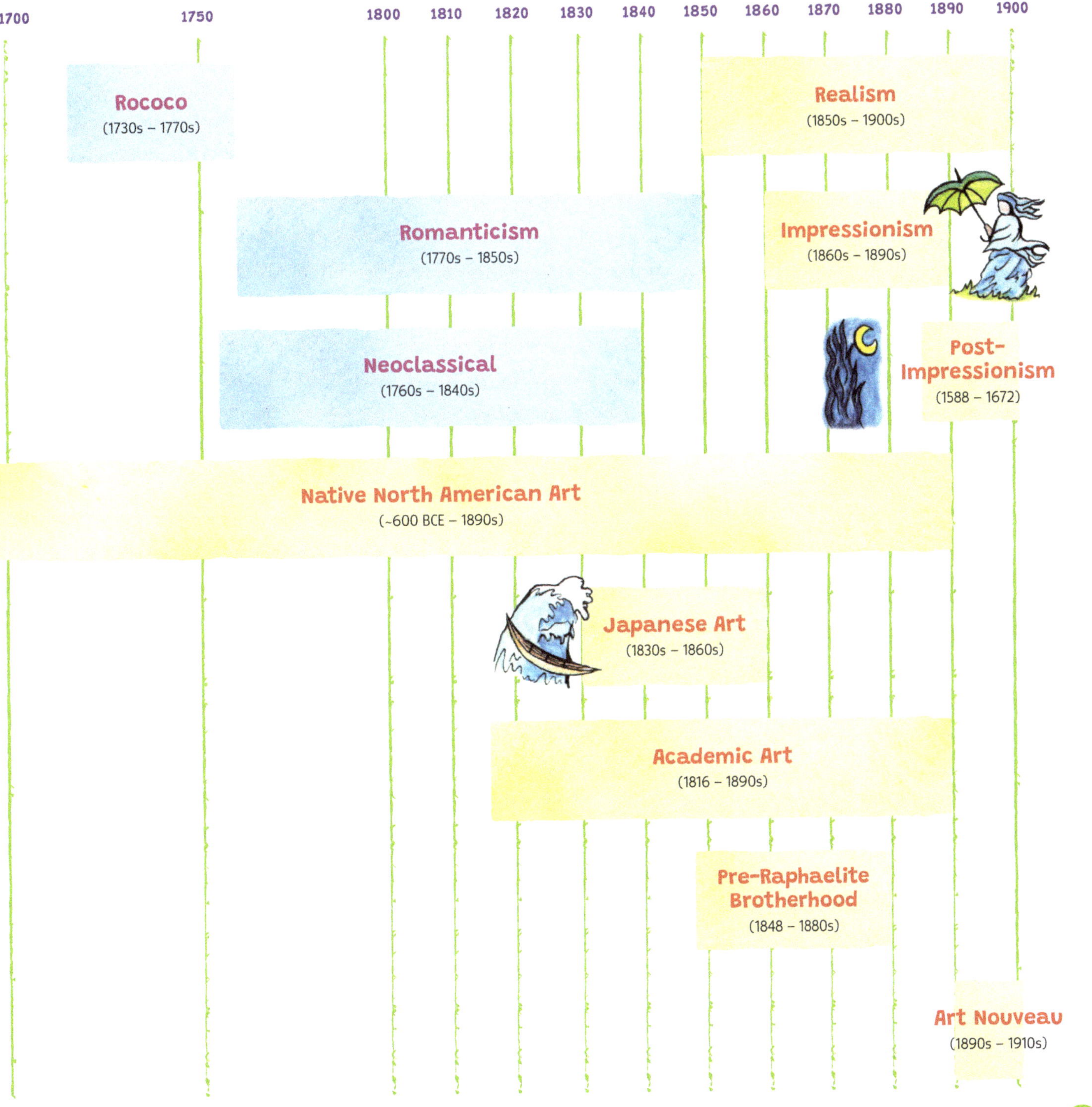
1700
1750
1800
1810
1820
1830
1840
1850
1860
1870
1880
1890
1900
Rococo
(1730s – 1770s)
Realism
(1850s – 1900s)
Romanticism
(1770s – 1850s)
Impressionism
(1860s – 1890s)
Neoclassical
(1760s – 1840s)
Post-Impressionism
(1588 – 1672)
Native North American Art
(~600 BCE – 1890s)
Japanese Art
(1830s – 1860s)
Academic Art
(1816 – 1890s)
Pre-Raphaelite Brotherhood
(1848 – 1880s)
Art Nouveau
(1890s – 1910s)

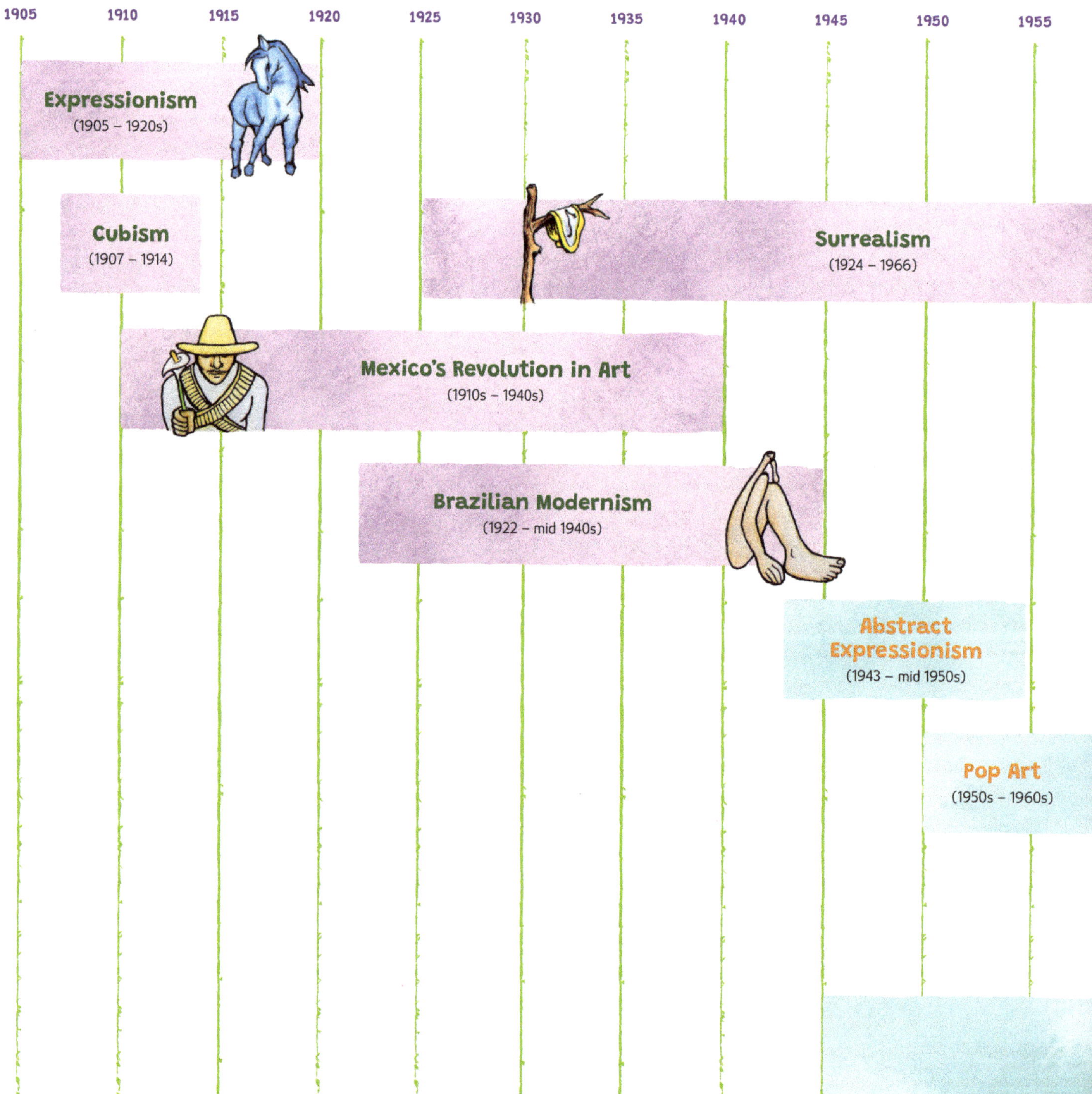
1905
1910
1915
1920
1925
1930
1935
1940
1945
1950
1955
Expressionism
(1905 – 1920s)
Cubism
(1907 – 1914)
Surrealism
(1924 – 1966)
Mexico's Revolution in Art
(1910s – 1940s)
Brazilian Modernism
(1922 – mid 1940s)
Abstract Expressionism
(1943 – mid 1950s)
Pop Art
(1950s – 1960s)

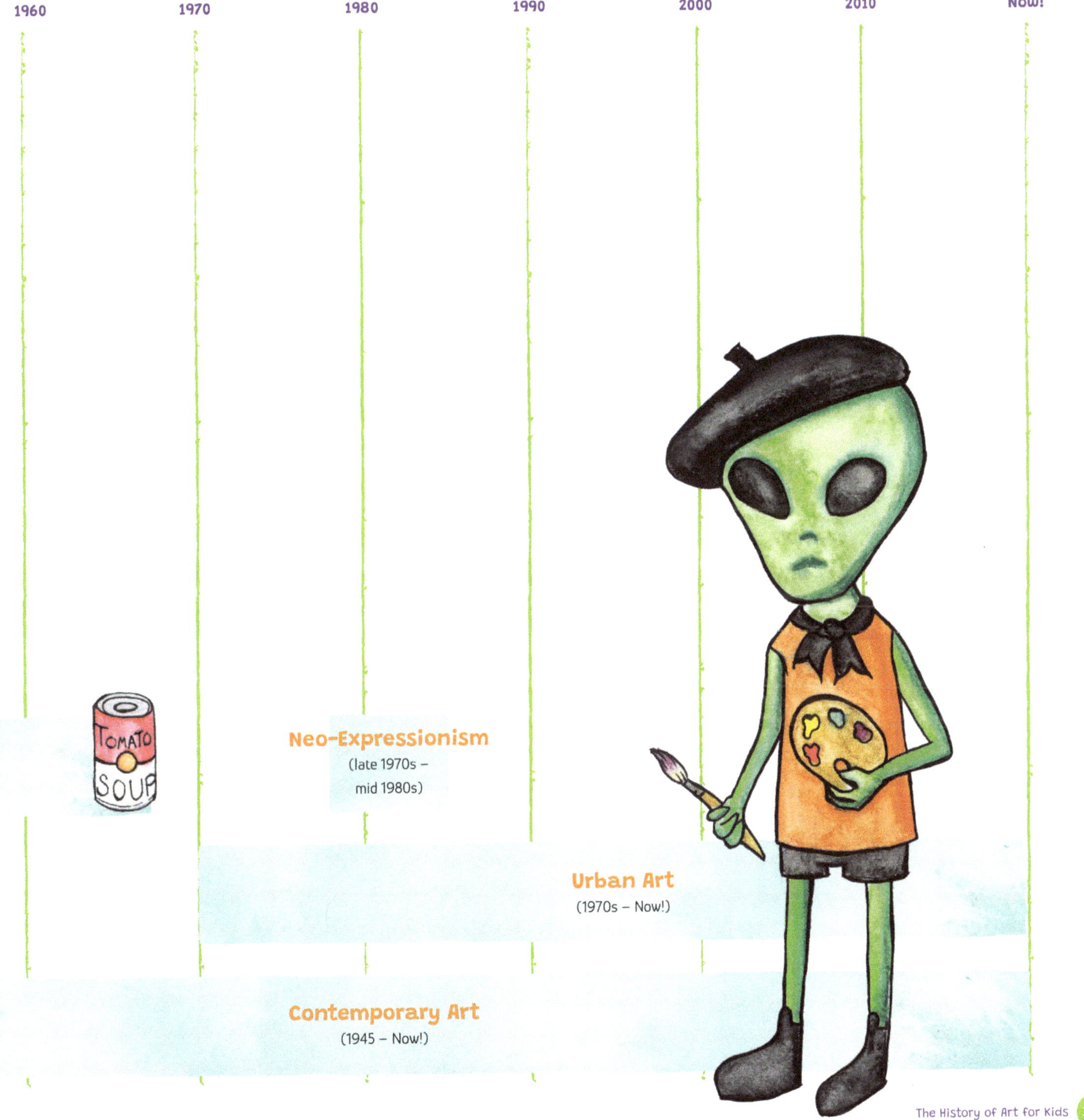
1960
1970
1980
1990
2000
2010
Now!
TOMATO
SOUP
Neo-Expressionism
(late 1970s – mid 1980s)
Urban Art
(1970s – Now!)
Contemporary Art
(1945 – Now!)

Thank you!

THANK YOU for reading this book. Want more art activities? Scan this QR code and share your e-mail address for more fun art projects!

cosmicclassbooks.com/bonus-activities/

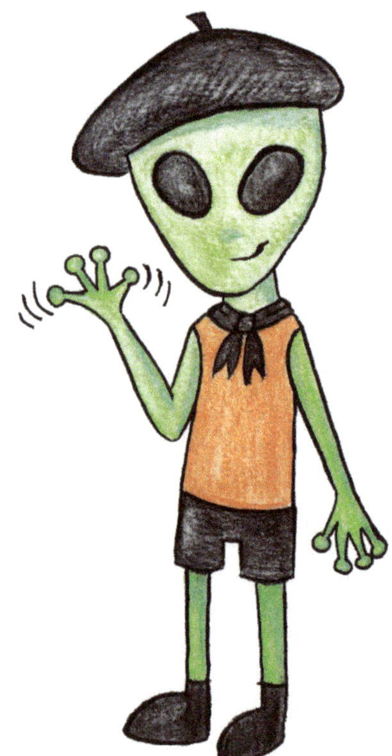

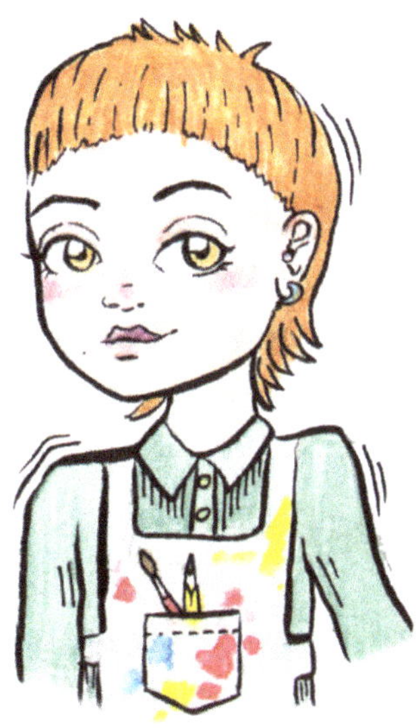

Meet the Artist

Julia Kobus is a Brazilian artist from the city of Curitiba, Paraná. At an early age, she uncovered a love of drawing and painting, following in the footsteps of her father, an artist and illustrator. As a child, Julia and her family moved to the United States, where she dove into the world of art schools and exhibits.

Julia attended U. B. Kinsey/Palmview Elementary School of the Arts and Armory Art Center in West Palm Beach, Florida. She later returned to her hometown, where she studied graphic design at The Pontifical Catholic University of Paraná. In 2017, Julia graduated with a degree in Visual Arts from the State University of Paraná.

Julia is a versatile visual artist whose expertise lies in many areas including drawings, paintings, engravings, and murals. As an art educator, she hopes her passion for art will inspire the next generation of artists and art lovers.

Meet the Author

Fred Alien (his real name can't be pronounced by Earthlings) is an extraterrestrial art history extraordinare. He has extensively traveled throughout space and time to study intergalactic history.

Fred holds a PhD in Planetary History from Universe University and has a passion for sharing the vast knowledge he has gained from his travels. Fred's love of history has compelled him to write countless books, but *The History of Art for Kids* is his first that is specially crafted for Earthlings.

When not exploring the cosmos, Fred enjoys cherishing his loving family. He has been happily married for over 300 (Earth) years and is a proud father of 18 incredible extraterrestrial children.

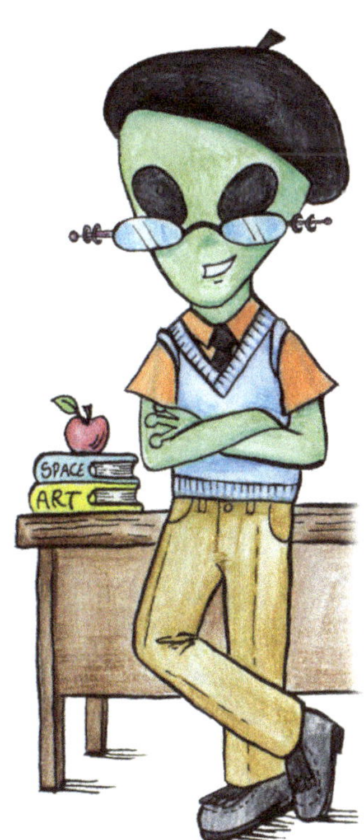

Index

Image Credits

Lascoux Cave Paintings - Page 14
Photo by Toshihiko Tanaka. Pexels.

Murujuga Petroglyph - Page 15
Wikimedia. Creative Commons CC0 1.0 Universal Public Domain Dedication.

Blombos Cave Art - Page 15
Photo by Chris S. Henshilwood. Wikimedia. Creative Commons Attribution-Share Alike 4.0 International license.

Nazca Lines - Page 16
Photo by Diego Delso. Wikimedia. Creative Commons Attribution-Share Alike 4.0 International license.

High Relief Featuring The Mushhushshu - Page 20
Photo by user Allie Caulfield. Wikimedia. Creative Commons Attribution 2.0 Generic license.

Terracotta Army - Page 22
Photo by Gary Lee Todd. Wikimedia. Creative Commons CC0 1.0 Universal Public Domain Dedication.

Terracotta Army 2 - Page 23
Photo by Gary Lee Todd. Wikimedia. Creative Commons CC0 1.0 Universal Public Domain Dedication.

Parthenon - Page 25
Photo by Steve Swayne. Wikimedia. Creative Commons Attribution-Share Alike 2.0 Generic license.

Trojan Archer from the Temple of Aphaia, Aegina - Page 26
Photo by Marsyas (real name not provided). Wikimedia. Creative Commons Attribution-Share Alike 2.5 Generic license.

Colosseum - Page 27
Photo by Kamran Salimi. Wikimedia. Creative Commons Attribution-Share Alike 4.0 International license.

Mosaic of Justinian I - Page 32
Photo by George E. Koronaios. Wikimedia. Creative Commons Attribution-Share Alike 4.0 International license.

Christ Pantocrator, 1180 – 1190 CE - Page 33
Photo by Gun Powder Ma (real name not provided). Wikimedia. Creative Commons Attribution-Share Alike 3.0 Unported license.

Nok Sculpture - Page 36
Photo by Sailko (real name not provided). Wikimedia. Creative Commons Attribution 3.0 Unported license.

Bronze Head from Ife - Page 37
Photo by Sailko (real name not provided). Wikimedia. Creative Commons Attribution-Share Alike 3.0 Unported license.

Picture of Shiva Nataraja Sculpture - Page 38
Photo by Yann (real name not provided). Wikimedia. Creative Commons CC0 1.0 Universal Public Domain Dedication.

Amitābha in Byōdō-in Temple - Page 39
Photo by Zairon (real name not provided). Wikimedia. Creative Commons Attribution-Share Alike 4.0 International.

Angkor Wat - Page 40
Photo by Jakub Hałun. Wikimedia. Creative Commons Attribution-Share Alike 4.0 International license.

Temple of Equality - Page 41
Photo by Martin Falbisoner. Wikimedia. Creative Commons Attribution-Share Alike 4.0 International license.

Interior of the Great Mosque of Damascus, Syria - Page 42
Photo by Dick Osseman. Wikimedia. Creative Commons Attribution-Share Alike 4.0 International license.
Dome of Soltaniyeh in Soltaniyeh - Page 43
Photo by Amir Hosein Nasooti, Fars Media Corporation. Wikimedia. Creative Commons Attribution-Share Alike 4.0 International license.

Hagia Sophia - Page 43
Photo by Arild Vågen. Wikimedia. Creative Commons Attribution-Share Alike 3.0 Unported license.

Taj Mahal - Page 44
Photo by A, Ocram. Wikimedia. Creative Commons CC0 1.0 Universal Public Domain Dedication.

Aztec Sun Stone - Page 46
Photo by Juan Carlos Fonseca Mata. Wikimedia. Creative Commons Attribution-Share Alike 4.0 International license.

Temple of Kukulcán - Page 47
Photo by Alastair Rae. Wikimedia. Creative Commons Attribution-Share Alike 2.0 Generic license.

Notre-Dame de Paris - Page 51
Photo by Peter Haas. Wikimedia. Creative Commons Attribution-Share Alike 3.0 Unported license.

Painted Porcelain Vase from Ming Dynasty - Page 53
Wikimedia. Creative Commons CC0 1.0 Universal Public Domain Dedication.

Bernini's Ecstasy of Saint Teresa - Page 76
Photo by Benjamín Núñez González. Wikimedia. Creative Commons Attribution-Share Alike 4.0 International license.

Modern and Contemporary Art Image Credits

"Bull" - Pablo Picasso, 1945 (FULL PAGE) - Page 127
© 2023 Estate of Pablo Picasso / Artists Rights Society (ARS), New York

"Violin and Candlestick" Georges Braque (1/2 page interior) - Page 125
© 2023 Artists Rights Society (ARS), New York / ADAGP, Paris

"The False Mirror" Rene Magritte - (1/2 PAGE INTERIOR) - Page 129
© 2023 C. Herscovici / Artists Rights Society (ARS), New York

"The Persistence of Memory" - Salvador Dali, 1931 (1/2 PAGE INTERIOR) - Page 130
© 2023 Salvador Dalí, Fundació Gala-Salvador Dalí, Artists Rights Society

"Paris Through the Window" Marc Chagall- (1/2 PAGE INTERIOR) - Page 131
© 2023 Artists Rights Society (ARS), New York / ADAGP, Paris

"North Wall" - Diego Rivera, 1933 (1/2 PAGE INTERIOR) - Page 133
© 2023 Banco de México Diego Rivera Frida Kahlo Museums Trust, Mexico, D.F. / Artists Rights Society (ARS), New York

"Self-Portrait with Necklace and Hummingbird" - Frida Kahlo, (1/4 PAGE INTERIOR) - Page 134
© 2023 Banco de México Diego Rivera Frida Kahlo Museums Trust, Mexico, D.F. / Artists Rights Society (ARS), New York

" The Scream " Edward Munch (1/4 INTERIOR) - Page 123
@ 2023 Artists Rights Society (ARS), New York

1940 "Vir Heroicus Sublimis" - Barnett Newman, 1950-1951 (1/2 PAGE INTERIOR) - Page 140
© 2023 The Barnett Newman Foundation / Artists Rights Society (ARS), New York

"Convergence" - Jackson Pollock, 1952 (1/2 PAGE INTERIOR) - Page 141
© 2023 The Pollock-Krasner Foundation / Artists Rights Society (ARS), New York

"Large Campbell's Soup Can" - Andy Warhol, 1964 (1/2 PAGE INTERIOR) - Page 144
© 2023 The Andy Warhol Foundation for the Visual Arts, Inc. / Licensed by Artists Rights Society (ARS), New york

"Old Couple on a Bench" - Duane Hanson, 1994 (1/4 PAGE INTERIOR) - Page 148
© 2023 Estate of Duane Hanson / Licensed by VAGA at Artists Rights Society (ARS), NY

"Untitled Mask" - Romuald Hazoumé, 1962 (1/4 PAGE INTERIOR) - Page 150
© 2023 Artists Rights Society (ARS), New York / ADAGP, Paris

L'Arc de Triomphe, Wrapped. Christo & Jeanne Claude (1/4 PAGE INTERIOR) - Page 146
© 2023 Artists Rights Society (ARS), New York / ADAG

All art projects and activities in this book are designed to be fun and educational. However, they involve the use of materials, tools, and techniques that require care and attention. Adult supervision is recommended for all activities, especially for children under 12 years old.

Cosmic Class Books and its contributors are not responsible or liable for any injuries, damages, or losses that may occur while engaging in the projects or activities described in this book. Please use your judgment and take necessary precautions to ensure a safe and enjoyable experience. Always follow safety guidelines for tools, materials, and equipment, and consult professionals when in doubt.

By participating in the activities outlined in this book, you agree to assume full responsibility for your actions and understand that Cosmic Class Books and its contributors disclaim all liability for any adverse outcomes.

www.ingramcontent.com/pod-product-compliance
Ingram Content Group UK Ltd.
Pitfield, Milton Keynes, MK11 3LW, UK
UKHW061951290726
14090UKWH00021B/1178

9 798991 239417